Lecture Notes in Artificial Intelligence   1535

Subseries of Lecture Notes in Computer Science
Edited by J. G. Carbonell and J. Siekmann

Lecture Notes in Computer Science

Edited by G. Goos, J. Hartmanis and J. van Leeuwen

T0242293

Springer
Berlin
Heidelberg
New York
Barcelona
Hong Kong
London
Milan
Paris
Singapore
Tokyo

Sascha Ossowski

Co-ordination in Artificial Agent Societies

Social Structures and Its Implications for Autonomous Problem-Solving Agents

 Springer

Series Editors

Jaime G. Carbonell, Carnegie Mellon University, Pittsburgh, PA, USA
Jörg Siekmann, University of Saarland, Saarbrücken, Germany

Author

Sascha Ossowski
Rey Juan Carlos University, School of Engineering (ESCET)
Campus de Móstoles
Calle Tulipan s/n, E-28933 Móstoles (Madrid), Spain
E-mail: S.Ossowski@escet.urjc.es

Cataloging-in-Publication Data applied for

Die Deutsche Bibliothek - CIP-Einheitsaufnahme

Ossowski, Sascha:
Co-ordination in artificial agent societies : social structures and its
implications for autonomous problem solving agents / Sascha Ossowski. - Berlin
; Heidelberg ; New York ; Barcelona ; Hong Kong ; London ; Milan ; Paris ;
Singapore ; Tokyo : Springer, 1999
  (Lecture notes in computer science ; 1535 : Lecture notes in artificial
intelligence)
  ISBN 3-540-65495-X

CR Subject Classification (1998): I.2.11, C.2.4, H.5.3

ISBN 3-540-65495-X Springer-Verlag Berlin Heidelberg New York

© Springer-Verlag Berlin Heidelberg 1999
Printed in Germany

Typesetting: Camera ready by author
SPIN 10692964   06/3142 – 5 4 3 2 1 0   Printed on acid-free paper

Für meine Eltern

Para Sandra

Foreword

Advances in Computer Science often arise from new ideas and concepts, that prove to be advantageous for the design of complex software systems. The conception of multi-agent systems is particularly attractive, as it promises *modularity* based on the conceptual speciality of an agent, as well as *flexibility* in their integration through appropriate interaction models. While early systems drew upon co-operative agents, recent developments have realised the importance of the notion of autonomy in the design of agent-based applications. The emergence of systems of autonomous problem-solving agents paves the way for complex Artificial Intelligence applications that allow for *scalability* and at the same time foster the *reusability* of their components.

In consequence, an intelligent multi-agent application can be seen as a collection of autonomous agents, usually specialised in different tasks, together with a social model of their interactions. This approach implies a dynamic generation of complex relational structures, that agents need to be knowledgeable of in order to successfully achieve their goals. Therefore, a multi-agent system designer needs to think carefully about conceptualisation, representation and enactment of the different types of knowledge that its agents rely on, for individual problem solving as well as for mutual co-ordination. A *knowledge-oriented* approach to agent system design will promote the emergence of methodologies and tools for building multi-agent applications, thereby providing evidence for the added value that agent technology provides over traditional approaches to the design of intelligent software systems.

The proposal that Sascha Ossowski presents in this book applies the above paradigm to artificial agent societies. A comprehensive survey of the different approaches to co-ordination in societies of (human and artificial) agents is given first. Setting out from a critical analysis of the state of the art, he suggests structuring multi-agent applications in line with a mechanism that he calls Structural Co-operation. Agents are provided with expertise about their environment in order to detect and overcome specific types of problem situations, make use of their social knowledge to mutually adjust their activities, and are coerced towards a coherent collective behaviour through normative rules. The proposed model is formalised theoretically within Game Theory, realised practically by means of an agent architecture, and assessed experimentally by building a prototype of a distributed decision support system for road traffic management and comparing it to an alternative model based on a centralised architecture.

Series Editors

Jaime G. Carbonell, Carnegie Mellon University, Pittsburgh, PA, USA
Jörg Siekmann, University of Saarland, Saarbrücken, Germany

Author

Sascha Ossowski
Rey Juan Carlos University, School of Engineering (ESCET)
Campus de Móstoles
Calle Tulipan s/n, E-28933 Móstoles (Madrid), Spain
E-mail: S.Ossowski@escet.urjc.es

Cataloging-in-Publication Data applied for

Die Deutsche Bibliothek - CIP-Einheitsaufnahme

Ossowski, Sascha:
Co-ordination in artificial agent societies : social structures and its
implications for autonomous problem solving agents / Sascha Ossowski. - Berlin
; Heidelberg ; New York ; Barcelona ; Hong Kong ; London ; Milan ; Paris ;
Singapore ; Tokyo : Springer, 1999
 (Lecture notes in computer science ; 1535 : Lecture notes in artificial
intelligence)
 ISBN 3-540-65495-X

CR Subject Classification (1998): I.2.11, C.2.4, H.5.3

ISBN 3-540-65495-X Springer-Verlag Berlin Heidelberg New York

© Springer-Verlag Berlin Heidelberg 1999
Printed in Germany

Typesetting: Camera ready by author
SPIN 10692964   06/3142 – 5 4 3 2 1 0   Printed on acid-free paper

Preface

In recent years the interest in agent technology – and agent-related publications – has risen enormously. There are books covering a wide range of recent research in the field: it is easy to find publications on particular agent theories and their underlying logics, on specific agent architectures and their dynamics, as well as on certain agent languages, their syntax and semantics. Although this huge amount of specialised publications makes available a large body of valuable knowledge and research experience, it may also appear unstructured and rather abstract to the reader. It becomes increasingly hard for an engineer to bridge the gap between particular theories, architectures or languages and their application to real-world problems.

This book is concerned with a broad and, as I believe, essential aspect of agent technology: how to achieve instrumental, co-ordinated behaviour among artificial agents for real-world applications? In the attempt to give an answer to this question, it has been necessary to draw on quite different strands of research. However, having in mind the aforementioned arguments, I have tried to pay special attention to show how these pieces fit together.

The book focuses on the nexus between theory and practice in multi-agent system research: setting out from a class of problems, it covers the whole process from the development of a multi-agent theory to the design of a multi-agent application. It reports how notions rooted in sociology can be adapted and transferred to societies of *artificial* agents; how they can be used to build and formalise a co-ordination mechanism within these societies, and how this mechanism is integrated in an experimental multi-agent system for urban road traffic management.

The history of this book dates back to when I left Germany, endowed with a "Human Capital and Mobility" grant of the European Union, in order to take on a research assistance at the Artificial Intelligence Department of the Technical University of Madrid (UPM). It compiles the essence of four years of research work that I carried out as a member of the Intelligent Systems research group at UPM, and in the course of which I defended my dissertation. During this time I had the chance to meet many people in different parts of the world, who have supported the realisation of my ideas in one or another way. I would like to thank them all. Still, I am particularly grateful...

— to professor José Cuena, director of the Artificial Intelligence Department of UPM and head of the Intelligent Systems research group, for the attention and the time he dedicated to me. He pushed me to do more than I thought I could. Without him, this book would not have reached its present shape.

— to associate professor Ana García-Serrano, my supervisor during my time at UPM. My esteem for her goes beyond the important contribution she provided for the formation of the work presented in this book. Through all this time, Ana has not just been a "boss", but also a friend.

— to all colleagues who took the trouble to review draft versions of my work: professor Alfons Crespo (UPV, Spain), professor Yves Demazeau (IMAG, France), professor Manuel Hermenegildo (UPM), assistant professor Josefa Hernández (UPM), associate professor Martín Molina (UPM), Dr. habil. David Pearce (DFKI, Germany), M.Sc. José-Luis Sierra (UPM), associate professor Juan Tejada (UCM, Spain) and many more... Their comments and criticisms did a great job in improving clarity and conciseness of this book. Special thanks to Yves Demazeau and David Pearce for encouraging me to submit the manuscript for publication in the LNAI series of Springer Verlag.

— to all members of the Intelligent Systems research group, for their help with many of the tiresome tasks that have come up in the course of the research that led to this book.

I am particularly indebted to my parents, for their moral and intellectual support. A very special "thank you" is owed to Sandra, for her infinite patience with me and my projects. Without her continuous assistance, encouragement and inspiration this book would not have come to a "happy end".

Madrid, August 1998   Sascha Ossowski

Contents

List of Figures

List of Tables

1 Introduction

1.1 Motivation

The notion of software agents has become increasingly popular over the last couple of years. Private companies as well as public entities spend a considerable amount of time, effort and money in research, development, and promotion of the idea of software agents. In some respect this is surprising, as software agents essentially do what one has always expected a reasonably intelligent computer program to do: they are artefacts capable of achieving certain tasks on behalf of their users. They enjoy a certain level of autonomy, as their activities need not be subjected to *constant* human guidance or intervention.

Most probably, the key to account for the proliferation of software agents lies in the variety of new applications that the growing connectivity in the frame of wide-area networks provides: in a future electronic marketplace a customer agent and a travel agency's vendor agent may negotiate the precise conditions of a journey; information agents roam through the Internet in search of documents that match a specific user query; personal assistant agents filter the flood of advertisements and announcements that companies and individuals broadcast on the basis of the user's interest profile; they remind him or her of deadlines, propose schedules for meetings and take over much of the "administrative" burden of everyday life.

Still, software agents "live" in a multi-agent world, so the successful completion of their tasks is subject to the decision and actions of others. On the one hand, agents may interfere with each other due to a mere side-effect of their activities, e.g. when one information agent has to wait for another to finish its library query. On the other hand, interaction can constitute an integral part of the agents' tasks, as in the example of journey negotiation.

Co-ordination, in a sense, occurs when agents adapt their activities in the face of those interactions. The coincidence with the common-sense connotations of the concept of co-ordination becomes clear when the agents' "interests" are not totally antagonistic. In such cases, agents may exploit synergy between their tasks by forming teams (or "coalitions") within which they co-ordinate their actions, so as to improve their joint "utility", i.e. their degree of task achievement. Just imagine information agents whose tasks give rise to identical sub-queries: both can benefit by "splitting up" work and sharing the results of the sub-queries.

So, interacting software agents essentially constitute a *distributed system*: from the stance of an external observer they constitute a group of interacting components that jointly achieve an *added value* (improved performance and/or task achievement) in a process of permanent mutual adaptation (co-ordination). This perspective might be easier to accept when recalling that software agents need not be mobile (as the above example of information agents that travel between libraries suggests), nor does a coalition necessarily have a short-term character. An example is given by software agents that support the flow of work within a company.

In short: co-ordination makes autonomous software agents act as a distributed system. So, an essential part of the question as to whether it is useful to design and co-ordinate groups of autonomous software agents comes down to the motivation for building distributed intelligent systems.

Despite this strong bet of the market for distributed solutions, in the AI community there is an ongoing discussion whether distribution is useful at all. In this controversy, a central argument of the party rejecting distribution is, that everything that can be done by a distributed system can be done with a centralised one as well – with at least the same degree of performance, but usually even more efficiently.

Imagine a distributed system, in which a set of agents (or "programs", "modules" etc.) co-ordinate their activities through a decentralised, distributed mechanism. In a corresponding centralised system, each agent might simply transmit its entire state (or those parts relevant to the co-ordination task) to a central processor, which could then do no worse than replicating the distributed mechanism: it could "simulate" the decentralised co-ordination process and implement its outcome as a central authority. Moreover, the central "co-ordinator" is usually provided with the potential of taking even better decisions than a distributed mechanism, as it can (but need not) ground its choices on a broader basis of knowledge and information.

However, this line of reasoning ignores an important fact: there are problems – and not few – that actually "call for" distributed solutions. Even more: in some classes of domains, the only possible solution is a distributed one.

The point lies in considering intelligent systems as being *situated*, embedded in some sort of environment. In order to cope with certain tasks, designers of traditional AI systems select specific *problem-solving methods* (Puppe 1993) based on certain task characteristics. For instance, for diagnosis tasks "cover-and-differentiate" or "establish-and-refine" methods may be chosen (Benjamins 1993). However, besides the functional characteristics of a task, the environment that a system is situated in implies additional task characteristics that need to be taken into consideration. Specific classes of environments show different forms of natural *a priori distribution*, which imposes additional requirements on both, the way tasks can be achieved as well as the evaluation of the quality of a solution:

- physical requirements
  Many environments show a natural spatial distribution. Intelligent systems embedded in an environment of this characteristic need to perceive their input by physically separated sensors, and to act upon it by means of effectors located at different sites. Telematics applications such as environmental emergency management or road traffic control constitute prominent examples of problem solving under the coercion of spatial distribution (Cuena and Ossowski 1998).

- organisational requirements
  Often, intelligent systems are implanted within the context of an existing human organisation. Human organisations are designed to have or evolve towards a set of structural relationships: power, authority, decision-making responsibility etc. are distributed among the different roles that individuals play within the organisation. Intelligent systems that perform or support tasks within existing organisations need to respect these relations (Vernadat 1996).

Such additional, a priori structures result in a set of constraints, that a designer must keep in mind when building an intelligent system. It is argued that distributed architectures can cope with both of the following types of design constraints:

- soft constraints
  Despite a priori distribution, a centralised solution is possible. However, a distributed architecture is a result of design decisions. Usually, this is justified by the fact that a distributed architecture can achieve a degree of performance that, though not as good as a centralised solution, is sufficient. Still, the cost of design and maintenance of distributed systems is generally much less.

- hard constraints
  The environment imposes exogenous constraints on the design process. Every design solution will have to obey them in order to be considered successful. This is the case when a priori structures require decentralised, distributed task achievement procedures.

This quite abstract line of reasoning will be pinpointed in the following. The potential of distributed intelligent systems is discussed in the light of their advantages in a number of prototypical settings, focusing on three types of restrictions.

Communication Restrictions

The a priori distribution of domains implies that parts of a system to be designed have to reside on different platforms at different locations. As these parts are interdependent, co-ordination is necessary which usually requires communication. However, real-world communication channels have limited bandwidth, a fact which sometimes becomes a decisive design variable.

Good examples of cases where the characteristics of an environment impose limits on communication are autonomous robotic outdoor vehicles. Such vehicles are predominantly acting in hostile environments, which makes communication difficult. Consider, for instance, underwater vehicles. The amount of information that can be exchanged between them is determined by the aquatic medium, which forces them to use low frequency communications offering only limited channel capacity. Furthermore, the case of a group of autonomous land vehicles can be highlighted, that jointly perform surveillance tasks for certain areas in a manoeuvre. They are not allowed to communicate explicitly by radio, as this would reveal their positions to the enemy (Gmytrasiewicz et al. 1991).

Another example is the spatial distribution of sensors and effectors in hydrology telematics domains. Consider, for instance, an intelligent system for predicting floods in a watershed basin. The basin comprises a collection of dams connected by several river links and interconnection channels. Dams offer limited storage capacity and are endowed with gates and spills by means of which water flows can be sent to the network. Rivers and channels are passive entities, at which an overflow occurs when the limits of their capacity are exceeded. In this domain, the task of a the system is to take dam management decisions, on the basis of water level data from measurement points, that prevent channels and rivers from overflowing, while keeping the dams' water storage within the limits of their capacity (Ossowski et al. 1996).

Here, a centralised solution is feasible: all water level data can be communicated from the different measurement points to a monolithic system that performs predictions respecting potential emergencies. Dam management decisions are generated to avoid such situations, and the corresponding commands are communicated to the dams' spill gates (e.g. the SIRAH system described in Cuena et al. 1992). However, an important factor for the overall cost of the system lies in the construction and maintenance of a radio communication network, which offers a sufficient bandwidth for the transmission of sensor data and commands. It is justified to believe that a distributed solution reduces this cost significantly.

Access Restrictions

Besides bandwidth limitations of communication channels, access restrictions constitute another reason for the unavailability of information relevant to co-ordination. Such a situation is present when enterprises seek synergies by limited co-operation, e.g. by jointly administering their logistics. This will be illustrated in the domain of multi-enterprise manufacturing scheduling (Sandholm 1996).

Imagine a situation in which several companies build up a (temporal) consortium for jointly producing certain goods that require massive capital investments and production capacities. They aim to design a computer system that builds up, co-ordinates and maintains (interdependent) production schedules for each involved production site of the different companies. This task includes choosing between alternative production variants as well as assigning human resources, lattices and execution times to production steps. The schedules need to be updated continuously due to the occurrence of unexpected events such as breakdowns of machines etc.

This problem cannot be solved in a way acceptable to the underlying organisations by building a centralised monolithic manufacturing scheduling system. Both companies will not provide each other with (potentially sensitive) information about their production program. They will neither permit the other to produce a complete schedule for their production factors, thus ceding an important power of influence about their production. The problem requires a distributed solution: the sites construct their own local schedules and adapt them via negotiation so as to obtain a co-ordinated global schedule.

A similar scenario illustrates the use of access restrictions as a design decision. In multi-site scheduling, one big manufacturing firm has the production of items dispersed over several sites. Often, in such an organisation, one plant is the supplier of items used in another one, so that, as in the above example, schedules need to be co-ordinated, taking into account transportation time and costs etc. (Bel and Thierry 1993).

Imagine the case where one old plant is already using a manufacturing scheduler in the frame of a traditional closed information system. It is expensive to modify such a closed application in order to make relevant data accessible to a new company-wide system: much effort and money need to be invested in order to translate between data models or to upgrade the information system. Instead, a designer might prefer not to touch existing information technology and to integrate and co-ordinate old and new schedulers by means of a distributed mechanism such as co-operative negotiation.

Decision-Making Restrictions

Finally, the structure of existing organisations imposes restrictions on the decision-making processes that an intelligent system might perform or take part in.

Consider, for instance, the case of a hospital. Patients reside in *units* that are organised by branches of medicine, such as orthopaedics or neurosurgery. Each day, physicians request certain tests and therapies to be performed as a part of the diagnosis and treatment of a patient. Tests are performed by separate, independent *ancillary departments* in the hospital. The radiology department, for example, provides X-ray services and may receive requests from a number of different units in the hospital. Furthermore, tests are interdependent: some of them may be preconditions for others; the completion of one test may invalidate the result of another etc. These interactions need to be taken into account when scheduling the activities within the hospital. Note, however, that the units are interested in minimising the patients' stays in the hospital, while the ancillary departments try to maximise equipment use (throughput) and minimise set-up times (Decker 1995, Decker and Li 1998).

The point is that no centralised computer system can provide an automated solution to that scheduling task because the humans involved try to preserve their autonomy, and will not cede their authority to a central administrator. Still, the groups they belong to are actually attempting to maximise different sets of (par-

Table 1.1. Distribution and design

	design constraint	design decision
communication	autonomous vehicles	flood prediction
access rights	multi-enterprise scheduling	multi-site scheduling
decision-making	hospital scheduling	traffic management
	workflow management	workflow management

tially conflicting) performance criteria. So, there is a need for finding a compromise in the frame of distributed co-ordination.

Another example domain is business process management. Workflow management systems, for instance, render support to the articulation of organisational work processes in order to foster the "smooth flow of work" within the organisation. Models of routine processes are usually instantiated before enactment by a centralised workflow engine, making binding commitments concerning all relevant aspects of the constituent tasks. The engine is then in charge of monitoring process enactment, transferring items between work cells etc.

The success of this approach has been limited, as in real organisations activities take place semi-autonomously, and centralised control is rarely possible or socially desirable. Firstly, workflow management systems are usually *too prescriptive* for human actors, as they "over-specify" their work. Support systems frequently impose new (presumably "better") ways of doing things, which is alien to the actors' own methods of organising their work. Secondly, they are *inflexible* with respect to exception handling and "on-line" adaptation to changing circumstances. As the work of all the actors needs to be specified in a fine-grained fashion, unexpected events imply a considerable amount of changes in the workflow, which may exceed the computational capacity of a central co-ordinator (Ossowski and García-Serrano 1996). Similar arguments hold for assisting humans doing concurrent engineering of hardware or software. No engineer will want to be told exactly what to do and exactly when, especially by a computer system (Bowers and Benford 1991).

A last example, illustrating distribution as the outcome of design decisions, draws on the domain of road transport telematics. Imagine a traffic network in a city where junctions, equipped with traffic lights, are connected by street sections with limited capacity. An intelligent control system influences traffic flows by modifying the traffic lights' green times for the different directions, as well as through messages on panels that inform drivers of the network situation downstream. The goal of such a system is to foster swift traffic flow and to guarantee upper limits to the sizes of queues at the accesses to junctions (Ossowski et al. 1996).

Again, decision-making by a monolithic controller is feasible and efficient as long as the number of traffic agents is small (Cuena et al. 1995, 1996). However, as the size of traffic control systems grows, building up and maintaining large knowledge bases for co-ordination becomes an extremely difficult and *expensive*

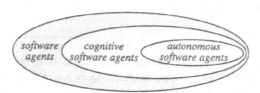

Figure 1.1. Agent types
(adapted from Conte and Castelfranchi, 1995)

task. A distributed mechanism constitutes an alternative: it may provide a basic level of "emergent" co-ordination on top of which refinements can be made, using explicit co-ordination knowledge.

Table 1.1 summarises the above examples: it outlines the potentials of distributed approach for building intelligent systems.

1.2 Scope

The work presented in this book is situated within the area of Distributed Artificial Intelligence (DAI). It is concerned with the problem of co-ordinating intelligent agents, which is one of *the* classical problems within DAI. Still, the area is rapidly expanding and a great variety of diverging currents have come up, so it is convenient to confine the scope of this work.

This section draws a line between those aspects of DAI to be tackled and research lines that are outside the scope of this book. We will do this by characterising the type of agents and the type of societies that we are studying. Table 1.2 resumes our (necessarily incomplete) classification, which will be discussed in the sequel.

The essentials of agenthood will not be discussed in this book, nor will we enter the controversy respecting the concise delimitation of agents and "non-agents" (e.g. mere programs). In much the same way, we will not join in the discussions respecting the use of the qualification "intelligent" with respect to agents. Still, some agent characteristics actually *are* useful. They are organised in a simple taxonomy depicted by Figure 1.1.

First of all, this work deals with *software* agents. It is concerned with programs, pieces of software, that perceive and manipulate some environment. This environment may be either the real world or some simulated setting.

It does *not* pay attention to embodied agents. It is not concerned with agents that have some "physical" existence such as robots. In particular, it does not intend to contribute to the solution of the "classical" problems of embodied agents, such as vision or navigation in real-world environments.

Table 1.2. Scope of this book

within scope	outside scope
software agents	embodied agents (e.g. robots)
cognitive agents	sub-cognitive agents (e.g. AL agents)
autonomous agents	pre-determined agents (e.g. DPS agents)
persistent society structure	dynamic society structure (e.g. open systems)

However, we will borrow from some results within this area, as many of the problems that embodied agents face also come up in the area of software agents, though in a much simpler fashion. Just consider, for example, the need of software agents to interpret "sensory" data from its environment or the need for timely reaction to environmental events.

Secondly, we are concerned with deliberative or *cognitive* agents. A cognitive agent uses its sensory input to build up and maintain a symbolic model of the world. It is endowed with an explicit representation of "goals" or tasks, which determine the agent's actions in the course of some logical reasoning processes.

So, this book does *not* deal with sub-cognitive agents, whose state cannot immediately be related to the situation of the outside world and whose state changes follow much simpler rules than those of "logical reasoning" (e.g. neuronal nets, parallel genetic algorithms etc.). Research in the area of Artificial Life (AL), which studies emergent properties of sub-cognitive agents, is outside the scope of this work.

However, the notion of *emergence* is relevant for this work[1]. We are concerned with how to design societies of cognitive agents, so as to endow the collective of agents with the capability of performing tasks that no single agent is able to attain by itself.

Thirdly, we study *autonomous* agents, i.e. agents that make "their own decisions" respecting which goals and tasks to attain and how to pursue them[2]. Needless to say, talking about choice in relation with machines is a dangerous issue: in the end, the actions that software agents take are governed by their "agent program" that simply unfolds the pre-compiled choice of its designer. Still, given a set of alternatives, we expect an autonomous agent to select the option that achieves the maximum expected benefit *for itself* (with respect to some measure

---

[1] The notion of emergence is being applied indiscriminately to denote a variety of different phenomena. In this book, we are concerned with "layered emergence": a property is emergent if it can be attributed to an entity at some level of complexity or abstraction, but cannot be detected at lower levels (Conte and Gilbert 1995).

[2] There are many connotations to the concept of autonomy, from adaptivity and belief-revision to the notion of "self-interested" choice presented here. Furthermore, a realistic determination of the term will probably not conceive it as an exclusive qualification but as a continuum: there are different degrees and levels of autonomy (Castelfranchi 1995). Still, the term is in steady use in the DAI community and it is useful to delimit the class of agents that we are interested in. Autonomous agenthood will be discussed at length in Chapter 3.

of utility such as the achievement of tasks or goals). The point is that such "self-interested" choice may be contrary to a certain functionality or welfare of a society of agents.

This becomes clearer when applied to the problem of co-ordination. This book is *not* primarily about designing patterns of agent interactions that achieve global co-ordination, and "building" such pre-compiled co-operative behaviour into the agents: agents are not assumed to be pre-determined to co-ordinate their behaviour. So, for instance, groups of benevolent agents, which are usually applied in traditional Distributed Problem Solving (DPS) systems, will not be studied.

Still, we are interested in mechanisms that constrain the agents' choice. Needless to say, in a multi-agent system the autonomy of an agent, however smart it may be, is not infinite but bounded by the choices and actions of other agents. This book is concerned with designing mechanisms that bias the choices of autonomous agents so as to make them instrumental for achieving co-ordination.

Finally, the present work assumes agent societies of *persistent* structure. The designer has full control over the "types" of agents that constitute a system and determines the structural relationships between them. These structural relationships shape the *problem-solving* capabilities of the society, so they are assumed to remain stable over time.

This book does *not* deal with designing conventions to assure desired properties within agent societies of *dynamic* structure. It is not concerned with protocols and incentive structures that make it "irrational" for autonomous agents to act malevolently. For instance, the question of regulations for open systems is not tackled: we do not study the circumstances under which it is counterproductive for a designer to endow its software agent with the capability to "lie", although it acts in an open environment where agents come and go and the chance to "meet again" is scarce.

Still, we *do* make use of prescriptions as part of a mechanism to attain desired global properties, namely co-ordinated task-achieving action. However, within the frame of this mechanism we assume agents to behave "sincerely" and "legally": agents neither try to manipulate others by deliberately emitting incorrect information, nor do they intend to transgress the imperatives that prescriptions impose on them.

1.3 Scientific Objectives

This book explores the potential of a distributed, agent-based approach to the design of intelligent systems: it aims at examining the characteristics of systems of software agents that interact in order to solve a given problem. The essential problem of such a setting is to ensure co-ordination of the activities of the agents that constitute the distributed system. Therefore, the fundamental interest lies in the study of distributed intelligent systems and their relation to agent co-ordination from the perspective of system design.

Although questions concerning distribution as an external a priori constraint are relevant to this work, its major concern is to examine distribution as a *design parameter*: we aim to find out as to how far an agent-based stance can provide an *added value* for application design. By making the decision to construct an intelligent application based on the multi-agent paradigm, we endeavour to achieve the following properties:

- economy
  In the previous section, we have provided examples of domains where a distributed agent-based approach leads to an economic design. This is due to the re-use of existing resources, of both physical (e.g. hardware) or immaterial (e.g. software) nature. In addition, an agent-based design can avoid investments in new resources; again, either due to physical (e.g. less communication bandwidth) or immaterial reasons (e.g. less knowledge acquisition). Note that this also favours a system's *scalability*.

- plausibility
  A distributed system of autonomous agents can be conceived as a society of agents, so that it is natural to seek its underpinning in human societies. By this it is possible to "rationalise" structure and dynamics of such a distributed system using concepts and theories that get a hold in reality, which helps to understand and communicate about its behaviour and architecture. So, among others, an increased plausibility contributes to the system's *maintainability*.

- efficiency
  A distributed system is structured in line with the set of agents that it comprises. These agents constitute a set of modules with well-defined interfaces; a fact that fosters *maintainability* and *reuse*. The same argument implies that modules can run simultaneously in order to increase system performance. This is especially true if the different modules execute on different machines.

- robustness
  A distributed approach shows graceful degradation of performance as certain functions are replicated among agents: in case of the breakdown of one agent, another can take over its tasks. By this, the existence of bottleneck components in the system can be avoided.

Still, this potential added value of a multi-agent design can only be evaluated in relation to the co-ordination overhead that a distributed approach implies. Characteristics such as economy, plausibility, efficiency and robustness are only relevant when a co-ordination model with similar properties assures a sufficient degree of problem-solving *quality*.

A model co-ordination must integrate both aspects: to attain an acceptable performance *and* to preserve the above characteristics. Consequently, it needs be:

- decentralised
  In order to maintain architectural advantages such as efficiency and robustness, the co-ordination task needs to be distributed among the agents in much the same way as the problem-solving activities. There shall be no distinguished agents in charge of (centralised) co-ordination.

- emergent
  Economic advantages can just be maintained when distributed co-ordination does not rely on great amounts of (centralised) co-ordination knowledge. So, the co-ordination model shall not replicate a central mechanism among many agents, but rely on a "conceptually distributed" mechanism. Just as in real societies, co-ordination shall *emerge* from such a mechanism. Consequently, the amount of knowledge acquisition that this mechanism requires shall not exceed the needs of a centralised co-ordination approach.

In short: we want to develop a decentralised mechanism that allows for emergent co-ordination among autonomous agents, so as to come up with an operational problem-solving society capable of attaining desired tasks. Let us nail down this aim in further detail, examining it from different perspectives:

- conceptual perspective
  The main *conceptual objective* of this work is to head towards a model of a *social intelligence*, a society of autonomous problem-solving agents from whose interactions co-ordinated activities emerge. So, at the macro-level, a social co-ordination mechanism is to be developed that involves autonomous agents in a decentralised co-ordination process; at the micro-level, a model of autonomous agent behaviour is to be given that reconciles co-ordination towards a global functionality and local autonomy.

- formal perspective
  We aim to ground our operational model of co-ordination on *descriptive* theories respecting co-ordination in human societies. So, in order to avoid conceptual fuzziness, the above conceptual model needs to be complemented with a certain degree of formalisation. At the micro-level, this requires a formal description of the behaviour laws that govern the individual agent's behaviour. In particular, a precise specification of the strategy that an agent applies in social interaction with others is to be given, as this is the decisive factor of co-ordination. Furthermore, a formal framework for analysing the co-ordination process at the macro-level is desirable.

- practical perspective
  Although our primary aim is not to solve a particular problem but to develop a model of decentralised and emergent co-ordination for a *class* of domains, it is important to make models operational in order to check their validity. So, at the micro-level, agents as the essential "material" part of the social intelligence need to be given a computational shape. An *agent architecture* is to be devel-

oped that implements the local behaviour rules of an agent so as to support the co-ordination process. At the macro-level, it has to be shown that the co-ordination mechanism achieves an adequate degree of co-ordination. For this purpose, the above agent architecture should be used as the fundament of a multi-agent system that attacks a real-world problem.

In the present work, the domain of intelligent traffic management has been chosen to validate our approach. A multi-agent system will be designed which makes use of the decentralised and emergent co-ordination mechanism in order to manage traffic flows within an urban motorway network.

1.4 Terminological Remarks

In this book, we will develop a co-ordination model of collections of intelligent agents. These agents will be implemented on networked computer systems, i.e. in the end they turn into pieces of computer software. The area of intelligent traffic control serves as an application domain to demonstrate the effectiveness of the co-ordination model: a "physical" domain whose basic ontology refers to quite "inanimate" entities such as loop detectors, streams of traffic flows and message panels. Nevertheless, we will describe the structure of the agent co-ordination model as well as its performance in traffic control using a "mentalistic" terminology including commitments, obligations, social interaction etc.. This deserves some explanation.

As an interdisciplinary discipline, research in AI has always suffered and profited from a dual character. On the one hand, AI research is done with *descriptive* objectives: cognitive scientists, physiologists, biologists, neuroscientists etc. observe the diverse phenomena related to the notion of intelligence and build up theories that account for relevant characteristics. It has become a common practice to simulate (parts of) those theories on computer systems in order to provide evidence in their favour or reasons for their falsification. On the other, AI research is driven by *prescriptive* motives: from an engineering point of view, the former theories are interesting as sources of mechanisms, tools and metaphors that contribute to the *design* of systems that actually *solve problems*. For instance, models from genetics constitute the basis of genetic algorithms and genetic programming; models from neuroscience have given rise to neuronal networks. This book takes the latter stance: we are concerned with co-ordinating autonomous agents to make them solve problems jointly.

Many AI architectures for individual agents draw on psychological findings. So, for instance, referring to the "goals" of an AI system is a common practice nowadays. McCarthy (1979) has been reflecting on the general question as to how far a rich mentalistic vocabulary can or should be applied to machines:

> To ascribe certain *beliefs, free will, intentions, consciousness, abilities* or *wants* to a machine or computer program is *legitimate* when such ascription expresses the same infor-

> mation about the machine that it expresses about a person. It is *useful* when the ascrip-
> tion helps us understand the structure of the machine, its past or future behaviour, or
> how to repair or improve it. It is perhaps never *logically required* even for humans, but
> expressing reasonably briefly what is actually known about the state of the machine in a
> particular situation may require mental qualities or qualities isomorphic to them.

The above quotation expresses quite well the motivation for using mentalistic notions within this book. Agents and co-ordination mechanisms are studied by taking an intentional stance (Dennet 1987): it is not relevant whether agents really have certain mental qualities (most probably they will not). The designer just takes the standpoint of an observer in order to model agents, *ascribing* mental qualities to them, as this is believed to be an adequate set of metaphors to characterise agent behaviour (Shoham 1993).

This book aims at studying autonomous agents ("social minds") in the frame of a society that shows certain functional characteristics: cognitive agents refer to others, so as to organise and solve problems which are beyond their individual capabilities. This objective determines the *type* of mentalistic terms that we will make use of. Throughout this book evidence will be provided for the appropriateness of using terms like commitment, obligations, conventions and norms for guiding the design of such agents and their interactions.

1.5 Organisation of the Book

The book comprises ten chapters and two appendices. This introduction is followed by the main body that comprises three major parts.

Part I describes the background of this work. Chapter 2 is dedicated to the phenomenon of co-ordination in human societies and its models in Social Science. Some formal and informal characterisations and models are sketched. Chapter 3 is concerned with the role of co-ordination in DAI. An overview of DAI research is given, paying special attention to aspects of co-ordination. Chapter 4 concludes Part I, presenting a critical analysis of the state of the art.

The second part presents the main theoretical contribution of this work. It is dedicated to the description, formalisation and instrumentation of the mechanism of structural co-operation, which allows for the emergence of co-ordination among autonomous problem-solving agents by designing adequate normative structures. Chapter 5 introduces the mechanism of structural co-operation with respect to the reactive co-ordination problem that we are concerned with. Chapter 6 provides a formal description by relating structural co-operation to bargaining theory. Chapter 7 presents the ProsA$_2$ agent architecture which supports the realisation of structural co-operation in societies of autonomous problem-solving agents. Special emphasis is put on the social interaction strategies of ProsA$_2$ agents, as they constitute the key aspect in the instrumentation of the mechanism.

Part III demonstrates structural co-operation in the domain of intelligent road transport management. Chapter 8 describes the TRYS family of traffic control systems, and outlines how the application of the ProsA$_2$ architecture to TRYS agents gives rise to a multi-agent traffic control architecture. Chapter 9 applies this architecture to a case study, the management of road traffic in a particular urban motorway network, and highlights the role of structural co-operation in the co-ordination of traffic agents.

The book is completed by Chapter 10, which discusses the contributions of the work and presents conclusions.

2 Co-ordination

Co-ordination is being studied by a variety of scientific disciplines. Sociologists observe the behaviour of groups of people, identify particular co-ordination mechanisms and explain how and why they emerge. Economists are concerned with structure and dynamics of the market as a particular co-ordination mechanism. In organisational theory, the emphasis is on predicting future behaviour and performance of an organisation, assuming the validity of a certain co-ordination mechanism. Finally, Distributed Artificial Intelligence is primarily concerned with *designing* co-ordination mechanisms for groups of artificial agents.

This chapter aims at providing a birds-eye-view of the phenomenon of co-ordination within *human* society. A detailed discussion of the role that co-ordination plays in Distributed Artificial Intelligence, which deals with societies of *artificial* agents, is postponed to the next chapter.

Section 2.1 approaches the subject under study providing an informal characterisation of the co-ordination problem. Section 2.2 is dedicated to descriptive models of co-ordination, drawing essentially on findings in organisational science. Finally, Section 2.3 is concerned with formal models of the phenomenon: basic game theoretic notions are introduced in order to pinpoint central problems of the co-ordination process.

2.1 An Informal Characterisation

Co-ordination is an elusive concept. Almost everybody has an intuitive sense of what the word co-ordination means, as it is present in almost every situation of our lives. Holt (1988) stresses that good co-ordination is almost invisible: watching a winning soccer team, people usually take the co-ordination of the players for granted, instead of wondering how well the players are co-ordinated. The effects of the absence of co-ordination, however, are immediately perceived by everyone: when people spend hours waiting for the bus or when they arrive at a hotel and their reservation has been given away, several, not always friendly comments come up.

Such intuitive notions of co-ordination are attractive but insufficient for scientific study; a definition of the concept of co-ordination is needed. Due to the different epistemological interests in different disciplines, it does not surprise that there is a variety of diverging viewpoints respecting when and how the term co-ordination should be used. In the following, some definitions are quoted in order to flesh out basic characteristics of co-ordination.

- With co-ordination some higher degree of complexity is achieved:

    Co-ordination is a kind of dynamic glue that binds tasks together into larger meaningful wholes (Holt 1988).

    The operation of complex systems made up of components (National Science Foundation, quoted in Malone and Crowston 1994).

- This complexity is achieved by structuring mutually constraining entities into a whole, whose salient features are instrumental with respect to some goal or functionality:

    The integration and harmonious adjustment of individual work efforts towards the accomplishment of a larger goal (B. Singh 1992).

    The act of managing interdependencies between activities performed to achieve a goal (Malone and Crowston 1990).

    Co-ordination is a way of adapting to the environment (von Martial 1992).

- Often (but not always) co-ordination involves multiple actors. It entails a certain overhead, which frequently manifests itself by communication between actors:

    The additional information processing performed when multiple, connected actors pursue goals that a single actor pursuing the same goal could not perform (Malone 1988).

On the basis of the above quotations, a first informal characterisation can be summarised as follows: the *co-ordination problem* consists in *composing* (relating, harmonising, adjusting, integrating) some *co-ordination objects* (tasks, goals, decisions, activities, plans) with respect to some *co-ordination direction* (goal, functionality). One or several actors are involved in the *co-ordination process,* which solve the co-ordination problem by composing co-ordination objects in line with the co-ordination direction.

2.2 Analytic Models

This section illustrates these rather abstract definitions by relating them to models of complex human activities. Such activities are based on two fundamental prerequisites: the division of labour into different tasks on the one hand, and their co-ordination on the other. An organisation is the framework within which co-ordination is realised. So, we will have a closer look at models from organisational theory.

Organisational theory focuses on the structure of human organisations and its effect on the co-ordination of organisational processes. On the one hand it is concerned with describing and classifying organisational co-ordination, on the other it aims to provide guidelines on how organisations should be designed (e.g. Mintzberg 1988) and to characterise their performance in different classes of situations (e.g. Malone 1987).

Decker (1995) identifies four major lines in organisation research, according to the organisational features that prevail in the analysis:

- The *rational systems view* highlights an organisation's normative structure with respect to the specific organisational goals. Individuals are supposed to behave in accordance with the rules of the normative structure, which determines roles and interactions separately from the attributes of the individuals occupying those roles.
- The *natural systems view* points out that organisations are made up of people, not norm abiding automatons. This fact has an important impact on the operation of every organisation, as informal structures emerge that often compete with formal prescriptions. However, apparently "irrational" behaviour within the informal structure is not always dysfunctional, but may lead to a more robust organisation.
- The *open systems view* stresses the environment that an organisation is embedded in. The organisation is in continuous interactions with the environment: organisation members come and go, resources are consumed and produced etc.. Differentiation and integration in the organisational structure are seen as the organisation's response to environmental features, uncertainties and contingencies.
- The *economic systems view* explains organisational structures in terms of the interests of the different individuals that comprise it. The driving force of co-ordination is the maximisation of the "utilities" of the different organisation members.

However, there is a common agreement that there is no best way to organise: the effectiveness of organisational structures and co-ordination mechanisms depends on the specific context in which the organisation is placed.

2.2.1 Organisational Interdependencies

A common approach towards organisational co-ordination is to consider the very problem of co-ordination as being caused by organisational interdependencies and to conceive co-ordination behaviour as the organisation's response to those problems (Crowston 1994). According to the objects between which they arise, Mintzberg (1988) proposes four classes of interdependencies:

- Workflow interdependencies refer to activities that achieve a task.
- Process interdependencies occur between activities that are part of different workflows.
- Interdependencies of scale are present between similar activities that might be more efficient if they were grouped together.

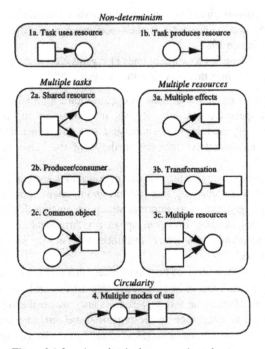

Figure 2.1. Interdependencies between tasks and resources

- Social interdependencies comprise subjective factors such as social needs or different personalities that determine the relation between workers.

An efficient organisational structure avoids harmful and exploits beneficial interdependencies, while providing the means to cope with interdependencies that emerge dynamically.

Much work has studied co-ordination from the perspective of managing interdependencies between activities. For instance, Thompson (1967) classifies interdependencies according to increasing strength in three classes: *pooled*, where activities access a common resource, *sequential*, where the initiation of some activity depends on the completion of another and *reciprocal*, where activities mutually serve each other as input. Crowston (1994) presents a semi-formal framework in which interdependencies arise between tasks (activities) and resources or vice versa: interrelation between two activities is conceived as the consequence of accessing a common limited resource.

Figure 2.1 shows Crowston's taxonomy of interdependencies in graphical terms: arrows depict the set of possible interdependencies between tasks (circles) and resources (boxes). In the same report, he illustrates the different types of interdependencies by examples and discusses their specific problems.

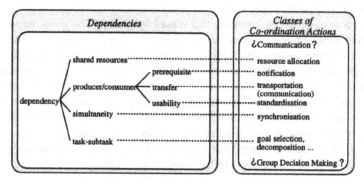

Figure 2.2. An abstract view of co-ordination

2.2.2   Organisational Co-ordination Mechanisms

There have also been many attempts to describe co-ordination mechanisms that manage interdependencies. Thompson (1967) sees three modes of co-ordinating work activities: *impersonal* (plans and rules), *personal* (vertical supervision) and *group* (formal and informal meetings). Van de Ven, Delbecq and Koenig add a fourth one, *team arrangements*, in which tasks are worked on simultaneously rather than being passed back and forth (see Crowston 1994). Mintzberg (1988) describes a similar set of co-ordination mechanisms: *mutual adjustment* between workers is achieved through informal communication. In *direct supervision*, one person is made responsible for the work of others. *Standardisation* provides norms concerning how things should be done typically; it may refer to work processes, to outcomes of tasks as well as to descriptions of posts. All these co-ordination mechanisms can also be used for managing groups of activities: sets of activities with strong interdependencies can be summarised in the same group, thus minimising inter-group dependencies.

Malone and Crowston (1994) present a good summary of the many works that adhere to this perspective of co-ordination. Setting out from examples from a variety of disciplines, different kinds of interdependencies between organisational activities are characterised, and different co-ordination processes are identified to manage them. Figure 2.2 depicts the above framework graphically. Dependencies are organised in four major groups:

- shared resources dependencies
  This dependency is present between multiple activities, if they need to access a common limited resource. It is managed by *resource allocation actions*. Malone and Crowston see task assignment as a special kind of resource allocation, because "the scarce time of actors" is allocated to the tasks they perform.

- producer/consumer dependencies
  One activity produces something that is used by another. This gives rise to different dependencies: *prerequisite constraints* are found when one activity has to end before another can begin. The corresponding co-ordination action is a *notification process*, by means of which the first activity informs the second about its termination. *Transfer relationships* arise when one activity produces something that is used by another. In these cases, *transportation actions* have to be performed, that move the resource between the activities. If the produced entity is information, this transfer act is called a *communication process*. *Usability constraints* determine that whatever is produced should be usable by the receiving activity. One way to achieve this is *standardisation*.

- simultaneity dependencies
  Often two activities are mutually exclusive in the sense that they cannot be performed at the same time. As a result, *synchronisation actions* should be undertaken, that restrict the periods in which the activities can occur.

- task/sub-task dependencies
  This dependency exists when a group of activities accomplishes sub-tasks that jointly attain some overall goal. Typical co-ordination actions include *goal selection, goal decomposition* etc.

Finally, important co-ordination processes are identified, that cannot be unambiguously assigned to specific dependencies:

- group decision making
  Many co-ordination processes require decision making that affects the activities of the group. This becomes apparent, for example, when there is a need to choose between several alternative co-ordination actions. Malone and Crowston subdivide group decision making in three classes: authority, voting or consensus (i.e. negotiation leading to mutual accord).

- communication
  Communication is present in almost every co-ordination process. By considering alternative forms of communication (paper vs. electronic etc.), different instances of co-ordination processes are generated.

2.2.3 Formal and Informal Organisation

Traditionally, research has focused on the formal structure of an organisation, aimed at optimising the organisational performance in a certain environment with respect to a set of objectives . However, organisational studies have revealed that informal structures usually arise analogous to the formal structure and that they change dynamically (e.g. Wöhe 1986).

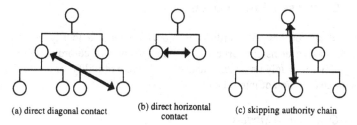

(a) direct diagonal contact   (b) direct horizontal contact   (c) skipping authority chain

Figure 2.3. Types of informal structures

There are essentially two reasons for informal structures to come up within an organisation. The first lies in the fact that organisational processes are too complicated to be controlled totally in advance, especially with concern to unexpected change: if reglementations are obeyed meticulously, the result is chaos. A second motive goes back to social needs of individuals: people need to relate to each other in order to be content with their work. Mintzberg (1988) identifies three types of informal structures, depicted in Figure 2.3.

Case (a) depicts the case where an individual with a certain level of authority directly communicates with the subordinate of an acquaintance of the same authority level. In case (b), two workers directly communicate with each other, instead of doing it through the authority, thus substituting formal authority by informal mutual adaptation. Finally, case (c) allows for the direct transmission of information by skipping the authority level of a directive.

The distinctions between formal and informal organisation go in lines with the notions of *bureaucracy* and *organic* structures. A bureaucracy provides norms for organisational behaviour, limiting its variability by prescribing standard procedures. By this, processes can be predicted and controlled. Contrary to this, organic structures determine open and informal relations, where problems are solved when they come up, in an "ad-hoc" fashion, through mutual adaptation. According to the environments an organisation is embedded in, bureaucratic or organic structures prevail. However, both are important for an organisation's effectiveness.

2.3 Formal Approaches

Ambiguity lies in the nature of informal characterisations presented in Section 2.1. For exact scientific work, this is an unsatisfactory situation. The descriptive models of the last section give an idea of what co-ordination in "real life" is about, but we still lack a formal definition of the essentials of co-ordination problems. In the sequel, we will characterise the problem at hand by relating it to well-known problems and mathematical frameworks.

2.3.1   Centralised Co-ordination

Centralised approaches to co-ordination model a central authority, which is in charge of making decisions respecting the composition of co-ordination objects. Usually, either they rely on some quantitative measure of utility, or they are based on a qualitative notion of interrelation.

2.3.1.1 Quantitative Models

The quantitative point of view sees co-ordination as a factor whose presence increases some abstract measure of value or utility. The underlying idea is that certain compositions of co-ordination objects are more useful than others with respect to the co-ordination direction and that this usefulness can be expressed in units of "utility".

Formally, such an account describes an *optimisation problem*. The co-ordination objects are represented by decision variables v_i, each with an associated domain D_i. The outcome of the co-ordination process (a composition of co-ordination objects) is modelled as an *instantiation* x of the decision variables v_i, i.e. as an assignment of a unique domain value out of D_i for each variable v_i. The *decision space* comprises all possible compositions of co-ordination objects and is thus defined as the set X of instantiations. A utility function models the co-ordination direction, by mapping each instantiation to a real number. So, the co-ordination problem can be defined as a triple (V,D,U), comprising

- a finite set of *variables* $V = \{v_1,...,v_n\}$,
- a set of *domains* $D = \{D_1,...,D_n\}$,
- a *utility function* $U : X \rightarrow \Re$.

A solution to the co-ordination problem consists in any instantiation $\hat{x} \in X$, such that

$$\forall x \in X. \quad U(x) \leq U(\hat{x}),$$

that is, in a composition of co-ordination objects that is "optimal" with respect to the utility function.

2.3.1.2 Qualitative Models

In the above model, the structure of the co-ordination problem is hidden in the shape of the utility function. Contrary to this, qualitative approaches explicitly model some of the "reasons" that underlie the varying adequacy of different compositions of co-ordination objects with respect to the co-ordination direction: when co-ordination objects are composed, they interact; and when this interaction has an effect on the co-ordination direction, it is termed *dependency*. These dependencies can foster or hamper co-ordination. Still, in the co-ordination process both classes of dependencies need to be taken into account.

It is straightforward to model this approach as a *Constraint Satisfaction Problem*, by substituting the utility function U by a set C of *constraints* that represent dependencies. Constraints are logical formulae over the decision variables. So, a dependency-based model is given by a triple (V,D,C), comprising

- a finite set of *variables* $V = \{v_1,...,v_n\}$,
- a set of *domains* $D = \{D_1,...,D_n\}$,
- a finite set of *constraints* $C = \{C_1,...,C_m\}$.

An instantiation x is *consistent*, if it complies with all dependencies, that is, if it is a model of the corresponding constraint formulae. The co-ordination process consists in finding a consistent instantiation of decision variables, i.e. an assignment $\hat{x} \in X$ of domain values to the variables, such that

$$\hat{x} \vDash C_1 \wedge ... \wedge C_m .$$

2.3.2 Decentralised Co-ordination

The above models set out from an ideal situation in which a central "authority" prescribes co-ordination towards some global objective. However, in real societies and organisations this is usually not the case, as co-ordination is further constrained by the fact that they are made up of self-interested individuals with (at least partially) conflicting interests. In such a situation, a solution to a co-ordination problem constitutes an *equilibrium*, a compromise that assures somehow "maximal" attainment of the different interests of all involved individuals. However, determining the meaning of this maximality in more detail turns out to be a tricky problem. Game theoretic frameworks provide the formal tools for such an enterprise.

2.3.2.1 The Notion of Games

Game theory aims to model individually rational choice in the presence of other rational agents (e.g. Owen 1995). It provides answers to the question which action is "best" for a self-interested individual, in relation to the potential actions of its acquaintances. The term *game* is used to characterise situations of rational interaction in a generic way. Co-ordination objects are modelled by *strategies*. Each individual involved in the game is provided with its personal *payoff* function. These functions assign utility values to sets of strategies, representing the individuals' degree of satisfaction with the corresponding composition of co-ordination objects.

For the purpose of this chapter, we define a game Γ in normal form as a triple (I,S,P), being

- I a set of n players ,
- S the space of joint strategies, $S = S_1 \times ... \times S_n$, where each player chooses from a finite set of individual strategies $S_i = \sigma_{i_1}, ..., \sigma_{i_m}$,
- P a set of payoff functions P_i for each player, each of which of the form $P_i : S \rightarrow \Re$.

Two-player games that allow only finite numbers of alternative strategies for each player can be summarised in a *game matrix*. This is achieved by explicitly listing the payoffs of each player for all the possible combination of strategies: rows represent the alternative strategies of the first player while columns denote the choices of the second player; matrix cells contain a pair of numbers, indicating the payoff for any one player.

The common-sense meaning of the term "game" is usually captured by *zero-sum games*, where one player always loses exactly what the other wins, that is

$$\forall \sigma \in S. \quad \sum_{i=1}^{n} P_i(\sigma) = 0 .$$

Looking at the payoff functions in two-person zero-sum games, it becomes obvious that in this class of games the players' interests are totally antagonistic:

$$\forall (\sigma_1, \sigma_2) \in S. \quad P_1(\sigma_1, \sigma_2) = -P_2(\sigma_1, \sigma_2) .$$

In two player zero-sum games it is rational for self-interested players to maximise their minimum payoff (maximin criterion): if one player takes a certain action, the opponent will react with its "best" actions, which, due to the zero-sum characteristics of the game, will result in the minimum outcome for the player.

2.3.2.2 Partially Conflictive Games

Co-ordination becomes relevant in *non-constant sum games*, as they represent situations in which the interests of the players are not totally antagonistic[1]. They are defined as follows:

$$\exists \sigma, \sigma' \in S. \quad \sum_{i=1}^{n} P_i(\sigma) \neq \sum_{i=1}^{n} P_i(\sigma').$$

So, from the point of view of the group, at least one strategy combination is better than another. Note that the optimisation problem of the previous section can be modelled as a non-constant sum game with perfect coincidence of the players' interests. This is the case when players are given identical payoff functions, i.e.

$$\forall i, j \in I \; \forall \sigma \in S. \quad P_i(\sigma) = P_j(\sigma) .[2]$$

---

[1] In fact, co-ordination already plays an important role in zero-sum games of more than two players.

[2] Team theory examines this case: agents share a common payoff function but do not have access to all relevant information about the world (Marshak and Radner 1972).

Partially conflictive scenarios with a potential for co-operation can be analysed from two different perspectives. One option is to assume that players mistrust others and try to get the best out of the situation despite the existence of others. As an alternative, one can assume that agents make a binding agreement to co-ordinate strategies.

Non-Cooperative Analysis

In the non-cooperative variant of non-constant sum games absolutely no pre-play communication is permitted to agree upon joint strategies and players' payoffs are unalterably determined by the rules of the games. In order to define "rational" solutions to these games, the maximin criterion is substituted by the following more appropriate notion: a set of strategies σ^* is called a *Nash equilibrium*, if the deviation of it by any one player will not increase that player's payoff. Formally:

$$\forall i \in I \, \forall \sigma_i \in S_i. \quad P_i\left(\sigma_1^*,...,\sigma_i,...,\sigma_n^*\right) \leq P_i\left(\sigma_1^*,...,\sigma_i^*,...,\sigma_n^*\right).$$

So, it is reasonable to consider a set of strategies that is a Nash equilibrium to be co-ordinated. Non-constant sum games can have many different Nash equilibria.

A problem arises in certain games with multiple Nash equilibria that appear equally good for each individual player: players need to agree on choosing the same equilibrium, as otherwise both will be worse off. However, non-cooperative frameworks do not allow pre-play communication to reach such an agreement. Another problem arises from non-cooperative games whose only equilibrium point corresponds to the individually rational attitude of distrusting the "opponent" and maximising its minimal payoff (e.g. the *Prisoners' Dilemma* discussed in the next section). However, if the players trusted each other and co-operated, they would be both better off.

Co-operative Analysis

The latter problems can be eluded by applying techniques of *Co-operative Non-constant Sum Games*, where it is *assumed* that players are free to make joint binding agreements. There are essentially two types of commitments: to co-ordinate strategies and to share payoffs. It is (individually) rational for an agent to commit to certain strategies that maximise the *joint* payoff of a certain coalition C, given that he or she believes to attain more "utility" (called *imputation*) in the redistribution of the joint payoff as if he or she acted alone[3].

A solution to this class of games is provided by the following notion: an imputation of a game is *Pareto-optimal* if no one can be made better off without making somebody worse off. However, Pareto-optimal imputations are not unique, so there is still a need for co-ordination in order to converge on a unique imputation. Several alternative techniques exist in Game Theory to overcome this difficulty, but all suffer from a high computational complexity (Shehory and Kraus 1995).

---

[3] It is assumed that utility is given in some kind of monetary unit that allows for side-payments.

2.3.2.3 Pitfalls of the Co-ordination Process

Although we have argued that any of the traditional analysis methods for partially conflictive games suffer from certain problematic aspects, co-ordination under realistic conditions is even harder. If all individuals involved in a co-ordination problem had complete knowledge about the world and about each other, as well as infinite computation and communication facilities in order to use that knowledge and to keep it up-to-date, co-ordination would be "easy". Still, in real-world situations none of these assumptions hold.

Individuals are usually neither completely aware of all action alternatives, nor of the precise outcomes of these actions. This may be equally true for their own actions, the actions of others, and the result of their interaction when performed together. Expressed in game-theoretic terms, uncertainty about the outcome of actions is reflected by the fact that the game matrix is only partially accessible to the players. Furthermore, decision-making in the outside world takes some time, and individuals act under time pressure. Therefore, their choices need not always be perfectly rational, which questions the analysis and solution concepts described so far. Furthermore, in real-world situations there is often no way to agree on a co-ordinated course of action. And if there is, mechanisms of enforcing agreements may not be in force.

These characteristics produce potential pitfalls for the co-ordination process, which can be observed frequently in the outside world. In the following, just two distinctive classes of problems will be outlined: we will introduce coherence problems and social dilemmas and characterise the situations in which they arise.

Coherence Problems

An important potential pitfall of the co-ordination process is an actor's uncertainty about the actions of others. It is usually implied by non-existent or insufficient means of communication, which make it impossible to agree on certain actions. The problem that people face in such situations is often called co-ordination problem (e.g. Ullmann-Margalit 1977, Fenster et al. 1995). However, as this term is used in a broader meaning within this book, we will refer to it as the coherence problem.

Ullmann-Margalit (1977) describes a typical situation in which a coherence problem arises: two persons are unexpectedly cut off in a telephone conversation. Both want to continue the conversation, and each of them has to choose whether to call back or to wait. It matters little to either of them whether he or she in fact calls back or waits, as long as the conversation is immediately restored. So each has to choose according to his expectation as to what the other will do: to call back if and only if the other is likely to wait. The success or failure of either person is the success or failure of both.

In the above situation, the persons' action alternatives and their outcomes are known to them, so we will analyse it in non-cooperative game-theoretic terms. Consider the game matrix shown in Table 2.1, where C denotes the action of

Table 2.1. Coherence problem

	C	W
C	(0,0)	(1,1)
W	(1,1)	(0,0)

calling back and W describes the attitudes of waiting for a call. Assume that managing to continue the conversation provides a utility of one to either person. Both achieve utility zero otherwise.

The matrix constitutes a prototypical example of a coherence problem. Its corresponding game structure presents two equilibria, (C,W) and (W,C) in the case of Table 2.1[4], i.e. several combinations of actions that result individually rational for all players. Each equilibrium appears equally good to any of them. However, if the players choose to go for different equilibria, everybody will be worse off. In the example, if one player aims at (C,W) while the other wants to achieve (W,C), both end up doing the same action, which results in a undesirable situation for both.

So, from a player's perspective the coherence problem consists in choosing one of several "good" equilibria, while being uncertain about the intentions of the other. A joint decision is to be brought about, either explicitly through communication or implicitly by convention, respecting which equilibrium to go for. For instance, experimental results show that in the face of coherence problems, people tend to go for *focal points*, i.e. they choose an option based on "uniqueness" features of action alternatives (e.g. symmetry and rarity). Fenster et al. (1995) provide a good example of how this phenomenon in human societies can be transferred to artificial agents.

Coherence problems are quite common in everyday life. Just think of the question on which side of the street to drive.

Social Dilemmas

Social dilemmas occur when the pursuit of self-interest by individuals in a group leads to less optimal collective outcomes for all of them. They are usually a consequence of an individual's *lack of confidence* in its acquaintances: if there were reasons to believe that its acquaintances chose a socially desirable option, a good, mutually beneficial degree of co-ordination could be achieved. However, since these reasons do not seem to exist, it appears rational to conservatively distrusted others, assuming the worst case, which leads to poor results for everybody.

The classical problem of this type is the so-called Prisoners' Dilemma (PD). Ullmann-Margalit (1977) presents it as follows: two guilty prisoners, against whom there is not enough incriminating evidence, are interrogated separately.

---

[4] We do not consider randomised choice here. An equally good (mixed) strategy would be to choose between C and W with equal probability.

Table 2.2. The Prisoners' Dilemma

	C	D
C	(-1,-1)	(-10,0)
D	(0,-10)	(-5,-5)

Each faces two alternative ways of acting: to confess a crime, or to keep silent. They both know that if neither confesses, they will be sentenced to a year in prison for a minor offence, for which there is sufficient evidence against them. If both confess, each will be condemned to five years of reclusion. However, if one confesses and the other keeps silent, the former is set free for his collaboration, while the latter receives a heavy term of ten years.

Expressed in game theoretic terms, we get the matrix shown in Table 2.2. The option C stands for co-operation, i.e. keeping silent, while D denotes defection, i.e. confessing. The payoffs reflect the duration of the corresponding offences for each prisoner.

From the perspective of safety, defection is always preferred to co-operation. Choosing C, a prisoner might by recluded for 10 years, while the maximum penalty for doing D is 5 years. An even stronger argument is provided by the fact that defection *dominates* co-operation: if the partner played D, the best thing for a prisoner is choosing D too, as in this case he or she goes to jail just 5 instead of 10 years. If C were played by the partner, the best option would also be D, as by confessing the potential penalty of one year vanishes to nothing.

Consequently, if both prisoners follow this reasoning, they both end up with five years of prison. However, if they trusted each other and co-operated, each of them would just be sentenced to one year in prison for a minor offence.

Social dilemmas underlie many manifestations of poor co-ordination in every-day life. Though in quite different appearances, they receive attention in a variety of disciplines. In political science and economy, for instance, they are usually identified with "public goods" problems: locally optimal choice is considered defection; a local sacrifice to improve global utility is associated with co-operation. Defection is also often interpreted as an attempt to "free-ride" on the efforts of others (Kurz 1994).

Bendor and Mookherjee (1990) underline that social interactions also have the structure of social dilemmas. If a set of mutually dependent individuals ask each other for help, the most secure choice for any of them is to deny it. Giving help to a partner implies a cost, which cannot be rationally justified if the partner does not reciprocate; and it is not sure whether he or she keeps the promise and grants help in return. On the other hand, realising the exchange is usually beneficial for both.

The counterpart of social dilemmas in mathematics is given by the simple fact that locally optimal actions often result in sub-optimal global performance. Examples of social dilemmas, which are often cited in Artificial Intelligence literature, include the Tragedy of the Commons and the Braess' Paradox (e.g. Glance and Hogg 1995).

Solutions to social dilemmas, i.e. co-operation in the support of group welfare, are only possible if there are selfish incentives that convert the social dilemma into a non-dilemma. Thus, in order to be effective, a co-ordination process must include such incentives, providing reasons for confidence in the involved individuals.

2.4 Bottom Line

Co-ordination problems are quite frequent in human society, and their different manifestations have been studied intensively in Social Sciences. However, the complexity of the problem in real-world contexts, and the different research interest of scientific disciplines, have led to a diverse use of the term, which makes it difficult to come up with a general-purpose definition.

The analytic models outlined in this chapter provide interesting insights in different aspects of co-ordination processes in human organisations and societies. They provide a valuable conceptual source for the construction of systems of artificial intelligent agents. The co-existence of a top-down perspective on co-ordination, implied by a priori designed structures, and a bottom-up view of organic, emergent co-ordination, sheds light on the dialectic, adaptive character of the co-ordination process.

Analytic models often try to capture *structural* elements of co-ordination problems, by taking into account the relational characteristics of the environment in which they arise. This is done by explicitly modelling either the environmental entities or the activities that modify these entities, in order to build up taxonomies of dependencies between them. Co-ordination behaviour is explained based on these taxonomies. However, there is no well-developed framework for formal analysis of decentralised co-ordination within the dependency-based approach.

There are also strands of work that model co-ordination within a game theoretic context. This is not surprising, as game theory provides a powerful formal framework for studying decentralised co-ordination among multiple rational actors: under a set of initial assumption, and given an exact specification of a problem situation, it determines the outcomes that the actors' interaction in the frame of the co-ordination process may result in. On this basis, many pitfalls of co-ordination in the outside world can be analysed.

Traditional game theory makes a set of unrealistic assumptions, that limit not only its applicability to real-world situations, but also its adequacy as a model for artificial agent societies. However, more recent research in the field tries to overcome these drawbacks: games with incomplete knowledge, models of limited rationality (e.g. Sandholm 1996), repeated evolutionary games (e.g. Axelrod 1984,

Casti 1994), as well as the possibility of learning (e.g. Shoham and Tennenholz 1994) are being considered.

More crucial for the purpose of the book is the difficulty to apply game theoretic tools to the *design* of an operational model of decentralised co-ordination among self-interested actors. This is largely due to the fact that the actors' individual reasoning processes are completely "hidden" within the players' utility functions. For complex settings, these functions are hard to design, and the effects of changing some parameters of the settings on the agents' utilities are difficult to predict.

For the construction of societies of artificial agents, a combination of structural notions of the dependency-based approach and formal conciseness of game theoretic frameworks seems desirable. Still, the above discussion suggests that it is still a long way from models of the co-ordination process in human society to the design of co-ordination mechanisms that are operational and effective in groups of artificial agents.

3 Distributed Artificial Intelligence

Distributed Artificial Intelligence (DAI) is concerned with systems of interacting artificial agents. Co-ordination provides the "control structures" in such a system. Hence, almost every DAI approach is somehow concerned with co-ordination. As the problem of co-ordination might be conceived in different ways, its importance may vary along with the different approaches. However, none of them can completely ignore it.

In line with the above insight, this chapter is structured in two parts. The first characterises research in DAI as a whole: Section 3.1 provides an overview over past and present research by describing and relating the different DAI currents. The second part focuses on co-ordination models in DAI. Section 3.2 gives an overview of the different classes of co-ordination mechanisms used in DAI. Section 3.3 provides examples of how different mechanisms are used in operational co-ordination frameworks. Section 3.4 wraps up our findings, providing a structured recompilation of the state of art that has been outlined in this chapter.

3.1 Overview of Research Fields

There is a broad variety of papers aiming at providing an overview over DAI and its different currents: Parunak (1988), Castillo-Hern (1988), Bond and Gasser (1992), Chaib-Draa and Moulin (1992), von Martial (1992), Gasser (1993), Moulin and Chaib-Draa (1996). Many recent overviews attempt to characterise particular aspects of DAI research, such as Wooldridge and Jennings (1995), Chaib-Draa (1995), Franklin and Graesser (1996), Nwana (1996) and Sycara (1998), as well as to relate them to each other (Durfee and Rosenschein 1994). However, there is no general agreement on how the different research lines should be classified. On the contrary, ultimately terms and notions become increasingly watered, so that the same term may refer to a very concrete technology or to almost every entity within DAI. A prominent example constitutes the term "agent" which may denominate everything from a computational "neurone" up to a complex expert system. Other examples include the concepts of "multi-agent systems" and "distributed problem solving", as well as qualifications such as "emergent" or "adaptive".

It is not the intention of this work to attack the Babylonian problems of DAI. Neither is it our attempt to give any general-purpose definition. However, for a book within the area of DAI it is indispensable to take a stance on the problem and outline what is meant when the above terms are used. By doing this, it is unavoidable that to some readers it might appear that some strands of work have been omitted, while others may argue that certain aspects are underestimated or reinterpreted. So, the following sections essentially constitute the conceptual fundament for this book. However, they may also be considered a platform for discussion concerning the structure of nowadays DAI research.

In the sequel, we set out from a short introduction to the history of DAI. Subsequently, the area of Autonomous Agents (AA) is described and related to the two classical areas of DAI, Multi-Agent Systems (MAS) and Distributed Problem Solving (DPS).

3.1.1   A Short History

Ever since the initials of Artificial Intelligence (AI) in the fifties, issues related to distribution and parallelism played an important role in AI research. However, the recognition of DAI as a separate discipline was a long process: much progress has been made in the seventies, but it took up to 1980 for the first outstanding DAI event to occur. In this year, the "Workshop on Distributed Artificial Intelligence" was held at the MIT in Boston. This event constitutes one of the landmarks of the evolution of DAI, as it gave testimony of the maturity of the discipline. Since then, DAI has found more and more interest along two decades: it gave rise to an increasingly vast variety of DAI events, that testify ongoing research interest in DAI up to our days.

In spite of early connectionist approaches, typified by Minsky and Papert's Perceptron (1969), (symbolic) mainstream AI constituted the basis for DAI in its beginnings. Interest in DAI was pushed by the shift from huge mainframe computer systems towards much smaller workstations and personal computers: interconnecting these information processing cells via communication channels provided a technically feasible and economically affordable basis for the design of distributed intelligent systems.

Almost simultaneously, attempts to build modular systems made one step beyond the notion of production systems, which advocated the representation of knowledge in small manipulable chunks. The metaphor of co-operating experts became popular, which gave rise to such well-known approaches as Hewitt's actor model (1977) and the Hearsay blackboard architecture (Erman et al. 1980).

So, it does not surprise that early DAI work concentrated on exploiting both, the power of parallelism and the advantages of modularity, by applying distributed, networked system architectures to the solution of AI problems, which were beyond the scope of existing approaches. These attempts were united under the umbrella of the term distributed problem solving. A paradigmatic example of this area is the contract net protocol (Smith 1980) for decomposing and allocating tasks in a network. These approaches also addressed harnessing the robustness provided by multiple sources of expertise, multiple capabilities and multiple perspectives, solving problems in inherently distributed domains, such as air traffic control (Steeb et al. 1981) and vehicle monitoring (Lesser and Corkhill 1983).

During the eighties there was a growing awareness that reuse is a key issue in computer science in general and in AI in particular. With respect to DAI, this trend implied a need to widen existing paradigms: while to-date distributed problem-solvers were constructed from the scratch by building a homogenous set of agents and making them co-operate in a coherent, robust and efficient manner, reusability required dealing with groups of heterogeneous agents, possibly endowed with different architectures, knowledge representation languages, communication languages etc. (Neches et al. 1991).

Still, problems did not end with questions of interoperability between pre-existing agents, as researchers aimed at constructing open systems (Hewitt and de Jong 1984): such systems permit agents to enter and to leave at almost any time, thereby leaving the co-ordination of agent activities to decentralised mechanisms. In accordance with assumptions made in other sciences, this stance diverges from traditional distributed problem-solving approaches, as the supposition of individuals, which always slavishly do what they are told to, does not hold anymore.

The area of multi-agent systems emerged, that deals with exactly these issues: what can be said about heterogeneous groups of agents that are constantly and dynamically changing? MAS research comprises a wide range of different agent types, from sophisticated, self-interested social agents, endowed with complex capabilities for reasoning about themselves and others, to quite simple reactive automatons. It draws heavily on the area of autonomous agents in order to formalise these agent models and to make them operational.

3.1.2 Autonomous Agents

The notion of Autonomous Agents (AA) originally goes back to robotics. The intention there was to endow physically "embodied" agents (Brooks 1986), robots, to do basic tasks in a real-world environment, such as moving from one place to another without colliding with an obstacle etc. Robotic agents should be endowed with capabilities to "survive" in real situations, which presupposes *autonomy* in order to react adequately to unexpected events.

Only recently, there is a growing awareness that the notion of autonomous agency is not necessarily linked to embodied agents. The idea of autonomous software agents as robots without a body has become popular[1]. The environment in which these software agents are supposed to "live" and "survive" is much like the Knowledge Medium envisioned by Stefik (1986): an emerging computational environment, by means of which people store and communicate their knowledge

---

[1] Etzioni (1993) highlights this by calling them *softbots* (software robots).

in a form, that is at least partially understandable by machines. In such a setting, software agents belong to a user, or a group of users, who grant a certain degree of autonomy to it, in order to perform tasks for them.

Software agents are to be used in a variety of tasks. Recently, a specific type of software agents, the so-called *information agents*, has received much attention. This is largely due to the rapid growth of wide area networks, especially the World Wide Web (WWW), and the potential that it provides for building up a real knowledge medium. Huge amounts of information and knowledge have become available on-line within seconds. However, the anarchic growth of the WWW leads to a vast amount of information sources which have only rudimentary structure, and often offer poor quality information: WWW users are "drowning in data but starved of knowledge" (Nwana 1996). Information agents are aimed at ameliorating this problem of information overload, by (actively) finding information that their users are interested in. They might be mobile agents in the future, capable of traversing the WWW, gathering information and reporting what they retrieve back to the home location; today's information agents contact some database, built up by particular indexers (e.g. Spiders), which report back the location of particular information sources. This type of agents is also of great interest in relation to a future electronic marketplace.

Interface agents are personal assistants that assist the user in handling a certain application. They "pro-actively" perform certain actions, based on the model they maintain of their user. For instance, an interface agent could filter out certain articles from a continuos stream of Usenet Netnews (Nwana 1996). Several other classes of software agents have been described, such as *believable agents*, that live in a virtual environment such as a video game and provide to their users "the illusion of life" (Wooldridge and Jennings 1994).

3.1.2.1 Characterisation

The term AA is widely used by many people working in closely related areas. Nevertheless, it is impossible to encounter a single universally accepted definition. This need not be a problem: after all, if many people are successfully developing interesting and useful applications, then it hardly matters that they do not agree on terminological details. However, the term agent has become overly "noisy", and sometimes its use creates more confusion than benefit. This section briefly discusses the notion of agenthood, biased by the particular stance taken in this book.

A minimal account of AA refers to them as *situated* systems (Russell and Norvig 1995). AA live in an environment that they perceive through their sensors and that they purposefully modify by acting upon it through their effectors (Franklin and Graesser 1996). AA may be embodied, as it is the case for mobile robots, or virtual, like software agents.

However, the above notions are still quite weak. In the following, the concept of AA will be pinpointed from three perspectives. Though not completely orthogonal, they give an idea of what is meant when we refer to AA.

First, as we are dealing with *cognitive* software agents that "live" in a *multi-agent world*, we are concerned with agents that fulfil the following characteristics:

- *Problem-solving capabilities*: agents can reason about their environment, which enables them to attain a set of tasks.
- *(Limited) rationality*: agents pursue tasks in a rational manner, i.e. they choose the action that they believe to be best in order to achieve a task. However, the optimality of these decisions is limited by time and resource constraints.
- *(Limited) autonomy*: agents operate without the direct intervention of humans and are able to devise certain tasks on their own. However, the existence of other agents puts limits to their capability of achieving their tasks individually.
- *Social ability*: agents are aware of the existence of other agents. They interact with other agents (and possibly humans) via a communication language.
- *Reactivity* and *pro-activity*: agents perceive their environment and respond to changes in a timely fashion. Furthermore, agents are capable of exhibiting goal directed behaviour, i.e. to act without a directly recognisable stimulus.

Secondly, as argued in the introduction, we will consider cognitive agents from an intentional stance (Dennet 1987): we ascribe a "mental state" to an agent and aim to predict or explain its actions on that basis. Wooldridge and Jennings (1994) argue that a mental state essentially consists of attitudes: *information* attitudes, such as belief and knowledge and *pro*-attitudes, such as desires, intentions, commitment, choice etc. Information attitudes are related to the information that an agent has about the world, whereas pro-attitudes guide the agent's action. Shoham (1993) notes that almost everything, from a light switch to a complex computer program, can be described in mentalistic terminology. However, we believe that it is useful to do this with AA, as it is an intuitive and simple way to provide a description of agent behaviour.

Thirdly, we are interested in agents that live in multi-agent worlds by providing a characterisation of an agent through its context, i.e. not centred on the individual agents, but based on the agent system. As shown above, it is obviously possible to call everything an agent, from light switches to software compilers, depending on how you interpret the context. So, one might define the context first and then derive the individual agent from that. From this perspective, an *agent system* is a system whose structure is determined by the dynamic interaction of its components (as opposed to a static and hierarchical structure). In consequence, the interacting components of such a system are called *AA*. As we will see in the sequel, this alternative perspective helps to relate AA and the areas of MAS and DPS.

3.1.2.2 Techniques

Wooldridge and Jennings (1994) identify three perspectives from which it is possible to study agents. They subdivide agent research in the following areas:

- agent theories
  This field essentially tackles the question how agents should be conceptualised. It provides specifications of what properties an agent should have and how to formally represent and to reason about them. Most agent theories regard agents as intentional systems, by ascribing mental attitudes such as goals, beliefs and intentions to them. Agent theories provide logical frameworks to characterise these attitudes, such as Cohen and Levesque's model of commitments (1990) or Rao and Georgeff's Belief–Desire–Intention logics (1995).

- agent languages
  The area of agent languages is concerned with programming languages and tools for building computational agents. Agent languages usually embody some of the principles proposed by agent theorists. Research in the field tackles the questions of what is an adequate set of constructs for building agents and how to ensure efficient execution of agent programs. Often, agent languages allow a system designer to program agents in terms of belief, desires and other similar concepts. Recent representatives in this area include Shoham's Agent-oriented Programming (1993), Thomas' PLACA (1995) and Steiner's MAIL (1996).

- agent architectures
  Agent architectures specify the internal structure of an agent. They usually commit to a specific "methodology" for agent design, encompassing guidelines for implementing the components of an agent and their interactions.

In the sequel, we will focus on agent architectures. Agents are conceived as situated systems, being in continuous interaction with the outside world. Consequently, the basic architecture of such an agent is then made up of three components: *sensors*, which transmit data to a *cognition* component, which communicates action commands to *effectors*. According to the structure of the cognition component, we will subdivide agent architectures in deliberate, reactive and hybrid approaches.

Deliberative Architectures

Deliberative architectures follow the paradigm of symbolic AI. They stick to the assumption that it is possible to modularise cognitive functionality in a top-down fashion, i.e. to study different cognitive functions separately and then put them together to form an intelligent agent. A deliberative agent maintains an explicitly represented symbolic model of the world on top of which it runs a sense-model-plan-act cycle: sensor data is used to update the world model; a planner uses this model within logical reasoning processes (based on pattern-matching and symbol manipulation) in order to decide which actions to undertake.

Most famous are BDI architectures, which go back to Bratman's (1987) model of human situated cognition: Beliefs, desires and intentions of an agent are taken as primitive notions. Beliefs refer to whatever is contained within an agent's model about the world or about itself. Desires and intentions refer both to a state of affairs that the agent aims to bring about, but while the former are abstract "wishes" that an agent may never set out to fulfil, the latter will lead the agent to attain the appropriate means for arriving at the intended state. Intentions imply a certain commitment of an agent to itself: they are conduct-controllers that guide future behaviour by delimiting sets of potential alternatives (Rao and Georgeff 1995).

Haddadi and Sundermeyer (1996) describe the Intelligent Resource-bounded Machine Architecture (IRMA) as one of the first BDI architectures. IRMA agents have four essential data structures: a plan library, and explicit representations of beliefs, desires and intentions. Five processes operate on these structures: a reasoner, that updates the agents current set of beliefs; a means-ends analyser which, given a set of beliefs, generates a set of options by determining which plans are apt to achieve the agent's intentions; an opportunity analyser, that monitors the environment in order to detect further options for the agent; a filtering process, which ensures that an option is consistent with the current set of intentions; finally, a deliberation process chooses between competing options. ARCHON agents (Cockburn and Jennings 1996) rely on an augmented BDI architecture, as they explicitly consider the existence of other agents in their reasoning.

Reactive Architectures

Reactive architectures emerged in the mid-eighties, driven by the idea that everyday activities mostly consist of presumably "simple" routine, instead of "complicated" abstract reasoning. However, deliberative architectures are notoriously weak achieving those basic behaviours. So, designers of reactive agents put the design process upside down and set out from a collection of simple behaviour schemes, which react to environmental changes in a stimulus-response fashion. Reactive agents continuously refer to their sensors rather than to an internal world model, because "the world is its best model" (Brooks 1995).

The behaviour-based approach to the bottom-up design of reactive agents has received much attention. It has first been implemented in Brooks' subsumption architecture (1986): A robot comprises a hierarchy of task-accomplishing behaviours that compete with each other in order to exercise control over the robot. Lower layers represent more primitive behaviours, such as obstacle avoidance. Higher levels can inhibit lower layers, by filtering their input data and preventing their output data from being sent to the effectors. Steels (1994) proposes an architecture within the same spirit, but applies co-operation instead of subsumption: the behaviours are not allowed to directly "inhibit" (control) one another, but co-operate or compete with each other, in order to achieve coherent behaviour. Other approaches within this branch include situated rules and situated automata (Agre and Chapman 1987).

Hybrid Architectures

Hybrid architectures aim to overcome the limitations of purely deliberative and purely reactive architectures by combining them. Seemingly simple time-bounded tasks (e.g. navigation) are performed by the reactive component. The deliberative component takes over, when "stimulus-free" activities are to be performed (e.g. reasoning with abstract notions in memory instead of sensory input) or when long-term strategic decision with irreversible effects have to be taken (e.g. committing to a coalition with other agents or not).

Horizontally layered hybrid architectures are similar to Brooks' subsumption architectures: all layers have access to both, perception and action component (J. Müller et al. 1995). For example, Ferguson's TouringMachines (1995) comprise three layers. A behaviour-based *reactive layer* provides the agent with fast, reactive capabilities for coping with events that the higher layers have not considered before. The *planning layer* generates, executes and repairs activity plans for the agent. The *modelling layer* is used as a platform for explaining observed behaviours of other agents and for making predictions about possible future behaviours. Each layer is an independently and concurrently operating, latency-bounded, task-achieving process. A (meta-) control framework mediates between the layers by means of two types of context-sensitive rules that the agent designer provides: censor rules prevent certain sensory objects from being fed as input to selected control layers, while suppressor rules prevent certain layers' output actions from being transmitted to the effectors.

In the above approach, the design of layer interaction schemes is rather complex, as each layer may theoretically interact with any other. This provides an argument in favour of layered architectures, where only "neighbouring" layers interact, such as J. Müller's InterRap architecture (1996). Each layer of an Inter-Rap agent represents a different level of abstraction of similar functionality: the *behaviour-based* component implements reactive behaviour and procedural knowledge of the agent on the basis of the world model; the *plan-based* component contains a mechanism which devises single-agent plans by using planning knowledge; finally the *co-operation* component is endowed with the capability of generating joint plans using special co-operation knowledge. The point is that each component can only access knowledge at the same or at lower levels, thereby constraining the possible interaction between the corresponding layers.

3.1.3   Distributed Problem Solving

Distributed Problem Solving (DPS) studies how a group of intelligent agents[2] can share their resources and co-ordinate their activities, so that the intelligence of the

---

[2] A variety of different terms are used to characterise the components of a DPS system: specialist, expert, knowledge source and problem-solver are just some of them. However, in line with the actual trend in DAI all of them will be subsumed under the term agent.

group is more than the sum of the individual agents' intelligence. Intelligence, in this context, is conceived as the capacity to solve a certain class of problems. In order to produce this synergetic effect, traditional DPS assumes that agents *co-operate*[3].

3.1.3.1 Characterisation

Durfee et al. (1991) compare the problem of designing a DPS system to the problem of building a house. Several agents are involved in this process, each expert in a different area: one might have expertise on the strength of structural materials, another on the space requirements for the different types of rooms, another on plumbing, another on electrical wiring, and so on. However, to build the house they need to co-operate, as this task is beyond their individual capabilities.

For instance, partial results have to be exchanged between agents, as in the case of the architect who passes the blueprints to a construction company; tasks may be delegated from one agent to another just like a construction company that engages subcontractors or a foreman that instructs the building-workers what to do. Information about the state of the problem-solving process has to be exchanged: Electricians should not start working before building-workers notify to have finished their job. Finally, unforeseen conflicts have to be solved: if electrical lines happen to pass close to water pipes, the plumber will have to negotiate with the electrician on how to solve that conflict.

The above example also sheds light on the delimitation between DPS and ordinary distributed systems. The latter solves well-defined problems in the frame of fixed control structures and rigid problem decomposition. Ordinary distributed systems are mainly concerned with issues like synchronisation and technical aspects of communication. On the contrary, DPS affronts complex tasks whose diverse aspects cannot be totally anticipated beforehand. The focus lies on aspects of co-operation within a dynamic problem-solving process. Setting out from the assumption of a limited bandwidth of communication channels that restricts the amount of information that can be exchanged, DPS studies how the agents' problem-solving activities can be co-ordinated to cope with the overall task. Questions include which agent shall perform what task, which partial results shall be exchanged, when shall such communication take place etc.

Overviews of DPS usually suffer from the fact that the term "co-operation" is only vaguely defined. Recently, there are attempts to characterise DPS without the need to refer to this ambiguous notion. Instead, a system is conceived to be DPS if its constituent agents show certain properties (Durfee and Rosenschein 1994). The following assumptions of agent properties are like to be made with respect to DPS systems:

---

[3] That is why this area has been termed Co-operative Distributed Problem Solving (CDPS) in the beginning.

- benevolence assumption
  Typically, benevolence implies that the agents help each other whenever they are requested to do so: benevolent agents slavishly do what they are told. However, this does not necessarily coincide with authority structures or any other kind of organisation between agents, as in groups of benevolent agents – depending on the task at hand – any one agent might tell others to do something. The point is that there is no sense of payments or any other kind of compensation. So to say, a benevolent agent obeys to a request "as an end in itself".

- common goals assumption
  One motivation for benevolence is given when agents are aware of the fact that they pursue a common goal. This is often expressed by the fact, that all agents aim to maximise the same global utility measure. Conflicts between agents are essentially subjective: they only arise as a consequence of incomplete or incorrect view of the state of the world, but not due to (objectively) contradictory interests.

- homogeneous agents assumption
  Homogeneity, within this book, refers to the fact that there is no "unnecessary" conflict or incongruity between the agents. So, homogenous agents will use compatible representation and communication languages. In general, they will not pursue (objectively) conflicting goals[4].

Adhering to this perspective, a system made up of benevolent agents, of agents with common goals or of homogeneous agents is considered a DPS system.

3.1.3.2 Techniques

The architecture of a traditional DPS consists of computational agents that co-operate in order to achieve some overall common goal. Co-operation is achieved through interaction that is mainly sustained by communication. So, besides the effort of achieving the individual problem-solving capacities of agents, DPS design activities focus on the generation of adequate co-operation protocols for a problem at hand.

Traditionally, reusability has not played a primary role in DPS research. Co-operation protocols have usually been designed from the scratch for each problem at hand. However, the general structure of a DPS problem-solving process is the following:

- task decomposition (TD)
  TD can be done in two ways: In a *qualitative* TD a task is decomposed into sub-tasks which are less complex, i.e. simpler to cope with. Most problem-

---

[4] In this book we see the assumption of homogeneity essentially as an attempt to capture the trails that a central designer leaves in the system architecture. Other authors conceive the term differently (e.g. Molin and Chaib-Draa 1996).

solving methods proposed in the area of (centralised) knowledge modelling make use of such a functional decomposition (Puppe 1993). A *quantitative* TD divides tasks into "smaller" partial tasks. This kind of decomposition is characteristic for distributed AI systems. It might be implied by a spatial distribution of the tasks (e.g. data sensed in geographically different regions). Alternatively, a quantitative TD can be implied by the distribution of capacity among agents (e.g. different manufacturing sites producing the same good).

- task allocation (TA)
  The TA step assigns (sub-) tasks to problem-solvers. A *unique* TA assigns a task to only one agent. This can be done through direct order as in standard architectures, or by means of some auction procedure like the contract net (Smith 1980). In a *multiple* TA two or more agents are allocated to the same task, in order to increase reliability or to avoid bias. For, instance, in collaborative engineering design a group of engineers, specialists in different areas, produce alternative solutions to the same task but from different perspectives (Bond 1989).

- problem solving (PS)
  During the PS phase each agent individually solves the (sub-) tasks that it has been attributed.

- solution integration (SI)
  The SI phase synthesises the results of the different problem-solving tasks. This has to be done in accordance with a set of constraints, due to domain characteristics, task interdependencies, agent authorities or user constraints. A *synthetical* SI combines several alternative solutions into one. It is usually preceded by a multiple TA. Synthetical SI tries to keeps the "good" features of every agent's solution while resolving potential conflicts. A *compositional* SI is the reverse of quantitative TD. Finally, *constructive* SI is usually present after a qualitative TD.

The above classification has been inspired by the work of Yang and Zhang (1995), that divide DPS techniques into four categories, DPS1 to DPS4, on the basis of different combinations of alternatives for the above process steps.

One might wonder what is so special about DPS as to become a specific current in AI: the structure of a DPS problem-solving process in general fits quite well into traditional AI frameworks. For distributed systems, in which the coordination of problem solving and solution integration is done by a centralised component (e.g. the TRYS system described by Cuena et al. 1996), this perspective might in fact be reasonable.

However, the characteristic feature of DPS is that the distribution of knowledge does not completely coincide with the (functional) structure of the task at hand. Borrowing from the model-based KADS methodology (Wielinga et al. 92), this will be called a *model mismatch*. This mismatch can be due to three reasons:

- Distribution of *case* knowledge: an agent cannot directly access a resource which is "controlled" by another agent, i.e. information from a sensor.
- Distribution of *domain* knowledge: an agent is not endowed with the knowledge to solve a task, but another agent is. For instance, an agent that detects traffic problems might not be endowed with knowledge on how to process noisy data.
- Distribution of *task* knowledge: an agent might be endowed with knowledge on how to solve several sub-tasks, but might not know how to combine them to cope with a more complex task. This is the case for a "worker" agent that needs a "manager" to co-ordinate its activities.

The model mismatch implies control uncertainty. Agents have to take decisions with global effects, but based on local, incomplete knowledge. If they knew about the global problem-solving state (which would be easily available in a centralised system), this would not be the case. So, DPS control uncertainty is not (or better: not only) the result of environmental contingency, but due to a "designed-in" model mismatch (Ossowski and García-Serrano 1995). There are essentially three co-ordination techniques used in DPS to overcome this uncertainty: organisational structuring, meta-level information exchange and multi-agent planning.

An Example

The famous Contract Net (CNET) protocol (Smith 1980, Davis and Smith 1983) makes use of the above DPS assumptions. CNET constitutes a mechanism for unique TA based on the notions of suitability and availability.

According to CNET, a manager agent, responsible for the achievement of a task, decomposes it into sub-tasks and sends task announcement messages, containing an abstract description of the characteristics of the sub-task at hand, to all other agents that might attack tasks of that type. Upon hearing the task announcement, eligible agents determine their adequacy for the task and send a bid back to the manager, including the result of that self-reflection process. When all the bids have arrived, the manager chooses the most adequate bidder and "contracts" it for a certain sub-task by sending an announced award message.

CNET heavily draws on the assumptions about agent properties outlined in Section 3.1.3.1. First of all, it assumes that bidders are *honest* in their bidding behaviour: they do not try to cheat the manager, e.g. by pretending to be busy or to be already overloaded with work. But, most important, it relies on agents to be *benevolent*. A bidder does not want to get anything in return for executing a task; there is no sense of payment or transfer of utility involved. In a world where these agent characteristics could not be assured, the original CNET protocol described in this example would not work.

However, neither assumption makes the design of a CNET-based system trivial. Even though agents want to do the best they can for each other, difficulties of timing and of local perspectives can lead to (unintended) distraction of acquaintances. For instance, important tasks could go unclaimed, because suitable agents are already busy with other tasks of lower importance: when they sent bids for these tasks, they did not know that later on a high priority job would be announced (Parunak 1988). In such cases the behaviour of a CNET-based system of benevolent agents appears uncoordinated.

3.1.4 Multi-Agent Systems

The area of Multi-Agent Systems (MAS) is concerned with the behaviour within groups of agents with varying characteristics: agents usually exist prior to the appearance of a specific task; their "existence" is not limited to a certain problem-solving context. So, instead of focusing on a specific problem, MAS approaches set out from an interaction-centred perspective: it takes a bottom-up approach and studies the properties that emerge from the interactions in such manifold collections of agents.

3.1.4.1 Characterisation

The motivation for studying the properties of such groups of agents is twofold. Firstly, heterogeneity is a necessary consequence of reusability. A designer, who has to compose a system out of pre-existing agents that have been designed at different times, by different people, and within different contexts, cannot completely control their properties. So, he or she somehow needs to harmonise the different architectures, representations and languages. Secondly, the need for more flexible and robust systems has pushed the idea of agents showing some kind of autonomous and self-interested behaviour.

Both motivations are captured by the Open Systems approach (Hewitt and de Jong 1984), which is one of the favourite metaphors in MAS research. An open system finds itself in continuous interaction with its environment: agents come and go, resources appear, become scarce and vanish etc. Obviously, making assumption about basic properties of the system (i.e. agents and resources) is a difficult job within such a context.

In fact, MAS research is especially interested in these "hard" cases where the agent features can vary uncontrollably within a group. This variability can be captured by assuming certain agent properties. One is inclined to label a group of agents as MAS, if some of the following assumptions hold:

- non-benevolence
  Agents are usually supposed to behave individually rational, that is trying to maximise their personal (instead of the system's) utility. The pursuit of self-interest makes agents less vulnerable to malevolent behaviour of others, but also protects them from distraction caused by ignorant or incompetent acquaintances. Furthermore, it is closer to human behaviour than pure benevolence, facilitating the collaboration between human and computational agents.

However, other guidelines of behaviour, such as altruism (Brainov 1996) or social responsibility (Jennings and Campos 1997), which lie "halfway" between benevolence and individual rationality, are being considered.

- multiple goals
  As a juxtaposition to the situation in DPS systems, the existence of multiple, at least partially conflicting goals is supposed. This is usually expressed by the fact that agents have different local utility measures. An important consequence of multiple goals is the existence of social dilemmas or of real (objective) conflict, which cannot be solved simply by increasing the agents' awareness of the situation on the basis of exchanging information.

- autonomy
  Agents are capable of creating and pursuing their own goals in a self-interested manner: based on some kind of "motivation" (some abstract desired state of the world), agents generate their own goals and decide whether to adopt goals of others. The latter decision is based on whether these goals contribute to bring the world in some state that is in line with *its personal* motivation. Autonomy in a group of agents with diverging goals implies non-benevolence: an agent will only help others if it gets something in return (Castelfranchi 1995).

- heterogeneity
  Heterogeneity among agents can appear in many different shapes. It frequently refers to different agent architectures, ontologies or knowledge representation and communication languages. In addition, it often implies different preference criteria among agents (i.e. multiple goals) as outlined above.

Research in MAS is interested in what can be said about *groups* of agents with the above characteristics, and how their dynamics can be influenced.

3.1.4.2 Techniques

The general structure of MAS can be seen as a setting of multiple agents whose states repeatedly undergo local changes. These changes are determined by behaviour rules, whose outcomes are influenced by the behaviour of other agents in their "vicinity". The interest of a MAS researcher concerns "interesting" properties of the system, e.g. the convergence on uniform behaviours that emerge among these mutually influencing local changes.[5]

In reactive DAI systems (Ferber 1996), the specification of behaviour rules is, in principle, the designer's concern. However, they are often inspired by concepts from other sciences: agents behaviour rules are intended to model certain aspects of the behaviour of animals, cells, genes or particles.

---

[5] Many MAS techniques rely on "sub-cognitive" agent models. So, for the sake of this overview will extent our area of interest to reactive DAI approaches.

The case of cognitive agents is somewhat different: the behaviour rules of cognitive agents are predetermined by the principle of rationality, which constrains action to be taken on the basis of the agents knowledge and beliefs. Unfortunately, in general not much can be said about the behaviour of collections of rational agents. However, a MAS researcher investigates under what conditions interesting global properties emerge; *mechanisms* are analysed and designed, that bias such rational action, so as to generate or explain global behaviour. Such mechanisms usually rely on some sort of common knowledge, which leads to incentives to foster certain behaviour and to discourage others.

In the sequel, we will first outline mechanisms for cognitive agents, inspired by models from social sciences. Subsequently, mechanisms for reactive agents are depicted that go back to theories from Natural Sciences.

As outlined in Chapter 2, game theory is a formal tool for modelling rational action in the presence of other rational actors. Many studies in social sciences rely on this framework (e.g. Bendor and Mookherjee 1990). MAS approaches, studying cognitive agents, usually do not constitute an exception. There are several studies concerning the emergence of co-operation in situations of the type of the Prisoners' Dilemma (e.g. Axelrod 1984, Mor and Rosenschein 1995). In addition, algorithms for coalition formation among rational agents are based on game-theoretic notions (e.g. Shehory and Kraus 1995).

Economics provides another source of inspiration for systems of cognitive agents. Neo-classical economic theory sets out from the assumption that economic actors aim to maximise their profit in an individually rational manner. So, many formal economic approaches rely on the application of models of rationality developed within specific branches of game theory. Many of them have found a reflection in MAS: auction models and taxation schemes have been applied to heterogeneous agent societies (Rosenschein and Zlotkin 1994). Models of voting procedures have found their way into multi-agent planning (Ephrati and Rosenschein 93). The applicability of related frameworks is discussed extensively by Sandholm (1996).

Other economic models focus on the market as a special co-ordination mechanism. By seeing an agent system as a virtual market, MAS designers hope to realise some desirable properties of real markets. To formulate problems as a computational economy, the activities of interest are usually cast in terms of the production and consumption of goods (Mullen and Wellman 1995). Consider, for instance, the WALRAS algorithm, which is the core of a market-oriented programming system (Wellman 1995). It implements a distributed auction mechanism for allocating resources ("goods") among multiple agents ("consumer" and "producers"). Agents can acquire resources at a certain price at different markets, which are managed by "auctioneers". Initially, agents send bids (demanded quantity of a good as a function of its potential price) to each market, on the basis of which the auctioneer computes the "clearing price", i.e. the point at which the aggregate excess demand is zero. Auctioneers then notify the bidders of the new price. The consumers adapt their demand functions to the new prices and send these updated bids to the auctions. The process terminates when the prices no longer change: the markets are in a general equilibrium, i.e. there is a perfect balance between demand and supply. In this situation, resources are "sold" to the agents according to their demands for the equilibrium price. Still, several conditions have to be met in order to assure that the process actually converges on a general equilibrium (Wellman 1995)

Within physics, Shoham and Tennenholz (1994) examine the potential of applying Ising Models from statistical mechanics to MAS, as they provide a powerful tool to analyse dynamic systems of an interesting structure. In such models there is a set of "spins" which can take different values. They are arranged into some fixed spatial arrangement within which they only interact with neighbouring spins. Ising models have proved useful for the investigation of various physical properties such as spontaneous magnetisation, that is the emergence of configurations in which the majority of spins end up with the same value.

Shehory and Kraus (1996) use mathematical models from classical mechanics as the basis for their *Physics-Agent-System*. Agents are modelled as dynamic particles within a non-ionic liquid system, and are mutually repulsive; goals correspond to static particles that attract agents. A goal is (partially) satisfied when a dynamic and a static particle collide. An algorithm is presented that determines agent behaviour based on physical equations describing the behaviour of dynamic particles. The Physics-Agent-System model is especially interesting for task allocation problems within domains with partially satisfiable goals and homogenous agents. In these domains the repeated partial satisfaction of goals by different agents gives rise to "emergent co-operation". The mutual repulsion of dynamic particles can be seen as one form of conflict avoidance.

The work by Shehory et al. (1998) is based on a metaphor from molecular genetics. The authors are concerned with load-balancing problems, where tasks have to be assigned to resource-limited agents, which reside on different machines that also offer only limited capacity. In order to overcome (predicted) overload situations, agents can pass tasks between each other. Still, another possibility for the overloaded agent is to *clone* itself: it may create an exact copy of itself and activate it locally or let it migrate to a remote machine. A variety of other work, such as the Computational Ecosystem framework presented by Kephart et al. (1989) or the many Artificial Life approaches, also rely on concepts and models rooted in biology.

An Example

Let us come back to our basic area of interest and present an example of MAS mechanisms in groups of cognitive, autonomous agents. Consider the following task assignment problem presented by Rosenschein and Zlotkin (1994): in a future electronic market intelligent telephone agents dynamically choose between several telephone companies in order to contract a carrier for a call that its user wishes to make. In the example shown in Figure 3.1, these are Telefónica, Deutsche Telekom and British Telecom. When the user lifts the handset, the telephone agent

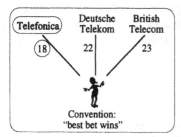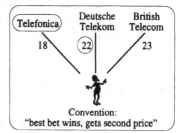

Figure 3.1. Example of a multi-agent telecom market
(adapted from Rosenschein and Zlotkin 1994)

sends call announcement messages to the companies. Each company runs bidding agents that evaluate the characteristics of the call, and declare a price per minute for which the company is willing to carry the call. In the example, this is 18 cents, 22 cents and 23 cents respectively. The telephone agent automatically collects these bids and selects one company according to a special decision convention, which is known to all bidders. Finally, the companies are informed about the outcome of the selection and the call is initiated automatically on the network of the winning company. Such a process is an example of an auction mechanism, where the telephone agent plays the role of the auctioneer and the companies represent the bidders.

A straightforward decision convention is shown on the left-hand side of Figure 3.1. The telephone agent grants the task to the bidder that offers the best (i.e. cheapest) price. In the example, Telefónica wins the call for 18 cents. However, this convention has a serious disadvantage: it promotes strategic behaviour among the companies. Instead of spending all their efforts in improving their services, companies might invest a great deal of resources to build up a model of their competitors' bidding strategies. If a Telefónica bidding agent were endowed with such a model, it would claim a price of 20 cents (i.e. overbid the "real" price by 2 cents), counting on it being less than the Deutsche Telekom bid. This strategy is risky, but the potential benefit constitutes a great incentive to do so.

The mechanism depicted on the right-hand part of Figure 3.1 overcomes such incentives for strategic behaviour. Now, the convention states that the cheapest company wins the call, but is paid the price of the second lowest bid, which is 22 cents in the example. If Telefónica requested a price higher than 18 cents it cannot win anything; its bid does never affect the price that it is paid. However, by overbidding it risks to lose the call in case that its model of Deutsche Telekom is imprecise and Deutsche Telekom just wants 19 cents. From the point of view of the customer, this mechanism has the disadvantage that he or she has to pay slightly more for each call; but the companies now have an incentive to put all their efforts in improving their services.

The above case outlines how a multi-agent system designer can enforce "efficient" behaviour by modifying incentive structures in an auction-like process on the basis of common knowledge about conventions.

3.2 Co-ordination Mechanisms

The specific co-ordination mechanism that is active within an artificial agent system determines its internal dynamics, i.e. the interactions between agents, as well as the external properties of society. Co-ordination mechanisms usually vary with the domains in which they unfold, depending on the *agents* and their inclination towards co-operation, the *environment* and its degree of stability and predictability as well as on the *tasks* and how decomposable and well defined they are. In this section, we will sketch the most important classes of co-ordination mechanisms that are used in DAI. Some particular mechanisms that are of special relevance for this book are described in more detail.

3.2.1   Organisation

In artificial agent systems organisation is usually seen as a metaphor for a set of long-term structural relationship between *roles*. When agents agree to play certain roles within an organisation, they commit to comply with the behaviour that these roles and their relations imply.

There are many proposals to classify organisational structures (e.g. Pattison et al. 1988, Durfee and Lesser 1987, Jennings 1996). Their coercive nature, i.e. the way they constrain the possible actions that an agent within a certain role can take, may manifest differently. For instance, *responsibility* structures may define which role is to attain certain tasks, thus reducing the agents' local uncertainty by providing them with expectations about the behaviour of their acquaintances. Another example are *authority* structures, indicating which role may convey orders to others, thereby avoiding certain conflicts or specifying standard ways to solve them. Structural relations between roles are supposed to change rather slowly (or not at all), so they are usually considered common knowledge among agents.

In general, there is some knowledge within an organisation respecting the tasks and subtasks by means of which its objectives are to be attained. Often, the authority and responsibility structures go in line with the task structure of the problem to be solved. In such a case, being responsible for a composite task means to be entitled to manage the co-ordination of sub-tasks, potentially giving orders to agents that are to achieve them. There are two extreme cases of this type of organisation. In *hierarchical organisation*, for every task there it is a manager that controls and co-ordinates its attainment. In *lateral organisation*, however, there are no unique managers and every task is to be achieved in a co-operative fashion.

As Decker (1995) stresses, it is a general agreement that no organisational form is appropriate for all circumstances. So, as a situation evolves, the organisational structures should be periodically reassessed to determine if it is still appropriate or whether a rearrangement would be beneficial. Some authors completely reject the notion of organisation as an external coercive entity, but conceive organisation to be embedded in the beliefs, intentions and commitments of the agents. From this perspective, an organisation only exists in the commitments and expectations of its members (Chaib-Draa and Moulin 1992). Carley and Gasser (1998) provide an extensive survey of how findings from organisation theory have been transferred to artificial agent systems.

3.2.2 Multi-Agent Planning

Multi-agent planning (MAP) is a co-ordination mechanism, where agents form plans that specify all their future actions and interactions with respect to a par-ticular objective: all agents involved in a multi-agent plan *commit* to behave in accordance with it. This may lead to efficient co-ordination, as agents know exactly what actions they will take, what actions their acquaintances will take, and what interactions will occur. Still, unforeseen events may prevent the multi-agent plan from being successfully executed, so this technique can be regarded as focusing on rather short-term issues of co-ordination.

With respect to single-agent planning research, traditional MAP assumes envi-ronment features that are somewhere between *static* and *dynamic* planning. In the former approach, a single planning agent is the only source of change in an environment considered completely static. In the latter, the agent assumes that sudden events may unexpectedly alter the world state, so it explicitly considers contingencies in its plans, monitors their execution and revises them in the face of relevant environmental events (e.g. Russell and Norvig 1995). In MAP, the environment is constantly changing due to the actions performed by other agents, but these changes are not real contingencies. The planning agent(s) can predict them, and even influence the way of their occurrence.

Traditional MAP approaches first generate complete detailed plans for every agents: all actions and interactions to perform during plan enactment are specified before the execution commences (Jennings 1996). A straightforward approach in this line is to use standard non-linear planning techniques to generate admissible partially ordered sequences of actions (for an overview see Russell and Norvig 1995). Subsequently, unordered sets of actions are sent to different agents, which can execute them in parallel without the need for further co-ordination, because all possible interactions have been previously eliminated. However, the approach has the disadvantage that the factor of parallelism is only dependent on goals and actions, and not on the available agents (Durfee 1996). Therefore, two classes of MAP approaches have come up, both coping with the fact that the agents and their capabilities are given a priori.

In *centralised* MAP, one agent is responsible for the recognition and repair of plans. In Georgeff's system (1983), the co-ordinator is statically defined. It identifies potentially conflictive interactions between individual plans, groups them together into critical regions, and inserts communication primitives to synchronise them appropriately. In the air-traffic control system of Steeb et al. (1981), the co-ordinating agent is chosen dynamically. It builds up (flight) plans for the agents, containing particular actions to remove interactions, i.e. to avoid collisions. By contrast, in *distributed* MAP the plan itself is developed by several agents, none of which has a complete view of the entire community's activities. In Corkhill's distributed NOAH system (1979) agents represent each other's activities by means of specific nodes, and plan execution is co-ordinated by explicit synchronisation primitives.

Recent MAP approaches allow for a deviation from the agreed course of action (e.g. Pollack 1992). If a situation has changed drastically, dynamic plan modifications need to be performed at execution time, thereby withdrawing some of the commitments that the original multi-agent plan implied (e.g. Levesque et al. 1990). Durfee (1996, 1998) provides good surveys of the different approaches to multi-agent planning.

3.2.3   Negotiation

Negotiation is a co-ordination mechanism, which is based on medium-term commitments within a group of agents. Negotiation processes dynamically generate agreements, which usually last shorter than the a priori commitments that organisational structures imply. Still, agreements can be re-negotiated, so they may last longer than multi-agent plans.

The term negotiation is often given a rather broad meaning, and few recent DAI systems do not claim to apply negotiation in one or another way. However, we prefer to conceive negotiation in a more specific context: it is just one of many ways to achieve co-ordination. Therefore, we will adhere to the definition of Pruitt (1981), who states that

> negotiation is a process by which a joint decision is made by two or more parties. The parties first verbalise contradictory demands and then move towards agreements by a process of concession or search for new alternatives.

A central issue for a negotiation model is to represent the topic concerning which there is disagreement among the agents. This *negotiation object* is strongly dependent on the application. The *Persuader* system mediator helps a company and its union to find a compromise concerning labour-conditions (Sycara 1989). In the office automation domain, a co-ordinator negotiates with other agents about the adaptation of their *plans* (von Martial 1992). In distributed transportation scheduling, shipping companies negotiate the exchange of *orders* and their prices (Fischer et al. 1995, 1996). During distributed business process management, agents discuss *service level agreements*, the conditions under which they provide services to each other (Norman et al. 1996).

However, simply communicating instantiations of negotiation objects is not enough: an agent needs to express how the other party shall interpret a message. The language/action perspective taken by Winograd (1988) emphasises these pragmatic aspects of communication, drawing on Searle's Speech Act Theory (1969). They present five fundamental illocutionary points, distinguishing between assertive, directive, commissive, declaration and expressive utterances. Following H.-J. Müller (1996), we will refer to speech acts that are used within a negotiation model as *negotiation primitives*. The number and names of negotiation primitives usually changes with the application at hand, but three groups can be identified:

- *Initiators* allow to start a negotiation process by presenting an initial proposal.
- *Reactors* indicate that the negotiation process should be continued, by refining an existing proposal or by presenting a counter-proposal.
- *Completers* express a desire to end the process, probably by accepting or rejecting a final proposal.

Finally, a *negotiation protocol* has to be defined which determines legal (or: meaningful) sequences of messages. The negotiation protocol is usually supposed to be common knowledge, i.e. a mutually known convention concerning the "public rules" of the negotiation. Note that a negotiation protocol need not only refer to negotiation primitives, but may also constrain the negotiation objects involved in a message. Rosenschein and Zlotkin's "monotonic concession protocol" (1994), for instance, requires each agent to "improve" its offer in every negotiation step.

Negotiation objects, primitives and protocols define a set of *permissible* negotiation processes. However, the specific development of the negotiation process in a particular situation is determined by the *negotiation strategies* of the involved parties. These strategies determine which of the permitted options an agent actually chooses. They are purely local decision criteria, which need not be constrained by any external convention[6]. Usually, an agent's negotiation strategy aims at the maximal satisfaction of its self-interest. In these cases, any model of individually rational decision-making in a multi-agent world can be applied. However, as information, knowledge and computation power are usually limited, negotiation strategies are often based on heuristics. For instance, a heuristic may state how to start a negotiation (e.g. to pick out the most important conflict, to take the less different one, or to negotiate a whole package of conflicts together). During the negotiation process, a heuristic could be to stay *competitive* (i.e. to stay firm and to choose the alternative that is closest to its self-interest) or be *co-operative* (i.e.

---

[6] Note that in groups of homogenous agents, where the local decision-making strategies are built by a single designer, there is no need for a (prescriptive) negotiation protocol: it is just defined to be the sum of all possible negotiations that the local strategies generate.

to prefer options that are closer to a presumably mutually acceptable solution). However, H.-J. Müller (1996) underlines that it is usually not possible to determine a priori which of the negotiation strategy is the best for a certain scenario.

3.2.4 Examples

In the sequel, we will present some examples of mechanisms by means of which co-ordination within artificial agent societies can be fostered. Their selection might appear arbitrary at the first glance. However, we do *not* present the approaches primarily to illustrate the above classes co-ordination mechanism. They have rather been chosen based on their relevance for the work that will be presented later in this book.

3.2.4.1 Shoham and Tennenholz: Social Laws

The effects of organisational prescriptions on multi-agent co-ordination within a framework of social metaphors has been studied by Shoham and Tennenholz (1992, 1995), introducing the idea of *social laws*. These are conceived as hard constraints on agent behaviour. Seen from a designer's perspective, the basic idea is that social laws filter out sets of action combinations in a MAS which are known a priori to be bad for the desired overall functionality. From an agent's perspective, social laws make the behaviour of other agents more predictable. A typical example of a social law is the convention to drive on the right.

Shoham and Tennenholz aim to answer the question when social laws are useful. They model an agent as a finite automaton. An agent is endowed with a finite set A of actions. Its history is compiled in its actual (local) state s. The result of an action a in state s is modelled by a transition function $T(s,a)$. This function is non-deterministic in order to account for the fact that the actual result of an action depends on the environment, especially on the actions that the other agents take. A social law is defined as a constraint on this transition function.

Shoham and Tennenholz define focal states, which model states in which every agent desires to be. A legal plan is a sequence of transitions that lead from one focal state to another (without violating any social law). The social law is useful if for all pairs of focal states there is such a legal plan. Otherwise, it is "too restrictive".

Recently, there are attempts to overcome the rigidity of social laws. The idea is to attach some "context" to social laws, stating as to what point agents need to comply with them, and when they can be transgressed. These flexible social laws only *bias* but never *determine* agent behaviour. Briggs and Cook (1995) use such an approach to co-ordinate deliberately planning agents: social laws reduce the branching factor within an agent's search space and the chance of interaction with another agent's plan. They use a ranking of sets of social laws, from strictest to most lenient (e.g. no law): if an agent cannot create a plan that achieves its local goal within the constraints of the social law currently in force, it switches to the next weaker law and tries again.

3.2.4.2 Goldman and Rosenschein: Co-operative Rules

Goldman and Rosenschein (1994) study the *effect* of organisational prescription among co-operative agents within a testbed environment. Agent behaviour follows "co-operative state-changing rules" (similar to social laws in a co-operative setting). The authors reach the conclusion that in order to achieve co-ordinated behaviour, state-changing rules should generally urge agents to prefer "unconstrained situations", i.e. to *avoid* situations in which agent activities interfere and to foster the existence of prototypical, "easy" situations.

Goldman and Rosenschein support this claim by experiments in the Tile World (Pollack and Ringuette 1990), an artificial environment built on top of the MICE testbed (Montgomery and Durfee 1990). It constitutes a two-dimensional grid, with tiles, holes, barriers and agents. Agents have the task to "push" tiles into holes, an enterprise which is obstructed by barriers. A co-operative rule is proposed that induces agents to prefer situations in which the degree of freedom of tiles is maximal: tiles are pushed away from barriers so as to make access to them easier for other agents.

It is highlighted that such co-operative behaviour often implies an overhead for an agent compared to purely self-interested choice. Behaving sociably and freeing tiles might produce a cost for the agent, leading to potentially sub-optimal outcome for it. In these situations, co-operative state-changing rules should make the agents obviate from the locally optimal plan. The question is as to how far that extra work should be fostered, hoping that the result is a better overall solution, or, in the Tile World, how far (how many steps) should an agent obviate from its original path in order to "free" a blocked tile. Goldman and Rosenschein specify this by a fixed value called *co-operation level*.

3.2.4.3 Sichman et al.: Dependence Situations

The approach presented by Sichman (1995) and Sichman et al. (1994) models the reasoning processes underlying self-interested agent interaction. This is done within a qualitative, dependency-based framework.

An agent holds a data structure, called *external description*, which contains several *entries*, one for each agent. The entry concerning agent a_j in agent a_i's external description contains the following information:

- a set of goals that a_j is pursuing,
- a set of plans that a_j knows of, and that may achieve certain goals given that certain actions and resources are available,
- a set of actions and a set of resources available to a_j.

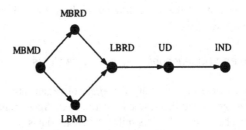

Figure 3.2. Criteria for the choice of partners

An agent a_i believes that there is a mutual dependence relation (MD) between itself and a_j for a common goal g and a plan p, if neither a_i nor a_j can achieve the goal alone, but using their action capacities and resource sets jointly, they can achieve g by executing p. A reciprocal dependence relation (RD) is weaker than a mutual dependence, as it does not require a_i and a_j to share a common goal. Agent a_i considers a dependence relation to be mutually believed (MB), if the plan that achieves the goal g belongs to a_j's entry. If it is contained in its self-description (its own entry in the external description), it is said to be locally believed (LB).[7]

Combining the above criteria there are four *dependence situations* in which a_j can be with regard to another agent a_j and its goal g: MBMD, MBRD, LBMD and LBRD respectively. This set is completed by the situation of independence (IND), where a_i is capable of achieving g using its own plans, actions and resources, and the situation of unilateral dependence (UD), where a_i depends on a_j but not the other way round.

In Sichman's model each agent is endowed with a social reasoning mechanism, that determines its dependence situation with respect to any other agent, setting out from the information included in its external description. Knowledge about dependence situations can be useful in various ways, e.g. in order to guide the choice of partners in social interactions. As Figure 3.2 outlines it determines a preference relation over partners for a future coalition. Partners in a MBMD are presumably more interested in accepting a proposal for a coalition than partners that may not know about it (LBMD), or that are aware of a mutual dependence but pursue a different goal (MBRD) etc.

Sichman and Demazeau (1995) present an extension to the above model that focuses on the effects of uncertainty on the social reasoning mechanism.

3.2.4.4 Rosenschein and Zlotkin: Rules of Encounter

Rosenschein and Zlotkin (1994) model interaction processes between heterogeneous self-interested agents within a quantitative, utility-based framework. Still,

---

[7] The qualification "locally believed" might also have been labelled "possibly locally believed", as it is based on agent a_i's ignorance concerning agent a_j's beliefs about it.

their aim is of constructive nature: they assume that a "committee" of agent designers agrees upon a set of prescriptions ("the rules of the game"), represented by the negotiation protocol. Within these limitations, each designer is completely free to endow its agents with the decision-making strategy that it considers convenient to maximise its agent's local utility. The idea is that by appropriately adjusting the prescriptive negotiation protocol, the private strategies that the designers put into their agents can be influenced: strategies with certain desirable characteristics simply become the best choices that designers can adopt.

A set of desirable properties of negotiation protocols is outlined. Firstly, the admissible deals should be *efficient*, in the sense that no utility is wasted (Pareto-optimality). Secondly, the strategies should be *stable*, i.e. no agent should have an incentive to deviate from agreed upon strategies (symmetric equilibria). Thirdly, the process should be *simple*: it should make low computational demands on the agents and require little communication overhead. Finally, *distribution* (no central decision-maker) and *symmetry* ("equal rights for everyone") are required. As these characteristics are interdependent, trade-offs have to be made between one attribute and another.

Different protocols and strategies are studied within a game-theoretic framework, which relies on a set of assumptions. Agents are utility-maximisers with symmetric abilities, capable of making binding agreements. No explicit utility transfer is possible (there is no money with which to compensate an agent for a disadvantaged agreement), but utility is comparable between the agents (i.e. an agent can compare its own gains/losses with the ones of others). Finally, only single two-agent encounters are considered; i.e. just two agents take part in the negotiations, which do not consider the possibility to meet again.

Zlotkin and Rosenschein perform their analysis in three classes of domains of increasing complexity: in *task-oriented* domains agents have non-conflicting jobs to do and the object of negotiation is to redistribute tasks to everyone's mutual benefit. In *state-oriented* domains agents pursue goals and actions which have side-effects, so that an agent doing one action might hinder or help another agent; they negotiate upon joint plans and schedules, i.e. when each of them should do which action. Finally, in *worth-oriented* domains, the degree of achievement of goals is determined by a utility function. The negotiation objects are the same as in task-oriented domains.

3.3 Co-ordination Frameworks

In this section, we provide examples of operational frameworks for multi-agent co-ordination. The approaches presented in the sequel are based on three different paradigms: centralised co-ordination of autonomous agents' plans, distributed co-ordination by co-operative negotiation and negotiated search.

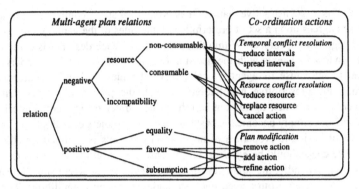

Figure 3.3. Plan relations and co-ordination actions

3.3.1   Von Martial: Co-ordination of Autonomous Agents' Plans

Von Martial (1992) presents a framework for the co-ordination of autonomous agents based on multi-agent plan relations. He sets out from a situation where each agent has already developed an abstract, individually admissible plan, which is supposed to contribute to the attainment of the agent's goals. Each agent's individual plan describes sequences of actions that it would like to perform in the future. Nevertheless, the nature of the actions makes plans interdependent; a fact that is captured by so-called *multi-agent plan relations*. A special planning agent detects these relations and modifies the agents' plans accordingly. Consequently, co-ordination is conceived as the process of handling multi-agent plan relations; plans are co-ordinated, if all plan relations are coped with.

Von Martial presents the taxonomy of multi-agent plan relations, which is depicted in Figure 3.3. Negative relations generally prevent individual plans from forming a globally consistent multi-agent plan. They arise either directly between actions, i.e. when agents plan to perform actions that are defined to be incompatible by some domain-dependent incompatibility scheme, or are induced by action-resource dependencies: two agents might need to simultaneously access the same scarce resource. Positive relations arise from a latent synergetic potential between plans: exploiting them means to produce a more efficient overall plan. Von Martial presents three types of positive relations. The *equality* relation is present, when two agents plan to perform the same action. A similar case is described by the *subsumption* relation, where the abstract actions of one individual plan imply the accomplishment of some abstract action of another. The *favour* relation indicates a somehow different situation. It states that actions of an agent *A*'s plan can be refined in a way, that "makes it easier" for an agent *B* to execute its plan. This can be done in two ways: either *A*'s refined action helps to establish a "precondition" for the execution of an action that B would be like to have performed, or it actually is that action.

Three classes of actions to handle plan relations are identified. *Temporal conflict resolution actions* manipulate the planned execution intervals of the conflicting actions. *Resource conflict resolution actions* include the use of alternative resources, the reduction of the necessary amount of a resource, or the cancellation of the planned action. *Plan modification actions* add, move or refine actions in one or several plans.

As Figure 3.3 shows, a mapping between plan relations and co-ordination actions is provided, which specifies alternative ways to handle dependencies. For example, a non-consumable resource conflict between two actions can be solved by reducing or spreading the execution intervals of a pair of actions, by replacing the resource etc. Agents make use of the favour relation by adequately removing, adding or refining their corresponding plans.

The detection and resolution of plan relations within the group of agents is achieved using a fixed communication protocol. The detection of plan relations and the evaluation of possible co-ordination actions is done in a centralised manner by a special agent who adopts the role of a *co-ordinator*: it detects plan relations using a set of specialised algorithms and then selects co-ordination actions by heuristically assigning cost values to the set of possible actions shown in Figure 3.3. These actions are proposed to the agents whose individual plans are involved in the dependency. Agents are supposed to be autonomous, so they can either change their plan accordingly or refuse the proposal, leaving plan relation unresolved. In the latter case, the co-ordinator generates alternative co-ordination proposals. This process hopefully leads to a set of co-ordinated individual plans; i.e. plans that are mutually unrelated respecting the dependencies of Figure 3.3.

3.3.2   Decker: TÆMS and GPGP

The approach presented by Decker (1995) is twofold. On the one hand, a general modelling language (TÆMS) has been developed whose major modelling power lies in the possibility to represent dependencies. On the other hand, a distributed multi-agent planning framework (GPGP) has been built, that generates and adapts agent plans with respect to the dependencies, which have been detected in a TÆMS description of a domain.

The *TÆMS* framework (Task Analysis, Environment Modelling and Simulation) is intended to model co-operative distributed systems and to analyse their performance by qualitative simulation. Problems are modelled under a task-centred perspective. *Tasks* are structured in a directed acyclic graph by the sub-task relation. Tasks that have no sub-tasks (the "leaves" of the task-graph) are regarded as primitive entities and are identified with the *methods* that cope with them. There is no independent notion of methods in TÆMS.

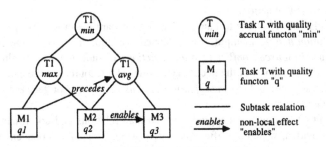

Figure 3.4. Example of a TÆMS model

Methods can achieve a certain "quality", which measures how well a task is done. It measures, for instance, up to which degree a task has been completed, or the certainty and precision of its outcome. The notion of method quality is modelled by a *quality function Q* that at each time t assigns a positive value $Q(M,t)$ to a method M. This kind of influence that a method's execution has on its own quality is called *local effect* of its execution. A *non-local effect* is present when the execution of one method affects the quality or the duration of another method, that will be executed later. This is modelled by a parameterised *effect function e*, that determines the changes in the influenced method's duration and quality at each time t. The parameters can be used to specify different classes of effects. Method quality is propagated "upwards" along the sub-task relation. A *quality accrual function* is assigned to each non-primitive task T, which determines at each time t, how T's quality is calculated from the quality of its sub-tasks. Figure 3.4 shows an example of a TÆMS model.

Interactions between two tasks with respect to temporal and quality aspects are modelled by non-local effects. When non-local effects occur between methods associated with different agents, they are called *co-ordination relationships*. Commonly found classes of non-local effects include:

- *A enables B*: B cannot start before method A has achieved a certain quality, i.e. up to that time A's quality is zero.
- *A facilitates B*: an increase in the quality of method A facilitates the execution of method B, i.e. augments its quality.
- *A hinders B*: constitutes the opposite relation of *facilitates*.
- *A precedes B*: method A must have achieved a certain quality before method B can start, and the better A is done, the more quality is achievable by B.

Generalised Partial Global Planning (GPGP) (Decker and Lesser 1992, Decker 1995) extents Durfee's PGP approach (1988) to general TÆMS models. The basic idea behind GPGP is to detect and respond appropriately to the TÆMS co-ordination relationships.

It is assumed that both, control and data, are distributed. Agents only "believe" portions of the task structure of a TÆMS model. These portions include the methods that an agent is responsible for, but generally also comprise "social information", i.e. methods that will be executed by other agents. This information is used to construct a (partial) model of the agent's acquaintances. When an agent detects a need for co-ordination, for instance because it believes that a non-local effect exists between one of its methods and a method believed to be executed by another agent, it should modify its individual plan and *inform* other related parties accordingly.

The GPGP agent architecture, that achieves the above behaviour, comprises two major components. The *local scheduler* takes as input the current, subjectively believed task structure and produces a schedule of problem-solving methods that are executable in that situation by ordering them in an attempt to maximise the schedule's overall quality. The *co-ordination component* provides additional constraints to prune the search space of the scheduler. It accomplishes this by passing information about commitments (e. g. to achieve quality for a task before a certain time t), which are established as a result of applying *co-ordination mechanisms*.

Co-ordination mechanisms are usually applied in response to co-ordination relationships and can be adapted to different problem-solving situation by means of a set of parameters:

- The *updating non-local viewpoints* mechanism exchanges useful private views of the task structure.
- The *communicating results* mechanism informs agents about the outcome of tasks as a result of commitments made earlier in the problem-solving process.
- The *avoiding redundancy* mechanism is present when an agent detects that an acquaintance plans to execute a method for the same task as itself. In this case, both negotiate to find out who will finally be responsible for that task.
- *Handling co-ordination relationships* requires that agents executing related tasks meet the constraints that co-ordination relationships between them imply. In order to do so, the involved agents enter a negotiation process, and subsequently commit to the agreed deadlines.

3.3.3 Lander: the TEAM Framework

The TEAM multi-agent framework presented by Lander (1994) is intended to support the integration of heterogeneous and reusable agents into functional agent sets. As agents can be complete knowledge-based systems, chosen from an agent library by the system designer, they may be endowed with disparate long-term knowledge and solution-evaluation criteria, as well as be based on different languages, algorithms, hardware requirements, etc.

Lander's work is mainly concerned with "high-level" issues of heterogeneity. The main interest lies in managing the knowledge inconsistencies that necessarily arise when knowledge systems, developed by different designers at different times and with different ends must co-operate in a single system. It is argued that the attempt to achieve global consistency within such a system is neither feasible nor desirable: computationally, maintaining global consistency is expensive, while seen from a philosophical stance different viewpoints can even be advantageous. Therefore, agents usually come up with different evaluations of situations and actions, which results in conflicts that need to be resolved.

Lander assumes agents benevolent and co-operative. They communicate via a shared data space (blackboard). Partial solutions are stored in this space and are incrementally specified by the agents.

Co-ordination is essentially achieved through conflict resolution, which is carried out within a distributed search procedure. An agent's *local search space* is modelled by n parameters with associated domains. The *local solution space* is constituted by n-tuples of value assignments to parameters, each of which satisfies a set of constraints, locally known by the agent. A *global solution space* is created by sets of parameters, each of which is either present in some local solution space or computable out of this information and compatible with all local constraints. Consequently, the agents' local problem-solving activities interfere when they refer to the same or to related parameters.

Lander presents an opportunistic search strategy called *Negotiated Search* (NS). NS essentially provides a mutually known protocol according to which local search operators are applied (represented as a graph whose nodes are global problem-solving states and whose arcs are labelled with admissible operators). There are four search operators: an agent invokes the *Initiate-Solution* operator, to generate a base proposal that satisfies its locally known set of constraints; *Extend-Solution* generates a proposal that extends and is compatible with an existing solution; *Critique-Solution* is similar to Extend-Solution except that it returns a critique rather than a proposal; finally, the *Relax-Solution-Requirement* operator weakens some constraints and propagates this change through any existing solution (possibly making unacceptable solutions acceptable).

In an initial step of NS some agents produce base proposals (*Initiate-Solution*) which are subject to the others' criticism (*Critique-Solution*). If a conflict is detected, the partial solution is either considered unacceptable or at least one of the implicated agents decides to relax some of its local constraints (*Relax-Solution-Requirement*). The process goes on (*Extend-Solution*) until a global solution is found or the search process is aborted unsuccessfully.

NS is refined by strategies that specify different protocols for negotiation in conflict situations, thus overcoming the opportunistic character of the general NS algorithm. A strategy is defined in terms of roles, which are associated with certain action capabilities. For instance, the *linear compromise* strategy, according to which a compromise is calculated as the intersection of the linear functions that two agents use in order to determine the utility of a value for a certain parameter, requires two roles: one to generate the functions and another to calculate the intersection points. When a conflict is detected, a strategy is chosen among the involved agents, it is instantiated (i.e. agents are assigned to the roles) and finally executed.

The architecture of the implementation of TEAM consists of three parts. Firstly, a blackboard stores problem definitions, strategies and (partial) solutions. The second part is given by a group of agents, each provided with a local inference engine (a set of Knowledge Sources), a local agenda (an ordered list of Knowledge Source activations) and a working memory. The Knowledge Sources of an agent represent search operators whose specific functionality is achieved by invoking abilities of the underlying knowledge-based system. Finally, the TEAM framework comprises a special team manager agent (TMan). TMan constitutes a set of Knowledge Sources that facilitate agent co-operation by mediating blackboard updates, sending notifications to agents etc. Concurrent (synchronous) action is simulated: during a TEAM execution cycle, each agent performs the action with the highest rating value in its local research agenda. Then, TMan becomes active and accomplishes the desired modifications on the blackboard etc.

The agents' benevolence and the low degree of local control uncertainty due to the global blackboard, facilitate the task of achieving globally coherent solutions within the TEAM framework. For instance, if in the aforementioned strategy the utility functions of the involved agents are mutually known, a compromise is not explicitly *negotiated* but can be directly *calculated*. Agents are so fully aware of the problem-solving state, that, when a conflict resolution strategy is agreed upon, the actual resolution is trivial. The conceptual framework of TEAM need not rely on a centralised co-ordinator: coherent action is achieved based on common knowledge and co-operative search.

3.4 Bottom Line

This chapter has given a survey of co-ordination models in artificial agent societies, drawing on work in the field of Distributed Artificial Intelligence. We have presented different classes of co-ordination mechanisms and have described examples of operational co-ordination frameworks.

DAI has been characterised as an aggregate of three main currents: AA, DPS, and MAS. An attempt has been made to characterise these currents by basic *endogenous* properties of agent systems: AA focuses on questions of autonomy of individual agents (often in a multi-agent environment), MAS is concerned with heterogeneous systems of non-benevolent agents with conflicting goals, while DPS aims at designing homogeneous systems whose functionality arises from the co-operation of benevolent agents pursuing common goals.

However, Durfee and Rosenschein (1994) point out that characterising DAI systems by *endogenous* properties draws a rather fuzzy border between the fields.

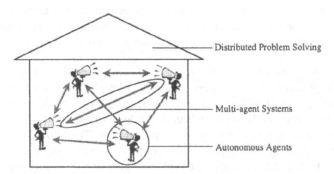

Figure 3.5. An integrative view of DAI

In Sycara's Persuader system (1989), for instance, agents representing a company's management and union agents negotiate about labour contracts. With respect to the contract, they have the common goal of finding an agreement (DPS style), while their interests are definitely contrary (MAS style).

This suggests a classification based on *exogenous* properties. Instead of conceiving AA, MAS and DPS as labels for particular kinds of systems, they might rather be considered descriptions of the different objectives that designers have when they build DAI systems (Durfee and Rosenschein 1994). A researcher in the area of AA aims at providing formalisms and architectures for designing agents endowed with autonomy, so as to enable them to "survive" in a certain class of environments; a MAS designer is interested in the emergence of desired properties of agent interactions from a fundament of groups of agents with uncontrollably varying characteristics. A DPS system designer, finally, aims at building agent systems that cope with a certain task; he or she is interested in generating a desired functionality among a group of agents with manipulable characteristics.

From this perspective AA, MAS and DPS appear as the different parts of a "divide and conquer" approach to DAI: a DPS designer is concerned with solving a certain problem by means of a distributed system, using methods that presuppose certain properties of agent interactions. For instance, in order to assure efficient and robust problem solving, a designer might decide to use a contract net mechanism. However, this relies on the existence of benevolent agents, a condition that cannot always be assured. So, he or she refers to the area of MAS in order to coerce self-interested decision-makers to interact in a benevolent fashion: taxation mechanisms may be used, for instance, providing incentives that harmonise the agents' interests. Finally, from the area of AA he or she borrows agent architectures or languages in order to make these models operational.

Figure 3.5 resumes this stance on DAI. At the risk of oversimplifying, it is nailed down to the following assertions:

- AA research is *agent-centred.* The attempt is to make it "survive" in real-world situations (including multi-agent worlds).
- MAS research is *interaction-centred.* It aims to assure internal properties such as stability, sincerity, etc. in a system of agents whose individual properties can vary.
- DPS research is *problem-centred.* It focuses on how to build a collective of agents that shows desired external properties, such as robustness and high performance. Setting out from certain properties of agents and interactions, some functionality is to be achieved in dynamic and uncontrollable environments.

4 Analysis

The first part of this book has compiled the various lines of research concerning the phenomenon of co-ordination: Chapter 2 has examined important aspects of co-ordination in human societies, while Chapter 3 has given an overview of DAI research with a special focus on co-ordination among artificial agents. At this point, it is convenient to relate the state of the art to our objectives listed in Chapter 1. Consequently, this chapter first analyses existing DAI from this perspective and then motivates the work that will be described in the rest of the book.

4.1 Limitations of Present Co-ordination Models

Some comments about the limitations of the previously described approaches to co-ordination are pertinent here. The first issue to be discussed is of quite general nature and refers to the growing divergence of DAI research.

Need for Holistic and Structured Models

The growing interest in DAI together with the broad extension of the field has led to increasingly specialised research efforts. Work on specific sub-problems is abundant, while efforts to integrate solutions for real-world applications have become rather rare. In the different DAI currents, this negligence of an overall view has led to the following situation:

- The area of AA is being "flooded" by ad-hoc agent architectures. A variety of them has been developed for robotic and for software agents (see J. Müller 1998). However, on the one hand, many approaches have just been tested in laboratory conditions or stick to their own, purposefully designed simulation testbeds. On the other hand, many efforts are concerned with stand-alone agents, whose performance is measured in how well they can perform a certain task (*despite* the potential existence of other agents). Less work has been done on autonomous agents that cope with real-world tasks as members of an (emerging) team.
- Research in MAS usually shows what Conte and Gilbert (1995) call a "sub-cognitive" bias: the emergence of desired properties from individual "agents" is associated with elementary entities such as neurones or simple automata. When cognitive agents are considered, utility-based models are stressed. However, game theoretic frameworks provide only limited support for the design of agent

systems, as they hide important features of the agents and their environment in the utility function(s). In order to account for complex phenomena such as co-ordination in many realistic scenarios, more "structured" models are desirable.

- DPS approaches do not clearly distinguish between co-ordination and local problem solving. As Jennings and Campos (1997) underline, effective problem solving requires agent interactions which are *between* co-operation (benevo-lence) and conflict ("pure" self interest): in some situations an agent better grants help to an acquaintance, while in others it contributes to the resolution of a problem giving preference to its own local goals. However, this decision is hard-wired in traditional DPS co-operation protocols, i.e. it is usually not sub-ject to reflective reasoning. Domain independent co-operation models that al-low for (a certain degree of) autonomy of the involved agents are still to come.

There is a need to take a holistic stance, and to integrate findings from the above fields, so as to come up with operational co-ordination mechanisms that allow groups of autonomous cognitive agents to attain some global functionality.

The above comment leads directly to the next two issues. They are concerned with *technical* questions respecting the design of co-ordination models.

Need for Reusable and Scaleable Co-ordination Models

The major interest with respect to the question of agent reuse has focused on how to integrate a priori existing agents into a functional system. Big research projects are under way, aiming at the interoperation of previously existing knowledge-based systems by converting them into "agents" (e.g. the ARPA knowledge sharing effort, described in Neches et al. 1991).

Less attention has been paid to how problem-solving agents should be designed so as to be reusable, although this question has recently received more attention (e.g. Lander 1994). The concept of autonomous agents constitutes an important contribution to this venture, as the notion of self-interest as a behaviour guideline encourages a separation between individual and collective problem solving.

Despite recent work on communication and negotiation protocols (e.g. Bar-buceanu and Fox 1996), the panorama is still worse with respect to the reusability of co-ordination models. Usually, even though an agent's problem-solving capa-bilities are encapsulated to be reused in different tasks, the co-ordination knowl-edge and mechanisms are usually designed ad hoc for every problem instance. A model of "baseline" co-ordination would be helpful, tailorable to different specific problem instances, and reusable for different tasks.

Need for Design Guidelines

Not just the terminology but also the mechanisms and architectures used within DAI are diverse. Therefore, when a certain problem is to be solved by DAI tech-niques, it is extremely difficult to make a justified choice for a particular ap-proach.

Solving problems by means of *reactive* agent systems is much of a "black art" (Jennings and Campos 1997). Iglesias et al. (1998) provide a survey of recent developments in the field of methodologies for *cognitive* agent systems. In general, the approaches set out from existing object-oriented approaches (e.g. OMT, Rumbaugh et al. 1991), or are based on model-based methodologies for knowledge system development (e.g. KADS, Wielinga et al. 1992). Still, most approaches are mainly "extensions" of existing approaches and are still in experimental stages (e.g. Glaser 1996, Kinney et al. 1996 or Iglesias et al. 1996). Furthermore, as long as DAI has not reached a state of greater stability and maturity, it seems difficult that any genuine agent-oriented methodology will be widely accepted.

For the time being, some simple guidelines will definitely be helpful. A concise separation between problem solving and co-ordination is a step in the right direction. Layered agent architectures might support such a guideline, as they allow stepwise design and evaluation.

The final two items of the list of remarks with respect to the state of the art are of *conceptual* nature. They refer to our objective of capturing essential characteristics of a "social intelligence" based on decentralised co-ordination within groups of autonomous agents.

Need for Social Co-ordination Architectures

This point concerns the "architecture", the structure of a social intelligence. Essentially two classes of approaches are commonly used in DAI:

- In a centralised architecture, an individual agent orchestrates co-ordination respecting a certain set of goals within a group of agents. It could be considered an *individual intelligence* that tries to make use of social resources. For instance, in von Martial's dependency-based approach (1992), a single co-ordinator is knowledgeable about potential interdependencies between individual plans, detects them and tries to resolve them, so as to satisfy the interests of the agents to be co-ordinated.
- A distributed architecture comprises several agents that intend to shape group co-ordination. However, this is usually done from the viewpoint of a *replication* of an individual intelligence: agents develop joint goals and pursue joint intentions, which constitute (potentially different views of) the same multi-agent plan *iterated* in the agents' belief and knowledge bases. Decker's GPGP approach (1995) falls into this class: each agent develops partial global plans for itself and for others. The problem lies in how to deal with uncertainty, i.e. when to exchange partial global plans and how to join them into one.

Both approaches take the traditional AI tack towards co-ordination. In the first, *one* sole agent co-ordinates the plans of others, while in the second *many* agents do the same thing. In any of them, the co-ordinating agent "wants" to harmonise group activity, it is (or: believes to be) completely aware of the situation and, on this basis, generates a model of how *it* would like others' to behave with respect to certain criteria.

So, it appears promising to consider models of *emergent* co-ordination based on metaphors and mechanisms found in human societies, or *social* co-ordination for short. In social life, people are neither entirely manipulated by society, nor are they fully conscious of the impacts of their behaviour in society. A mechanism is needed that influences the self-centred cognition of autonomous agents so as to make their behaviour instrumental for the "functioning" of the group. Such a mechanism will capture important peculiarities of co-ordination in artificial agent societies: social co-ordination becomes different from the distributed replication of centralised co-ordination models under uncertainty.

Need for Flexible, Operational and Understandable Biasing Mechanisms

This final remark is closely related to the previous: it concerns the *scope* of the mechanisms used to design a purposeful social intelligence. Many approaches coerce agent behaviour by means of a fixed set of regimentations (e.g. the social law approach described in Shoham and Tennenholz 1992, 1995), which has turned out to be constraining, thus limiting their applicability to rather static environments. By contrast, descriptive models of mechanisms in human societies are more flexible, but often not fully formalised and usually not operational (e.g., the work presented in Conte and Castelfranchi 1995). Both types of approaches generally do not provide evidence to foresee the impact that the coercion of any one agent will have on society level.

A sufficiently flexible, understandable and operational biasing mechanism seems appropriate. It will be the key part of any social co-ordination that is to be apt for complex applications.

4.2 The Approach of this Book

The approach taken in this book, to be presented in the following chapters, has been developed with the above analysis in mind. We will treat any of the above issues in the sequel, although not all of them in the extension that they deserve. Discussing any of the above questions in depth would most probably require a book of its own. However, our paramount interest resides in providing an operational model of decentralised co-ordination for real-world multi-agent systems. In line with this "holistic" stance, this book highlights the *integration* of models and mechanisms of the different areas of DAI.

First, the mechanism of structural co-operation is introduced. Structural co-operation allows for emergent social co-ordination, borrowing from theories concerning simple human societies. In this mechanism, the self-interested action of autonomous agents is biased by means of "social structure". These concepts are defined concisely and the mechanism is described within a precise model. Subsequently, the ProsA$_2$ agent architecture is presented. The architecture comprises several layers, that can be built upon incrementally in order to achieve desired behaviour: an individual layer is concerned with local problem solving, a social layer achieves basic co-ordination, while a normative layer biases the outcome of the latter. A social interaction strategy for each agent is presented that complies with the requirement of self-interest as implied by the concept of autonomous agenthood, but at the same time makes it possible to achieve a sufficient level of co-ordination in society. Therefore, the work to be presented comprises all three aspects of DAI research:

- distributed problem solving
  A framework is presented that allows a central designer to co-ordinate the activities of autonomous agents so as to solve the problem at hand. Co-ordination is achieved through the mechanism of structural co-operation.

- multi-agent systems
  Within the framework of structural co-operation, social interaction strategies for autonomous agents are designed. The global outcome of the social interaction process within the society of agents is analysed.

- autonomous agents
  A layered architecture for autonomous agents is presented. This architecture provides the operational basis for structural co-operation.

The approach will be validated in the domain of road traffic control. An experimental multi-agent traffic management system will be presented and applied to a real-world road network.

5 Emergent Co-ordination by Structural Co-operation

The present second part of the book is dedicated to the mechanism of structural co-operation, one of the main contributions of the work. This chapter introduces the mechanism. It is organised as follows: first, we present theories from social science underlying the development of structural co-operation. It is shown how observed social phenomena can be explained in terms of their social finality, and what role social structure plays in such rationalisations. Section 5.2 describes the reactive co-ordination settings that we are interested in. Subsequently, we show how the notion of social structure can be applied to these settings, giving rise to the mechanism of structural co-operation. Finally, we conclude this chapter by discussing issues respecting structural co-operation and multi-agent system design.

5.1 The Metaphor: Functionality of Social Structure

This section aims at motivating the conceptual framework within which a mechanism that allows for the emergence of co-ordination within a society of autonomous agents will be developed. It is subdivided in two parts. We will first make a short detour to the area of social science and examine the type of analysis that a particular school, structural functionalism, applies in order to explain observed characteristics of human societies. In the second part, we analyse as to how far structural functionalist explanations of social phenomena can provide us with conceptual metaphors for constructing co-ordination mechanisms for multi-agent systems.

5.1.1 Structural Functionalism

The conceptual basis of research in multi-agent systems has been largely influenced by economy. Terms such as negotiation, contract, marginal costs etc. are in heavy use within the MAS community. All these metaphors are borrowed from a discipline that describes a developed society where the division of labour is predominant and where the exchange of "goods" is realised within the frame of some monetary system. As the sociologist Durkheim noticed around the turn of the century, the behaviour of the agents that comprise such complex social systems is mainly determined by individuality. The influence of socialisation on the self-interested behaviour of individuals decreases with the complexity of society. By contrast, within simpler societies the socially conditioned sphere of individual consciousness is predominant. In the sequel, we will examine as to how far this argument, and the study of "primitive" societies in general, can provide ideas for the design of co-ordination mechanisms within multi-agent problem-solving systems.

Up to the early days of our century sociology, and social anthropology in particular, was approached on the basis of the paradigm of evolutionism. Social phenomena were often analysed in rather simplistic schemes, as Darwin's ideas respecting biological evolution were rigidly transferred to human societies. Habits and customs were deterred from their cultural context to be compared indiscriminately, and often conjectures about the societies' histories were presented in order to "explain" them by their supposed genesis.

Structural Functionalism became popular especially in the United Kingdom as a response to conjectural reconstructions of evolutionists. Radcliffe-Brown, one of the major defenders of this school, conceived social anthropology as a natural science that applies inductive methods. Large amounts of data were gathered in field-works and common structural principles were abstracted that allowed for a classification of societies (Kuper 1973). The point lies in a shift from diachronic to synchronic explanations of phenomena. The reasons for certain observed patterns of behaviour are sought in the present, not in the past: instead of speculations about past origins which are necessarily opaque to the scientist it is asked for the "purpose" or the "meaning" of a specific custom in the contemporary situation. In structural functionalism, this type of explanation is organised around three basic concepts: *process* and *structure*, whose relation is referred to as *function*.

The object of anthropological study is identified as the *process* of social life. This concept comprises the multitude of actions and interactions of human beings acting within a particular group and in a particular place. It constitutes the concrete, observable phenomenological reality.

Social structure is seen as "an arrangement of persons in institutionally controlled or defined relationships" (Radcliffe-Brown 1952). Social relations arise either from person to person (father and son) or between social roles (king and subjects). It exists "between two of more individual organisms when there is some adjustment of their respective interests, by convergence of interest, or by limitation of conflict that might arise from divergence of interests" (p. 199). Any relationship "is one in which the conduct of persons in their interactions is controlled by norms, rules or patterns" (p. 10). The established moral codes, norms of conduct, the rights and the duties pertaining to a particular social structure are referred to as *institutions*.

Function is conceived as the "functioning of its structure". The function of a particular set of norms is the contribution it makes to the continuity of society and the maintenance of its structure: normative standardised behaviour gives rise to recurrent social processes whose effects correspond to the conditions of persistence (or the "needs") of society. The basic need of all societies has been termed *co-aptation* by structural functionalists, meaning the mutual adjustment of members of society: morals, etiquette, religion, government, and education are all parts of the complex mechanism by which a social structure exists and persists.

Within the above conceptual framework, observed phenomena are explained by means of a *functional* analysis. It sets out from the assumption that all parts of a social structure work together with a sufficient degree of harmony or internal consistency, that is, without producing persistent conflicts: the social structure as a whole is considered *a priori* to be "functioning", i.e. to be apt to meet the necessary conditions for the existence and the reproduction (or "survival") of society. On this background a particular institution is analysed with respect to its instrumentality: the structural functionalist aims to show how it fits in the network of different interests and conflicts that exist within a society, so as to contribute to an *equilibrium* of force which leads to a stable social structure. Social processes, a religious ritual for instance, are not explained by their evolution, but by their "objectives" or functions, which, in the end, are always assumed to promote the maintenance of a social equilibrium.

Although the main interest lies in the description and comparison of social structure, it is acknowledged that norms and institutions "work or 'function' only through their effects in life, i.e. in the thoughts, sentiments and actions of individuals" (Radcliffe-Brown 1952, p. 185). Social institutions are characterised by being external to individuals and coercive in nature and are thus an instance of Durkheim's notion of *social facts*: they exist before an individual's birth and endure after its death. The individual cannot freely choose to adopt them but just has to live in a society where a set of norms is in force (i.e. being generally recognised as binding and widely observed). So, society and its structure are seen as influencing individual behaviour by creating external constraints: norms and values, rules of descent and residence are just social facts, that contribute to maintain the society in equilibrium, that is, to ensure its survival.

It is accepted that the explanations, that individuals in society provide for their own behaviour and for their abidance to social norms, are different from structural functionalist interpretations, as such "apparent" functions of social structure are believed to be analytically insignificant. The interest of the structural functionalist lies in the *latent* functions, which the individual ignores or is unaware of. These can only be analysed from the outside, taking a holistic stance: it is argued that the function of a norm can only be explained in its relation to the social structure and the external conditions of society, i.e. by taking the entire system into consideration.

Structural functionalism within social anthropology was strongly tied to the study of indigenous societies during the context of colonialism. The relative rigidity of these societies in colonial regions gave the (false) impression of harmonious, internally consistent social structures with stable social equilibria. So, it is not surprising that the decline of colonialism after the Second World War accelerated the transition from structural functionalism to more diachronic, process-oriented theories which underline the dynamic aspects of human society[1].

5.1.2   A Constructive Perspective

At first glance, the above excursion into social anthropology, which aims to build an analytical model of phenomena observed in reality, appears to have little relation to our attempt to engineer intelligent computer systems that efficiently solve problems. Still, the key problem of applying the paradigm of multi-agent systems to problem solving is to coerce autonomous agents to mutually adjust their behaviour so as to achieve a certain task. There is a growing awareness in the DAI community that "pure individualism", as reflected by the principle of individual rationality, is not a good choice as a guideline for decision-making of autonomous agents that make up those systems (Jennings and Campos 1997).

Structural functionalism provides a model of how society, or social structure, "moulds" individual behaviour so as to achieve globally functional behaviour. Still, in order to use this model as a metaphor in the design of artificial agent societies, we need to turn structural functionalist analysis upside down: instead of explaining observed behaviour in terms of social structure, we would like to *design* a "social structure", so as to achieve the "co-aptation" of the behaviour of autonomous agents towards a "social equilibrium" that leads to a satisfying achievement of a global task. There are two ideas in structural functionalism that are of special interest for this enterprise:

- the *biasing* effect of social structure
  Norms and social institutions impose external constraints on an agent's freedom of choice. They are primitive notions, not reducible to any other, that actually *influence* the behaviour of a "socialised" autonomous agent. Still, they are not assumed to completely determine agent behaviour, but just bias self-interested action in a certain ("socially desired") direction.

- the *teleological* character of social structure
  Seen from the outside, social structure induces the *co-ordination* of the behaviour of autonomous agents towards a global function of society. From an agent's perspective social structure induces a specific form of *co-operation* in the sense of mutual adjustment of individual action.

We will term *structural co-operation* such a mechanism that makes the co-ordination of autonomous agents emerge from social structure. Figure 5.1 graphically depicts the notion of the functionality of social structure, that structural co-operation is based on, from a constructive perspective. It sets out from autono-

---

[1] In fact, an essentially synchronic analysis of *human* societies in the tradition of structural functionalism is strongly discouraged. It must be underlined once again that we are concerned with *artificial* agent societies: we are seeking guidelines for constructing computational mechanisms to be applied within an *engineering* process.

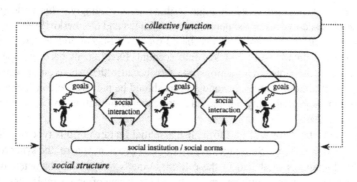

Figure 5.1. Emergent co-ordination by structural co-operation

mous agents that pursue their individual goals upon the background of a common social structure. The bold arrows indicate social interaction processes that the agents are involved in and that influence the characteristics and the achievement of their goals. Thin arrows denote functional effects. A chain of *functional effects* can be recognised: norms influence social interactions, which modify the individual goals of the agents so that their actions become instrumental with respect to a collective function. It is the task of the multi-agent system designer to establish a social structure that induces co-ordination with respect to the problem to be solved. He or she has to develop a "legislation" or a "code of moral behaviour" so as to make the collective function coincide with the desired functionality of the system.

In order to make these quite abstract ideas more precise and to turn structural co-operation into an operational mechanism, two key questions must be tackled: we need a model of how an autonomous agent acts in the presence of other agents and how social structure influences this process. The following sections are dedicated to this enterprise.

5.2 The Problem: Reactive Co-ordination

Before we transform the above metaphor into a mechanism that supports the co-ordination of autonomous problem-solving agents, we need to outline the class of problems that are to be affronted. In doing so, we also clarify the meaning of terms such as "reactive co-ordination" or "multi-plan", which will be essential throughout the remaining chapters of this book.

The domains that we are interested in share the characteristic of being highly dynamic: perceptions are error-prone, actions fail, contingencies occur. A common way to deal with this problem is to build systems that only plan their actions for a short time horizon, in order to assess the effects of their interventions as early as possible, and to adapt future behaviour accordingly. This paradigm is frequently used in decision-support domains (Cuena and Ossowski 1998).

When such systems are modelled based on a multi-agent architecture, two essential constraints have to be taken into account. First, agents need to cope with the fact that their plans and actions interfere because they share an environment with only limited resources. Second, agents should be prepared to consider actions that attain their goals only *partially* due to resource limitation and environmental contingencies.

In this section, we will first formalise essential features of this type of reactive co-ordination settings. Subsequently, a particular problem sphere, the synchronous blocks domain, is modelled in these terms. Finally, important characteristics of reactive co-ordination settings are illustrated by means of an example scenario in the synchronous blocks domain.

5.2.1   A Formal Model

We will describe the setting that we are interested in by means of a state-based model based on first-order logic augmented with negation as failure. Unless stated otherwise, set-theoretic notation is used as a shortcut for the corresponding logical expressions.

Let S be a set of *world states* and Π a finite set of *plans*. The execution of a plan π changes the state of the world, which is modelled as a partially defined mapping

$$res : \Pi \times S \rightarrow S .$$

A plan is *executable* in s, if only if *res* is defined for a certain world state s. At least one *empty plan* π_ε is required to be included in the set of plans Π; it is modelled as identity.

There is a finite set of agents A, each of which can act in the world thereby modifying its state. An agent $\alpha \in A$ is characterised by the following notions:

- capability
  The predicate $can(\alpha, \pi)$ determines the *individual plans* $\pi \in \Pi$ that α is able to execute. An agent α is always capable of executing the empty plan π_ε.

- ideal states
  The predicate $ideal(\alpha, s)$ expresses the states $s \in S$ that the agent $\alpha \in A$ would ideally like to bring about. We denote the set of ideal states of α by S_α^{ideal}.

- distance measure
  The metric function d_α maps a state and an ideal state to a real number:

$$d_\alpha : S \times S_\alpha^{ideal} \rightarrow \Re .$$

This number represents α's estimation of how far a state is away from an ideal state. It usually models the notion of relative difficulty to improve world states.

In the scenarios that we are interested in, an agent usually cannot fully reach any of its ideal states. So, we will use the notion of ideal states together with the distance measure d_α to describe an agent's preferences respecting world states. As these preferences are supposed to guide the agent's behaviour, the ideal states together with the distance measure are called the agent's *motivation*.

Note that the agents in A will usually have diverging motivations: they may be endowed with different (partially conflicting) ideal states and may even measure the distance to ideal states in different scales. So, for instance, even though two functions d_α and $d_{\alpha'}$ map one and the same state to the same real number, this number may actually express different degrees of preference for the agents.

We now introduce a notion of interdependent action. The set M of *multi-plans* comprises all multi-sets over the individual plans Π [2]:

$$M = bagof(\Pi) \, .$$

A multi-plan $\mu \in M$ models the simultaneous execution of all its *component plans*, i.e. of the individual plans $\pi \in \mu$ that are contained in the multi-set μ. If all component plans of a multi-plan are empty plans, it is called an empty multi-plan μ_ε.

In the sequel, we identify an individual plan π with a multi-plan $\{\pi\}$ that contains it as its only element. Based on this idea, the partial function *res* is extended to multi-plans:

$$res : M \times S \to S \, .$$

The extension of the function *res* compiles the outcome of interactions between the *component plans* of a multi-plan. So, for instance, the result of a multi-plan need not coincide with the "conjunction" of the effects of its component individual plans. The function *res* is undefined for a multi-plan μ and a state s, if some of the individual plans that it contains are *incompatible*, i.e. in case it is impossible to execute them simultaneously in a state s of the modelled domain. Otherwise, μ is said to be *executable* in s. The empty plan π_ε is compatible with every plan and does not affect its individual outcome when they are executed together within a multi-plan.

Multi-plans can be "constructed" from simpler multi-plans and/or individual plans by means of the commutative operator $\circ$. It expresses that its operands are executed together

$$\circ : \quad M \times M \to M \, .$$

The semantics of the operator is given by multi-set union: an individual plan appears as many times in the resulting multi-set as the sum of its appearances in any of the operands [3].

---

[2] The "composition" of agent plans within a multi-agent system is often referred to as "joint plans". Authors usually apply this term to denote situations where agents have formed a coalition and pursue a common goal (e.g. Cohen and Levesque 1990). Still, in our model agents do *not* share goals. A multi-plan just describes the simultaneous enactment of the agents' plans as perceived by an external observer.

[3] Again, we use a multi-set of cardinality one and its only element indiscriminately. So, for instance, we write $\mu = \pi \circ \pi' = \pi' \circ \pi = \{\pi, \pi'\}$ and $\mu \circ \pi = \pi \circ \mu = \{\pi, \pi, \pi'\}$.

Note that the result of a multi-plan may coincide with the result of a plan $\pi \in \Pi$. Still, the distinction between both is deliberate. It highlights that the agents that we endeavour to build do not deal with global plans, but are interested in the interaction of simultaneously executed local plans.

The notion of capability for executing a multi-plan is also a natural extension of the single agent case. We define the set of groups Γ as the powerset of the set of agents:

$$\Gamma = \wp(A).$$

Just like in the case of plans, an individual agent α is identified with the group $\{\alpha\}$ that contains it as its only element.

A group $\gamma \in \Gamma$ is capable of executing a multi-plan μ, if there is an assignment such that every agent is to execute exactly one individual plan and this agent is capable of doing so, i.e. there is a *bijective* mapping ψ from μ (a multi-set of individual plans) to γ (a set of agents), such that

$$can(\gamma, \mu) \equiv \forall \pi \in \mu.\ can(\psi(\pi), \pi).$$

In particular, this means that we need precisely n agents to enact a multi-plan μ comprising n individual plans, even though μ contains some individual plans more than once.

We are now in the position to give a precise definition of the scenario within which we will develop the mechanism of structural co-operation:

Definition 5.1. A *reactive co-ordination setting* R is defined by the sets of individuals S, Π, A, M and Γ, the functions *res*, d_α and $\circ$ as well as the predicates *can* and *ideal*.

5.2.2   The Synchronous Blocks Domain

The above definitions will be illustrated within the synchronous blocks domain, which is an extension of the well-known blocks world[4]. There is a table of unlimited size and a finite set of blocks B. Each block has one of a finite set of possible colours C. Blocks can be placed either directly on the table or on top of another block, and there is no limit to the height of a stack of blocks.

Let $x, y \in B$ be blocks, $c \in C$ denote a colour and *table* a simple constant. The predicate *colour* is used to relate both sets, i.e. by *colour*(x,c) we denote that Block x has the colour c. The following assertions are available to describe properties of a state s in the synchronous blocks domain:

---

[4] The use of "toy domains" such as the different variants of the blocks world is often criticised, as they do not capture genuine aspects of real-world problems. However, the scenario presented in this section is intended to provide illustrative examples of reactive co-ordination settings and the mechanism of structural co-operation. We will confirm the adequacy of our model for complex applications later, when structural co-operation is applied to the problem of road traffic management in a real-world motorway network.

- $On_s(x,y)$: in a state s, Block x is located (directly) on top of Block y.
- $On_s(x, table)$: in a state s, Block x is located on the table.
- $Clear_s(x)$: in a state s, there is no block on top of Block x.

Several constraints hold among the above predicates, in order to capture the intuitive relations between them. These constraints are represented by additional axioms. For instance, in order to express that a block is clear if only if no block is on top of it we write:

$$clear_s(x) \leftrightarrow \forall y \in B. \neg on_s(y,x) .$$

Closed first order formulae over the predicates and the individuals out of B and C are used to characterise world states. In the synchronous blocks domain, just two *operations* can be performed:

- *Move(x,y)*: Block x is placed on top of Block y.
- *NOP*: do nothing.

The precondition for the application of the first operation obviously is that x and y are clear. Its execution changes the world state, thereby modifying the truth value of the predicates that determine x's location and y's property of being clear. In the resulting state s, the predicate $on_s(x,y)$ is true and, consequently, $clear_s(y)$ is false. Obviously, *NOP* has no preconditions and does not alter the world.

An instantiated sequence of operations is called a *plan* π, and the set of all plans is denoted by Π. A plan is *executable* in a situation s, if initially the preconditions of the first operation are fulfilled, and if after the execution of each operation the preconditions of its successor operation hold. In this case, the result *res* of the enactment of plan π corresponds to the world state after the execution of its last action. If π is not executable in s, $res(\pi,s)$ is undefined.

So far, our model is a special case of the classical blocks world. Still, we now introduce a notion of time into the model: there is a clock that marks each instant of time by a tick. During plan execution, the different operations are successively performed each at one tick. The *duration* $dur(\pi)$ of a plan π equals the number of operations it contains.

There is a finite set of agents A in this domain. Each $\alpha \in A$ is an autonomous robot, endowed with an "arm" to move blocks. The basic difference between the domain described here and the standard blocks world is that operations may fail and contingencies occur. Therefore, as it cannot be assured that after plan execution the world really is in the state that it was expected to be, the agents stick to the following reactivity paradigm. Agents develop individual plans for a period of t *ticks*, and evaluate them in relation to their expected outcome, i.e. based on the world state that would be reached if all actions were successful and no sudden events occurred. On this basis, a plan is chosen and executed. Then, the whole process is reinitiated without any reference to the previous plan.

In short: plans are executed *en bloc*, they cannot be interrupted, and the history of previously executed plans does *not* influence in present choice. To model this paradigm, the agent's capabilities are restricted to all plans of duration t:

$$\forall \alpha \in A. \ \forall \pi \in \Pi. \ \ can(\alpha, \pi) \rightarrow dur(\pi) = t.$$

The empty plan π_ε, that every agent is capable of executing, is given by a sequence of t *NOP*-operations.

The *ideal states* of agents are described by formulae as above. Many different metric measures can be defined to determine the distance between pairs of states within the synchronous blocks domain. In the following, we assume that "time is money" (e.g. that our robotic agents discharge their batteries at each tick), and connote distance with the minimum cost that an agent needs to incur in order to reach one state from another. So, we define the distance between the states s and s' as the duration of the "shortest" plan π, that transforms s into s', i.e.

$$d_\alpha(s, s') = min\left\{ dur(\pi) \mid \pi \in \Pi \land res(\pi, s) = s' \right\}.$$

In the synchronous blocks domain each state can be reached from any other by means of some plan, so the minimum over the durations of plans is always well-defined. The above definition maps identical states to zero (by means of the plan that does not contain any operation), it is symmetric (every plan has an inverse of the same length) and the triangle inequality holds. Note that it is completely independent of the agents' actual capabilities.

With relation to reactive co-ordination settings, agents only need to express the distance between ordinary states and their *ideal* states based on the above definition. So, by the sets of ideal states and the above distance measure, the agents' motivations are defined. Note that although all agents use the same distance measure, their motivations are different if they maintain diverging ideal states.

The function *res*, which has been used to determine the result of enacting individual plans in a situation s, can be easily extended to multi-plans[5]. In the synchronous blocks domain agents execute their individual plans synchronously. They start plan execution at the same time and perform one action at each tick. Therefore, in general the result of multi-plan execution is the "sum" of the results of the component plans. However, in some multi-plans the component plans mutually affect their executability. In these cases the following rules apply:

- action incompatibility
  At one tick, two component plans access the same block, either by moving it away or by stacking another block on top of it (this includes the case of two identical individual plans). This is fatal for the agents that might enact them (one might think of the robots damaging their arms), so the plans are incompatible and the result function is undefined for the multi-plan.

---

[5] Rosenschein and Zlotkin (1994) use the term "joint plan" in a similar scenario. Still, they set out from a given joint multi-agent plan, and agents just disagree with respect to the *role* that each of them plays in it. By contrast, our approach highlights co-operation and conflict in the *emergent generation* of composite plans. The term "multi-plan" underlines this difference.

- state incompatibility
  One component plan obstructs a block that another uses at a *later* tick, i.e. it invalidates the precondition of some action included in another component plan. Again, the corresponding multi-plan is considered incompatible and the result function is undefined for it.

- compatibility
  In much the same way, a component plan can move blocks in a manner that makes it possible to enact another component plan, which would not have been executable individually. Being subject to the restrictions outlined above, the multi-plan can be executed and the resulting world state is the "sum" of operations of the agents' plans.

In line with the definitions of the reactive co-ordination setting, a group of n robotic agents in the synchronous blocks domain is capable of executing a multi-plan with n component plans, if it is possible to assign one component plan to any of them, such that every agent *can* execute its individual plan.

5.2.3 An Example Setting

In this section, the above definitions will be illustrated by an example. A setting in the synchronous blocks domain is presented, and the possibilities for co-ordination of two agents that live together in that world are outlined.

In our example, the blocks are numbered from one to four and are coloured dark grey, black, white and light grey respectively:

$$B = \{1,2,3,4\} \qquad C = \{white, light, dark, black\}$$
$$colour(1,dark) \wedge colour(2,black) \wedge colour(3,white) \wedge colour(4,light).$$

We assume the existence of just two agents α_1 and α_2, which use a time horizon of $t=2$ ticks, i.e. they just consider plans of duration two. Agent α_1 can move all blocks but the light grey ones, while α_2 is capable of manipulating all types of blocks except the white ones.

$$can(\alpha_1,\pi) \quad \equiv \quad dur(\pi) = 2 \wedge \forall x, y \in B.(move(x,y) \in \pi \rightarrow colour(x) \neq light)$$
$$can(\alpha_2,\pi) \quad \equiv \quad dur(\pi) = 2 \wedge \forall x, y \in B.(move(x,y) \in \pi \rightarrow colour(x) \neq white)$$

Figure 5.2 depicts the remaining information necessary to specify a scenario in the synchronous blocks world. In the initial state s_0, Block 1 is on top of Block 4 and Block 2 on top of Block 3, while the latter are located on the table:

$$on_{s_0}(1,4) \wedge on_{s_0}(4,table) \wedge on_{s_0}(2,3) \wedge on_{s_0}(3,table) \ .$$

Agent α_1 would ideally like to bring about a state in which there is a stack of black, white and dark grey blocks, while agent α_2's ideal states contain a tower of black, light grey and dark grey blocks. Obviously, the ideal states are incompatible in a situation such as s_0, where black and dark grey blocks are scarce resources.

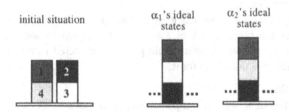

Figure 5.2. An example scenario

$$ideal(\alpha_1, s) \equiv \begin{array}{l} \exists x, y, z \in B. \; on_s(x, table) \wedge on_s(y, x) \wedge on_s(z, y) \wedge \\ colour(x, black) \wedge colour(y, white) \wedge colour(z, dark) \end{array}$$

$$ideal(\alpha_2, s) \equiv \begin{array}{l} \exists x, y, z \in B. \; on_s(x, table) \wedge on_s(y, x) \wedge on_s(z, y) \wedge \\ colour(x, black) \wedge colour(y, light) \wedge colour(z, dark) \end{array}$$

Recall that in this example setting, there is just one block of each colour, so each of the above descriptions can only be fulfilled by one situation.

Both agents use the metric distance measure over world states defined in the previous section. We illustrate its effects by determining the distance between the current state s_0 and the ideal states $\overline{s}_1$ and $\overline{s}_2$ of agent α_1 and α_2 respectively. The shortest plans that transform s_0 into the states $\overline{s}_1$ or $\overline{s}_2$ are

$$\pi'_{\alpha_1} = [move(2, table), move(3,2), move(1,3)]$$

$$\pi'_{\alpha_2} = [move(2, table), move(1, table), move(4,2), move(1,4)]$$

So, we get the following distance measures:

$$d_{\alpha_1}(s_0, \overline{s}_1) = 3 \text{ and } d_{\alpha_2}(s_0, \overline{s}_2) = 4 \; .$$

In spite of the rather simple scenario and the short time horizon, both agents are capable of executing a considerable amount of plans. Each agent can move three blocks and put them on three others plus the table, so that, including the *NOP* operation, 13 actions are possible in each step. Simple combinatorics suggest that there are 169 plans of two ticks, but fortunately just a small portion is executable in the initial situation s_0.

Table 5.1 shows the set of plans that we will refer to in later sections. Every plan *can* be executed either by α_1, by α_2 or by both agents. Still, in the given situation s_0 the plans π_2 and π_9 are not executable. The empty plan π_ε consists of a sequence of two *NOPs*.

Any pair of the above plans constitutes a multi-plan. The outcome of a multi-plan is determined by means of the plan interaction rules presented in the last section. For instance, in situation s_0 the combination of π_{10} and π_{11} results in an incompatible multi-plan:

$$res(\pi_{10} \circ \pi_{11}, s_0) = undefined \; .$$

Table 5.1. Some example plans and their properties

Plan	Operations	Capability	Executability
π_1	[move(2,table),move(3,2)]	α_1	true
π_2	[move(1,table),move(3,2)]	α_1	false
π_3	[move(2,table),NOP]	α_1, α_2	true
π_4	[move(1,table),NOP]	α_1, α_2	true
π_5	[NOP,move(2,table)]	α_1, α_2	true
π_6	[NOP,move(1,table)]	α_1, α_2	true
π_7	[move(1,table),move(2,table)]	α_1, α_2	true
π_8	[move(2,table),move(1,table)]	α_1, α_2	true
π_9	[move(2,table),move(4,2)]	α_2	false
π_{10}	[move(1,2),move(4,1)]	α_2	true
π_{11}	[move(2,1), move(3,2)]	α_1	true
π_{12}	[move(1,2),NOP]	α_1, α_2	true
π_ε	[NOP,NOP]	α_1, α_2	true

If the concurrent execution of plans π_1 and π_4 by the agents α_1 and α_2 leads to a certain state s_1, i.e.

$$res(\pi_1 \circ \pi_4, s_0) = s_1 ,$$

then in this state s_1 the blocks 1, 2 and 4 are on the table, while Block 3 is located on top of Block 2.

5.3 The Mechanism: Structural Co-operation

In this section, the notion of the functionality of social structure is transformed into a mechanism called *structural co-operation*. At the beginning of this chapter we have presented how given behaviours in a society of agents can be explained in terms of the functionality of its social structure. This explanation has been based on a *pre-established* notion of the processes that develop within society and their relation to social structure. In order to convert the metaphor of the function-ality of social structure into a mechanism, it must be shown how these processes are generated among autonomous agents[6]. We must focus on the micro-level and model how and why an autonomous agent chooses to co-operate with others and what role social structure plays in the resulting interactions.

This section is dedicated to modelling such behaviour of an autonomous agent, which is involved in structural co-operation within a reactive co-ordination set-ting. We first give an overview of the different contexts within which the actions

---

[6] With respect to *human* societies, this means to switch from the structural perspective, mostly pursued by social anthropologists, to the motivational perspective which is largely associated with social psychologists, as discussed in depth by Befu (1980).

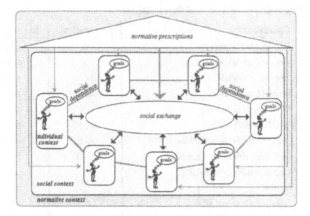

Figure 5.3. The mechanism of structural co-operation

of the agent are taken. Subsequently, the influence of each of these contexts on the agent's self-interested behaviour is described in detail.

5.3.1 Overview

The fundamental idea of structural co-operation is that social structure modifies the self-interested actions and interactions of autonomous agents in a certain functional way. So, from a motivational perspective, we need to clarify two questions. First, a model of the process of self-interested choice by means of which an autonomous agent selects its actions is to be given. Second, we need to show how social structure influences this process.

Figure 5.3 graphically depicts a society of agents from a single agent's perspective. We analyse the emergence of structural co-operation by examining an autonomous agent's behaviour successively in different comprehensive contexts. In each context, the outcome of self-interested action changes.

The *individual context* just comprises statements concerning an autonomous agent's individual characteristics and its relation to the (passive) objects in the world. An agent's behaviour is guided by its motivation (implied by the reactive co-ordination setting): it generates goals so as to bring the state of the world in line with its motivation. Furthermore, our notion of autonomy requires that goals are generated and deliberately pursued on the basis of individual rationality: plans are only executed if they *improve* the world state in the eyes of the agent, i.e. if they bring the world closer to an ideal state. Under this restriction, an agent analyses the set of individual plans that it can choose from. Within the individual context, a self-interested agent will select the plan that contributes most to the achievement of its goals, regardless of the effect that this may have on other agents. Self-motivated behaviour in the local context consists in framing the situation in the light of its motivations and changing it in accordance with the resulting goals as if the agent was alone in the world.

However, as member of an artificial society an autonomous agent is *not* alone in the world, but is condemned to coexist with its acquaintances in the same environment. In the *social context*, this fact is taken into account: it comprises all agents that share the environment with it. Within the social context, the degree of an agent's autonomy changes. On the one hand, it is *bounded* by the existence of others, as its goal and plans may conflict with those of others: they might have to compete for scarce resources etc. On the other hand, it is *enhanced*, when knowledge and capabilities happen to be complementary with respect to goals: with the help of its acquaintances, an agent may attain goals that it cannot cope with individually. Self-interested behaviour in the social context differs from the local context in so far that both phenomena need to be taken into account when choosing a plan to execute.

This fact motivates an autonomous agent to maintain interactions with its acquaintances. The result of these interactions are (partial) agreements concerning which plans an agent will (not) enact. Obviously, the agent as well as its partners will only support an agreement that they consider beneficial for themselves. So, agreements appear as *social exchanges*. In the social context, these exchanges are governed by the structure of *social dependence* between agents, which reflects what an agent needs from others and what it can offer them. Type and degree of an agent's social dependence is a measure of its social strength, that determines which exchanges are rational and, in the end, which agreements the agents will end up with.

Finally, besides the existence of its acquaintances and the notions of social exchange and social dependence the *normative context* comprises a set of norms. Norms influence the agents' self-interested choice by issuing *normative prescriptions*. These prescriptions permit or prohibit the agents to perform certain plans. As a consequence, the social context (or more precisely: the network of social dependence) is modified, which is reflected by a change in the agents' social strength. The outcomes of social exchanges are altered and the agent society may converge on a different agreement. So, in the normative context the outcome of self-interested action is biased in a certain direction.

Structural co-operation is the result of self-interested action of norm-abiding agents within the aforementioned contexts. When the normative context is purposefully designed, the agreements that self-interested agents converge upon are co-ordinated towards some desired global functionality. Although the agents are just interested in fulfilling their self-interest deliberately, the normative prescriptions imply a global functionality that the agents are not "aware" of.

In the following sections, the three different contexts within which structural co-operation arises will be further described. We will pay special attention to what self-interested action means within them. For this purpose, we map reactive co-ordination settings onto a qualitative model that provides an intuitive interpretation of social structure as a set of relations.

5.3.2   The Individual Context

The notion of self-interested action of an agent in a single-agent world is straight-forward, and definitions differ essentially in their terminological framework. An intuitive description of rational action in an individual context has been given by Newell (1982) with respect to his theory on the knowledge level. It states that

> if an agent has knowledge that one of its actions will lead to one of its goals, then it will select that action.

So, the first thing to do is to introduce some notion of goal with respect to an agent.

5.3.2.1 On the Conception of Goal

A straightforward approach to the notion of goals in reactive co-ordination settings is to identify the ideal states of an agent as its goals. Just like a goal, a self-interested agent would like to choose plans that are expected to reach some ideal state. However, the synchronous blocks world example has shown that most probably agents will *not* fully reach their ideal states. Therefore, we run into problems with the above notion of rationality, which is based on a distinction between actions or plans that achieve a goal and those that do not.

In consequence, we stick to a weaker notion of the term: an agent's goal is to come as close as possible to an ideal state. It can reasonably be argued that this conception coincides with a set of alternative and potentially competing goals, each corresponding to a world state to be achieved, and a partial ordering relation on it. A self-interested agent will then choose the action by means of which it expects to attain its most preferred goal. This is precisely what the notion of self-interested action in the individual context will come down to.

Still, we use the concept of goals not as an end in itself that needs to be char-acterised, but as a means to guide the definition of a notion preference over states and plans. Therefore, we will stick to the intuitive characterisation of a goal provided in the beginning of this section, which allows us to interpret rational action in the individual context based on Newell's definition. The reader may keep in mind that, although we will not use the term goal in the sequel, it is implicit in this definition of preference.

5.3.2.2 Basic Notions

The first basic notion that is needed in order to define self-interested action in the individual context of structural co-operation, is the *executability* of a plan. This notion is directly derivable from the description of reactive co-ordination settings, i.e. a plan is executable in a state if the function *res* is defined for it in that state:

$$exec(\pi, s) \quad \equiv \quad res(\pi, s) \ is \ defined \ . \qquad\qquad (A_1)$$

Secondly, in order to build up a qualitative model of the setting in which autonomous agents act within structural co-operation, we first need to come up with a notion of *preference*. For this purpose, we use the distance measure between a state and an ideal state to construct a preference relation over world states. From the point of view of an agent α, a world state s is at least as good as s', if it is equally close or closer to some ideal state than s'. Formally:

$$ s' \prec_\alpha s \Leftrightarrow \exists \bar{s} \, \forall \bar{s}' \, ideal(\alpha, \bar{s}) \wedge ideal(\alpha, \bar{s}') \wedge d_\alpha(s, \bar{s}) \le d_\alpha(s', \bar{s}') . \qquad (A_2) $$

Strong preference of the states s over s' is given when s is definitely closer to some ideal state than s. We can define this based on the above notion, stating that in this case in the eyes of agent α the state s is preferred to s', but s' is *not* preferred to s:

$$ s' \prec\!\!\prec_\alpha s \Leftrightarrow (s' \prec_\alpha s) \wedge \neg (s \prec_\alpha s') . \qquad (A_3) $$

This preference over world states can be transferred to the agents' plans, as these are employed to bring about desired states. So, in some situation s a plan is (weakly) preferred to another, if both are executable and the former brings about a world state which is at least as preferred as the state that the latter achieves. In addition, every plan is at least as preferred as a non-executable plan. Formally, this boils down to:

$$ \pi' \prec_\alpha \pi \Leftrightarrow (exec(\pi, s) \wedge exec(\pi', s) \wedge res(\pi', s) \prec_\alpha res(\pi, s)) \vee \neg exec(\pi', s) . $$

5.3.2.3 Self-Interested Action

In the light of the above denotations, self-interested action is described easily. In a certain situation s, it is individually rational for an agent to select some plan π^* out of the set of most preferred plans that the agent is capable of performing. Formally, we get:

$$ \pi^* \in \max_{\prec_\alpha} \{ \pi \in \Pi \mid can(\alpha, \pi) \} . $$

The maximum always exists as an agent is always capable of enacting the empty plan π_ε. In addition, π_ε is always executable, so the notion of preference over plans implies that π^* is also executable. However, π^* need not be unique. Still, for our purposes it does not matter which of the most preferred plans the agent actually chooses. As long as the agent is capable of enacting that plan, it can expect to achieve its goal to come as close as possible to some ideal state.

In the example of Figure 5.2, the agents will choose to execute the initial sequence of actions of the plans that lead directly to ideal states. So, in the individual context agent α_1's self-interested choice will be plan π_1 while agent α_2 acts individually rational if it executes π_7 or π_8.

5.3.3   The Social Context

In a multi-agent system, an autonomous agent needs to make decisions within a social context: it is forced to share its environment with its acquaintances and, independent of whether it welcomes or dislikes the existence of others, it needs to take them into account as other active subjects when making its decisions. By consequence, the outcome of self-interest in the social context is different from the individual context.

This shift of outcome will be modelled based on the notion of social dependence. We aim to express the following idea: an agent *socially depends* (in different degrees) on a group of acquaintances with respect to its plan, if the latter can take decisions that influence the feasibility or the degree of success of that plan.

In the following, we first extend the basic definitions made in Section 5.3.2 to account for multiple active agents. Subsequently, different relations between plans are introduced, which provide the basis of a characterisation of classes of social dependence relations between agents. Finally, some issues concerning social exchange as the foundation of a strategic model of self-interested action in the social context are sketched.

5.3.3.1 Basic Notions

As a prerequisite for any description of the behaviour of an autonomous agent in the social context, the above notion of executability needs to be transferred to multi-plans. Again, executability is derived directly from the description of reactive co-ordination settings. We define the notion formally by extending the predicate *exec* to multi-plans. A multi-plan μ in a state s is executable if the function *res* is defined for μ and s:

$$exec(\mu, s) \equiv res(\mu, s) \text{ is defined} . \tag{A_4}$$

A second prerequisite concerns the notion of capability, which reactive co-ordination settings define by the binary predicate *can*. We will need to distinguish between different kinds of "disposition to act" when an agent finds itself in the normative context. They will be subsumed under the notion of *preparedness*. In the social context, however, we will consider preparedness to be equivalent to capability, i.e.

$$prep_s(\alpha, \pi) \Leftrightarrow can(\alpha, \pi) . \tag{C}$$

5.3.3.2 Relations between Plans

Setting out from the above notions, the relations between plans in a reactive co-ordination setting can be modelled. In a situation s a plan π can be in four mutually exclusive qualitative relations to a multi-plan μ:

Definition 5.2. Plan relations

$$indifferent_s(\pi,\mu) \quad\Leftrightarrow\quad \big(exec(\pi,s) \wedge exec(\pi \circ \mu,s) \wedge res(\pi \circ \mu,s) = res(\pi,s)\big)$$
$$\vee \big(\neg exec(\pi,s) \wedge \neg exec(\pi \circ \mu,s)\big)$$

$$interferent_s(\pi,\mu) \quad\Leftrightarrow\quad exec(\pi,s) \wedge exec(\pi \circ \mu,s) \wedge res(\pi \circ \mu,s) \neq res(\pi,s) \quad (A_s)$$

$$complementary_s(\pi,\mu) \quad\Leftrightarrow\quad \neg exec(\pi,s) \wedge exec(\pi \circ \mu,s)$$

$$inconsistent_s(\pi,\mu) \quad\Leftrightarrow\quad exec(\pi,s) \wedge \neg exec(\pi \circ \mu,s)$$

The multi-plan μ is *indifferent* with respect to π if the execution of μ does not affect at all the outcome of π. This is obviously the case when both are executable and the parallel enactment leads to the same state of the world. Alternatively, π is indifferent to μ if the former is not executable and the execution of the latter does not remedy this problem.

In the synchronous blocks domain example, the empty plan π_ε is indifferent with respect to π_1 as the former just performs two *NOP* operations, which obviously influence neither the executability nor the outcome of π_1. Plans π_9 is also in an *indifferent* relation with π_6: in order to execute π_9 it is necessary to make Block 4 clear in the first step, but π_6 does not provide that condition.

The plan μ is *interferent* with π if π is executable alone as well as in conjunction with μ, but the two alternatives lead to different world states. This captures the notion that μ has side-effects which interfere in the normal execution of π. It changes π's result but does not make its execution impossible. The state resulting from performing both plans together is most probably closer or further away from an ideal state of some agent. Still, we cannot distinguish between positive and negative interference here, because the relations described are objective, while the comparison of two states on the basis of preference is the result of a subjective attitude pertinent only to agents.

In the example of Figure 5.2 plans that make agents keep still in the first step are usually interferent with plans that require a *NOP* in the second step. For instance, π_5 and π_6 are interferent with π_4 and π_3 respectively. Compatibility is assured as those plans manipulate unrelated blocks at different ticks, but the actions performed in the second step by π_6 (π_5) change the outcome of π_3 (π_4). Another example of a multi-plan made up of interferent individual plans is $(\pi_1 \circ \pi_4)$, where the former manipulates the right stack, while the latter refers to blocks in the left stack.

Complementarity of μ with respect to π is given, when π is not executable alone, but in conjunction with μ it is. The idea is that there is a "gap" in the plan π, i.e. some action is missing or the preconditions of some action are not achieved within the plan, and μ fills that gap by executing the missing action and bringing about the lacking world features.

In the synchronous blocks domain example plan π_9 is in an *complementary*-relation with π_4. The missing action of π_9, unstacking Block 1 from Block 4, is contributed to the multi-plan by π_4. In much the same way π_2 is complementary respecting π_3.

Finally, the plan μ is *inconsistent* with π if π is executable alone but not in conjunction with μ. This is the case, for instance, when both plans need to access the same non-sharable resource or when they lead to incompatible world states.

A large amount of plans are in *inconsistent* relations in the example domain, as they try to move the same block to different positions or just because they access the same stack simultaneously. In particular, note that the plans that the agents choose in the individual context (π_1 and π_7 or π_8 respectively) are inconsistent in the social context.

It is worthwhile pointing out that these relations between the possible plans go back to "objective" characteristics of a reactive co-ordination setting. They are a fact that co-ordination in every system (even in a centralised one) needs to take into account. Plan relations are *not* affected by the agents' attitude towards them.

Note that the above set of relations is limited to the reactive co-ordination settings that we are concerned with. In general, a more fine-grained specification of objective plan relations may be used. A genuine planning application will probably model plans as complex and structured objects, composed by a (partial) temporal sequence of actions. The actions will have preconditions that make reference to (scarce) resources and post-conditions that modify certain aspects of the world. Plan relations will then be defined with respect to actions, making reference to temporal, resource and other aspects of their interdependence. In such a setting, a taxonomy of plan relations needs to be developed, and efficient algorithms that exploit the plan structure in order to detect them are of major importance.

Still, the problems that this book is concerned with do belong to the class of reactive co-ordination settings. Furthermore, our primary interest does not lie in the detection of plan interdependencies[7], but in the decisions of how to handle them. The aim of this paragraph is to provide a simple set of objective plan relations in order to develop a classification of the *social* relations they imply. The latter are used to devise the "social strength" of an agent, which finally determines the above decision. For this objective, the degree of detail of the above conception is convenient.

5.3.3.3 Dependence Relations between Agents

This paragraph turns the attention to the social side of the above notions: we endeavour to derive social relations between agents from objective relations between plans. Of course, such a deduction is sensitive to the agents' capability of performing certain plans.

An agent is in a social relation with others, if the outcome of its plans is influenced by the options that the latter choose. The agent depends on its acquaintances in order to assure a certain level of effectiveness of its plans. The social relations

---

[7] This has been done elsewhere. See, for instance, the work by von Martial (1992) or Decker (1995) described in the first part of this book.

developed in the following are intended to capture different types and degrees of such social dependence. The essential idea is that the less an agent depends on its acquaintances, the more *social strength* it has in the group. When agents find an agreement, it will be biased towards the stronger agent: its preferences will have more weight than the one of its weaker partner. So, social dependence is the basis for a decision on how to solve potential conflicts.

Concerning its individual plan π an agent α can be in four mutually exclusive social relations with a group γ of acquaintances, $\alpha \notin \gamma$, and their multi-plan μ.

Definition 5.3. Dependence relations between agents

$$prevents_s(\alpha, \pi, \gamma, \mu) \quad \Leftrightarrow \quad prep_s(\alpha, \pi) \wedge prep_s(\gamma, \mu) \wedge inconsistent_s(\pi, \mu)$$

$$enables_s(\alpha, \pi, \gamma, \mu) \quad \Leftrightarrow \quad prep_s(\alpha, \pi) \wedge prep_s(\gamma, \mu) \wedge complementary_s(\pi, \mu)$$

$$hinders_s(\alpha, \pi, \gamma, \mu) \quad \Leftrightarrow \quad prep_s(\alpha, \pi) \wedge prep_s(\gamma, \mu) \wedge interferent_s(\pi, \mu) \wedge$$
$$res(\pi \circ \mu, s) \prec\!\!\prec_\alpha res(\pi, s) \qquad (A_6)$$

$$favours_s(\alpha, \pi, \gamma, \mu) \quad \Leftrightarrow \quad prep_s(\alpha, \pi) \wedge prep_s(\gamma, \mu) \wedge interferent_s(\pi, \mu) \wedge$$
$$res(\pi, s) \prec\!\!\prec_\alpha res(\pi \circ \mu, s)$$

It can be easily checked that both, agent α and the group γ, need to be prepared to execute their plans so that a social relation exists between them[8]. Under this condition, the different types of relations are given as follows:

- prevention
  The execution of agent α's plan π can be prevented by the concurrent execution of the multi-plan μ. So, decisions of the agents in γ concern α as they can turn down its individual plan π. For instance, in the initial state s of our example the relation $prevents_s(\alpha_2, \pi_{10}, \alpha_1, \pi_{11})$ holds.

- enabling
  The execution of agent α's plan π can be enabled by the simultaneous execution of the multi-plan μ. So, decisions of the agents in γ can make it possible for α to enact its individual plan π, which is impossible for it individually. For instance, in the initial state s of the synchronous blocks world example the relation $enables_s(\alpha_2, \pi_9, \alpha_1, \pi_4)$ holds.

- hindrance
  The execution of agent α's plan π interferes with the execution of the multi-plan μ by the agents in γ. The decisions of the agents in γ can hinder π to be fully effective in the eyes of α. In the initial state s of the synchronous blocks world example the relation $hinders_s(\alpha_1, \pi_{12}, \alpha_2, \pi_{10})$ holds.

---

[8] If we do not require preparedness for a dependence relation to exist, an additional "enabling" relation can be defined based of the agents' complementary capabilities. However, throughout this book we are interested in social dependence implied by plan relations.

- favour
  Again, the execution of agent α's plan π interferes with the concurrent execution of the multi-plan μ by the agents in γ. Still, in the case of this relation the decisions of the agents in γ can influence positively in the effectiveness of π. In the initial state s of our example the relation $favours_s(\alpha_2, \pi_3, \alpha_1, \pi_4)$ holds.

For convenience, we define three compound relations that aggregate primitive social relations with respect to different criteria. The *invalidates* relation is "hard", i.e. the agents in γ settle the *possibility* of the execution of π by α. In contrast, the *interferes* relation is "weak", as the agents in γ can only affect the *effectiveness* of the execution of π. Finally, the *disturbs* relation describes a negative influence on the feasibility or the result of a plan π.

Definition 5.4. Aggregate dependence relations

$$interferes_s(\alpha, \pi, \gamma, \mu) \quad \Leftrightarrow \quad favours_s(\alpha, \pi, \gamma, \mu) \vee hinders_s(\alpha, \pi, \gamma, \mu)$$

$$invalidates_s(\alpha, \pi, \gamma, \mu) \quad \Leftrightarrow \quad enables_s(\alpha, \pi, \gamma, \mu) \vee prevents_s(\alpha, \pi, \gamma, \mu) \quad (A_7)$$

$$disturbs_s(\alpha, \pi, \gamma, \mu) \quad \Leftrightarrow \quad hinders_s(\alpha, \pi, \gamma, \mu) \vee prevents_s(\alpha, \pi, \gamma, \mu)$$

Note that all these relations are defined from the point of an agent α. In principle, social relations can be both, unilateral and bilateral. When the individual plans of two agents are incompatible with each other, each of them is in a *prevents*-relation with the other. Still, if an agent needs the help of an acquaintance to execute a plan, for instance because it cannot execute a certain action, just the former is in an *enables*-relation with the latter. In general, multi-lateral dependence within a set of agents is expressed by various of the above social dependence relations.

We are now in the position to define the different *types* of social dependence that an agent can have respecting a plan and a group of acquaintances. Again, the following definitions cover important relations between an agent α, its plan π and some group γ of acquaintances, $\alpha \notin \gamma$.

Definition 5.5. Types of dependence relations

$$feas-dep_s(\alpha, \pi, \gamma) \quad \Leftrightarrow \quad \exists \mu. invalidates_s(\alpha, \pi, \gamma, \mu)$$

$$neg-dep_s(\alpha, \pi, \gamma) \quad \Leftrightarrow \quad \exists \mu. hinders_s(\alpha, \pi, \gamma, \mu) \quad (A_8)$$

$$pos-dep_s(\alpha, \pi, \gamma) \quad \Leftrightarrow \quad \exists \mu. favours_s(\alpha, \pi, \gamma, \mu)$$

There is a feasibility-dependence (*feas-dep*) of agent α for a plan π with respect to γ, if the group can invalidate the plan, i.e. in case they can make the execution of π impossible. Agent α is negatively dependent (*neg-dep*) for a plan π with respect to γ, if the group can deviate the outcome of the plan to a state that is less preferred by α. If the group γ can bring about a change in the outcome of α's plan π that α welcomes, then α is positively-dependent (*pos-dep*) on γ. If none of the above types of relations is present, agent α is said to be independent for a plan π with respect to γ, as the group cannot influence the outcome of the plan. Note that we do not distinguish between enabling and preventing dependence, because in both cases the group γ can decide to make it impossible for α to execute π.

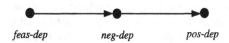

feas-dep　　　　　*neg-dep*　　　　　*pos-dep*

Figure 5.4. Degrees of social dependence

Figure 5.4 depicts our intuitive notion of the *degree* of dependence of an agent α on a group of acquaintances γ with respect to a plan π. Feasibility-dependence is the strongest relation as the agents in γ can turn down the execution of π; *neg-dep* implies a social dependence of medium level, because the acquaintances can do something "bad" to the effectiveness of the plan; finally, positive dependence is the weakest, as the worst option that the acquaintances can choose is *not* to do something "good" to plan effectiveness.

The dependence structure comprises all three types and degrees of dependence. In any state s, it is determined by all literals of the predicates *feas-dep*, *neg-dep*, and *pos-dep* that can be derived from a reactive co-ordination setting (R) based on the aforementioned axioms (A_1 to A_8) and on the notion of preparedness in the social context (C).

Definition 5.6. The dependence structure in a state s is determined by

$$A_1 - A_8, C \models_R feas - dep_s(\alpha, \pi, \gamma) \wedge neg - dep_s(\alpha', \pi', \gamma') \wedge pos - dep_s(\alpha'', \pi'', \gamma'') \ .$$

The dependence structure describes the agents' attitude towards actions of their acquaintances and is thus a *social* relation. Within a reactive co-ordination setting any multi-agent system gives rise to such a structure. Of course, whether and as to how far the structure is actually exploited is a different question.

Finally, we have a look at the attitude of each agent towards its plans. Especially two sets of plans are interesting:

- The set of *feasible plans* of agent α contains all the individual plans that are executable and that α is prepared to execute in situation s. The executability of a feasible plan π of α cannot be invalidated by any group of acquaintances, i.e. π can be enacted independently of what α's acquaintances do.

$$FEAS_s(\alpha) \ = \ \left\{ \pi \in \Pi \ \middle| \begin{array}{l} exec(\pi, s) \wedge prep_s(\alpha, \pi) \wedge \\ \forall \gamma \in \Gamma, \alpha \notin \gamma. \neg feas - dep_s(\alpha, \pi, \gamma) \end{array} \right\}$$

- The set of *autonomous* plans of agent α contains all individual plans that are executable that α is prepared to execute in situation s. The result of an autonomous plan π of α cannot be negatively affected by any group of acquaintances, i.e. by enacting π the agent α achieves a result that is at least as good as what it would have obtained alone, independently of what its acquaintances do.

$$AUT_s(\alpha) = \left\{ \pi \in \Pi \ \middle| \begin{array}{l} exec(\pi, s) \wedge prep_s(\alpha, \pi) \wedge \\ \forall \gamma \in \Gamma, \alpha \notin \gamma. \neg feas - dep_s(\alpha, \pi, \gamma) \wedge \neg neg - dep_s(\alpha, \pi, \gamma) \end{array} \right\}$$

A feasible plan π of agent α can be executed together with any multi-plan μ of a group γ of acquaintances, $\alpha \notin \gamma$, given that γ is prepared enact μ. In order to justify this, we point to two facts. Firstly, setting out from the fact that π is a feasible plan of α and that γ is prepared enact μ, it can be shown that the multi-plan $\pi \circ \mu$ is *executable*. Secondly, the definition of the predicate *can* ensures that on the basis of the above assumptions the group $\alpha \cup \gamma$ is *capable* of enacting $\pi \circ \mu$ and that in the social context this is equivalent to affirm that $\alpha \cup \gamma$ is *prepared* to enact $\pi \circ \mu$. As we will see later, our definition of the normative context does not change this property.

Note that the set of feasible plans is never empty, as in reactive co-ordination settings an agent is always capable of enacting the empty plan π_e. In addition, the definition of reactive co-ordination settings implies that the validity of the empty plan cannot be prevented by any group of agents. As we will see in the next chapter, feasible and autonomous plans of an agent play an important role in the dynamics of structural co-operation.

5.3.3.4 Social Exchange

So far, the dependence structure between agents in a particular situation has been defined. It remains to be shown how this structure shapes self-interested action, i.e. as to how far rational action is different in the social and in the individual context. The reader be warned that the final instrumentation of structural co-operation proposed in this book will *not* follow these ideas step by step. Instead, it will directly determine the result of this process. Still, the following paragraphs depict the essentials of a model of self-interested action in the social context and illustrate the difficulties that an explicit "simulation" approach sets off.

An agent involved in a social dependence relation is subject to the influence of its acquaintances, which restricts its freedom of choice. For instance, in the case of a *prevents* relation, an agent is actually forced to reach an agreement with its partners, as this is the only way to avoid fatal consequences (remember that in the synchronous blocks domain robots that intend to enact incompatible plans will damage their arms). In addition, it might only want to choose a certain option if it is sure that its acquaintances execute plans that *favour* or that at least do not *hinder* it.

There are many types of social interactions with which agents try to influence each other (e.g. Conte and Castelfranchi 1995). In the sequel, we will just consider *social exchange*. In social exchange, an agent tries to induce potential partners to behave in a certain way by offering something as reciprocation. Consequently, social exchange occurs in situations of reciprocal dependence, where all involved agents have the potential to influence the outcome of the others' plans. In the simplest case, there are two agents tied together by two social dependence relations: one relation is necessary for an agent α to be interested in an exchange while the other enables it to offer something in return to its partner α'. The object of exchange is "immaterial": agents mutually make commitments respecting properties of the individual plans that they will execute. So, what is actually commuted are self-imposed constraints on an agent's behaviour.

This kind of co-ordination will usually be done incrementally, i.e. the agents will successively augment the set of their commitments through exchanges. If we model this process step by step, every exchange will have to appear individually rational to our autonomous agents and, in addition, should reflect the social strengths of the involved agents in a certain way. Still, from the problem-solving perspective of structural co-operation, this extensive "simulation" of social exchanges essentially constitutes a particular strategy in a *distributed search* for the final outcome of the sequence of exchanges. Therefore, besides the "social plausibility" of exchanges, we also need to be concerned with particular properties of the distributed search method such as locality and termination. In the sequel, we sketch just some of the questions that arise when we tackle the problem from this perspective:

- The "exchange value" of commitments is to be defined. For instance, is the promise not to make use of two *hinders* relation more valuable than the commitment to refrain from realising an *invalidates* relation?
- In case of cyclic dependence, apparently irrational bilateral exchanges can become beneficial in the frame of a "bigger" exchange involving many agents. The question is whether every time an agent aims to make a bilateral exchange it needs to consider all other possible exchanges with k agents before.
- An agent may want to revoke previously made commitments, when it notices that it may get a "better" reciprocation from another agent. The question is when an agent should try to de-commit and how much it will have to "pay" for this.

We will not pursue this idea further. The above arguments suggest that it is rather complicated to present a plausible and efficient model of self-interested social action by extensively simulating the sequences of exchanges among autonomous agents based on the dependence structure. This is especially true for societies consisting of more than two or three agents. Instead, in the next chapter we map the dependence structure to a bargaining framework, and characterise the outcome of social exchanges in terms of solutions to the corresponding bargaining scenario. The objective of this section has been to characterise the notion of social exchange and to give the reader an idea of what we mean by *sequences* of social exchanges and their *outcome*.

5.3.4 The Normative Context

In the social context, an agent's self-interested action is shaped by the relations of social dependence that it is involved in. It can "win" or "lose" with respect to the individual context as a function of its social strength within the dependence structure. Still, by adhering to the metaphor of Section 5.1, we suspect that it need not always be the best "for society" to concede more weight to the preferences of stronger agents. In fact, a multi-agent system that shall achieve certain global functionality needs to be endowed with a means to modify the results of the dependence structure. This is precisely the finality of the normative structure presented in this section. In conjunction with a given dependence structure a carefully designed normative structure constitutes a social structure, within which self-interested choice of autonomous agents creates a global functionality.

5.3.4.1 Deontic Notions

Normative discourses are usually based on three essential notions: obligation, permission and prohibition (von Wright 1970). These notions may refer to a variety of different objects. They may qualify arbitrary formulae, world states ("ought-to-be norms"), actions ("ought-to-do norms"), etc. In addition, many different sets of axioms have been presented to characterise the different deontic notions and their interrelation.

Standard Deontic Logic (SDL), for instance, defines permission and prohibition for arbitrary formulae based on the notion of obligation (e.g. Krogh 1996). Suppose that the formula φ describes an action. If it is obligatory to do φ (formally: $O\varphi$) this is equivalent to the fact that it is forbidden not do φ (formally: $F\neg\varphi$) as well as that it is not permitted that not to do φ (formally: $\neg P\neg\varphi$).

In reactive co-ordination settings the normative context of structural co-operation has a quite limited frame of discourse. Firstly, we are interested in prescriptions that refer to the agents' decisions to execute plans. So, in the sequel deontic notions will just be considered with respect to plans. Secondly, we want to bias the outcome of social interaction towards particular agents. Therefore, *general* prescriptions, which state what is ideal for every member of society, are of no use to us. Instead, we will model what certain agents should (not) do, so we are interested in *specialised* obligations that pertain to particular individuals or groups of individuals.

The above comments suggest the use of the standard deontic notions defined over plans and pertaining to (groups of) agents. Still, prescriptions are *not* intended to enforce directly a certain action, but rather to constrain (or augment) the agents' choice sets. So, we will not directly rely on a notion of obligation, stating what certain agents ideally should do, but rather base our model on prohibition and permission. We set out from the notion of prohibition: the predicate *forbidden* states what multi-plan μ a group γ should not enact:

$$forbidden_s\,(\gamma,\mu) \equiv \text{ it is forbidden for the group } \gamma \text{ to execute } \mu \text{ in a state } s. \quad (F)$$

First of all, we require that it cannot be forbidden to enact empty plans. So, for the empty plan and all empty multi-plans we require that:

$$\textbf{not } forbidden_s(\gamma,\mu_\varepsilon)\,. \quad\quad (D_1)$$

The bold "not" in the formula represents "negation as failure". It requires it cannot be proved that $forbidden_s(\gamma, \mu_\varepsilon)$ is true. As we will see later, it is important to keep in mind that this does *not* mean that $\neg forbidden_s(\gamma, \mu_\varepsilon)$ has to be true.

For structural co-operation, we require a certain "coherence" between prohibitions pertaining to an agent α and those pertaining to a group of acquaintances γ, $\alpha \notin \gamma$.

$$forbidden_s(\alpha \cup \gamma, \pi \circ \mu) \Rightarrow$$
$$(can(\alpha, \pi) \wedge can(\gamma, \mu)) \rightarrow forbidden_s(\alpha, \pi) \vee forbidden_s(\gamma, \mu) \qquad (D_2)$$

In particular, the above states that if a plan μ is forbidden for a group γ, then for every possible unique assignment of individual plans $\pi \in \mu$ to agents $\alpha \in \gamma$ such that every agent is capable of enacting its plan, there is at least one agent for which it is forbidden to execute its "part" in the multi-plan μ.

We now introduce the individualised deontic notion of *permission* that complements to the above notion of prohibition. It is defined for single agents and individual plans by the following predicate:

$permitted_s(\alpha, \pi) \equiv$ it is permitted for the agent α to execute π in a state s. (P)

We define the relation of permission and prohibition in the usual fashion. The following axiom requires that a state should be free of intuitively "contradictory" imperatives:

$$permitted_s(\alpha, \pi) \Leftrightarrow \neg forbidden_s(\alpha, \pi) . \qquad (D_3)$$

Note that permission is *not* equivalent to the absence of prohibition. In Axiom D_3, we explicitly require that $\neg forbidden_s(\alpha, \pi)$ can be proved.

So far, we can express what agents *should not do* or *are allowed to do* in a certain situation. Together with an adequate model of the influence of prescriptions on agent behaviour, such specialised imperatives can be used to restrict the set of plans that agents are allowed to choose from.

Still, a set of prohibitions for certain agents may imply a *qualitative* change in the position of another. If all plans μ that some group of acquaintances γ can execute and that affect negatively the plan π of agent α are forbidden for γ, then α can execute π without the need to make any agreement. We will capture such interdependence between the deontic notions pertaining to individuals and groups by stating the following axiom concerning permission:

$$permitted_s(\alpha, \pi) \Leftrightarrow$$
$$\forall \gamma \in \Gamma, \alpha \notin \gamma \; \forall \mu \in M . (can(\gamma, \mu) \wedge disturbs_s(\alpha, \pi, \gamma, \mu) \rightarrow forbidden_s(\gamma, \mu)) \qquad (D_4)$$

A permission gives the agent a right to execute a plan without being influenced negatively by its acquaintances. This entails that for all groups of acquaintances it is forbidden to take actions that may turn down the permitted plan or just hinder its effectiveness. Still, our notion of permission does not imply that the acquaintances are urged to help, i.e. there is no obligation to execute plans that *enable* or *favour* the permitted plan.

A set of normative prescriptions, represented by the predicates *forbidden* and *permitted*, is called *deontically consistent*, if the above axioms D_1 to D_4 hold. Given that normative prescriptions are deontically consistent normative prescriptions, an agent can be in three deontic relations with respect to a plan π. Firstly, it can be *permitted* for agent α to execute π. Secondly, it may be a *forbidden* for the agent to enact it. Thirdly, it is possible that no deontic notion refers to the execution of π, in which case we say that the normative context is *silent* about π.

5.3.4.2 The Effect of Normative Prescriptions

The above discussion has introduced some deontic notions and characterised their correlation. Still, they must influence autonomous agent behaviour in order to become effective. Considering that deontic notions are prescriptive entities, there are essentially two ways of modelling their function in the normative context.

A simple approach sees normative prescriptions as *regimentations*: under no circumstances will an autonomous agent dare to violate them (Krogh 1996). Such prescriptions are usually built as "reflexes" into the action description of an agent: certain goals, actions or plans are "directly" excluded, without being filtered by some cognitive decision process.

As an alternative, normative prescriptions can be modelled as defeasible entities. They do not directly constrain an agent's behaviour, but leave the agent some normative choice with respect to its attitude towards the deontic statements (Conte and Castelfranchi 1995). In the end, an agent will have to determine the cost of norm abidance and the cost of norm transgression, and will comply only if this balance is inclined towards abidance.

In the sequel, we will be concerned with the first option. This is problematic if the cognitive processes of human agents regarding norms are to be modelled. Still, we are concerned with societies of problem-solving agents. Recall that human societies just serve as a *metaphor* to build a distributed intelligent system. We are *not* concerned with computer simulations of human societies.

Let us model an autonomous but *moral* agent[9], which unalterably does what "should be done". So, the notion of preparedness changes from the social to the normative context. In the normative context, we model the sufficient and necessary condition for the preparedness of agents to enact a plan by the fact that they can execute it *and* it is "legal" for them to do so. Formally, this comes down to:

$$prep_s(\gamma, \mu) \Leftrightarrow can(\gamma, \mu) \wedge \textbf{not } forbidden_s(\gamma, \mu) . \qquad (C')$$

---

[9] Taking into account that normative prescriptions are seen as contributing to social welfare, norm-abiding behaviour is also "beneficial for society", and thus might as well be termed *responsible*. Responsibility is a term that has been largely used in the DAI community (e.g. Jennings and Campos 1997). Still, in accordance with the metaphor that underlies structural co-operation, agents are not "aware" of the functionality of norms and thus do not deliberately make a responsible choice. Agents comply with norms because this is what *ideally should* be done, and it seems preferable to qualify such behaviour as "moral".

Recall that the bold "not" in the formula represents "negation as failure" over prohibitions. It is "legal" for an agent α to execute a plan π in the state s if it cannot be proved that it is forbidden for α to execute a plan π. By this, we introduce non-monotonicity into out model: by *adding* new prohibitions, the preparedness of agents with respect to certain plans (and all the structural relations that have been derived from that) can be *withdrawn*.

Given that normative prescriptions are deontically consistent, the notion of preparedness in the normative context has the same important properties as in the social context. Recall that in case an agent α can enact a plan π and of a group γ of acquaintances $(\alpha \notin \gamma)$ is capable of enacting a multi-plan μ, the group $\alpha \cup \gamma$ is *capable* of enacting $\pi \circ \mu$. Due to Axiom D_2, the definition of preparedness in the normative context also assures that if α is prepared to do π, and the group γ of acquaintances, $\alpha \notin \gamma$, is prepared to execute μ, then the group $\alpha \cup \gamma$ is prepared to enact $\pi \circ \mu$. In particular, this means that the properties of the set $FEAS_s(\alpha)$ of feasible plans do not change in the normative context. A feasible plan π of agent α can be executed together with any multi-plan μ of a group γ of acquaintances, $\alpha \notin \gamma$, given that γ is prepared enact μ. Axiom D_1 assures that the set of feasible plans of an agent is never empty, as also in the normative context every agent is prepared to enact the empty plan π_ε.

Note that the above definition requires as a necessary condition for preparedness that an agent's or a group's deontic relation with respect to a plan is either *permitted* or *silent*. In general, the three deontic relations of agent α with respect to an executable plan π, which α can enact, influence its co-ordination with its acquaintances:

- If it is *permitted* for agent α to execute π, then α is autonomous for π. Agent α need not reach an agreement with its acquaintances in order to execute π, while a certain minimum result of π is assured.

- If it is *forbidden* for agent α to execute π, an agreement is also unnecessary, as α is not prepared to execute π.

- If it is *silent*, i.e. no deontic notion refers to the execution of π by α, the agent is interested in reaching an agreement with others in order to avoid negative or even fatal plan interactions.

By substituting the above specification of preparedness in the definition of social dependence relations, it becomes clear that normative prescriptions actually "switch off" certain dependence relations. For instance, when an agent is no longer prepared to execute a certain plan that hinders the execution of an acquaintance's plan, the corresponding relation is not "valid" anymore. By this, the "level of security" of the latter may be augmented, as less agents may take injurious actions, or its "degree of independence" is augmented, as it depends less on the choices of others.

Note that normative prescriptions are primarily a means to influence agent behaviour. So, we do *not* aim to prescribe how every single potential conflict is to be solved. Therefore, we consider the use of normative prescriptions to be the exception, not the rule. Furthermore, in practical applications deontic notions will usually not apply to single plans. They may refer, for instance, to some resource or some action. As a consequence, all plans that need such resource or action are subject to the prescription. This reduces significantly the complexity of designing sets of prohibitions and permissions within the framework of structural co-operation.

5.3.4.3 Social Structure

In the previous paragraphs a model of the "dynamics" of the normative context has been given. Its result is determined by what we call the normative structure of society: the deontically consistent set of imperatives pertaining to its constituent agents. The "structural" property of normative prescriptions is induced by the interdependence between permission and prohibition as defined by the axioms.

Definition 5.7. The normative structure in a state s is determined by

$$D_1 - D_4 \models_{R,F,P} forbidden_s(\gamma, \mu) \wedge permitted_s(\gamma', \mu') .$$

In any state s, the normative structure is determined by all literals of the predicates *forbidden* and *permitted* that are consistent with the axioms D_1 to D_4 in a particular reactive co-ordination setting R. Note that, in principle, we account for a different normative structure in every state. In practise, these normative structures will have to be generated by some kind of "normative grammar". One might think of *norms*, being represented as generally applicable rules: if the antecedent matches a specific situation, the deontic statements in the consequent pertain.

We are now endowed with all the ingredients to present a precise definition of what we understand by social structure in relation to our mechanism. Just like in the dependence structure, the social structure is determined by feasibility, negative and positive dependence relations within society. Still, the social structure also considers the normative prescriptions pertaining to agents and groups. Therefore, as the type and the amount of dependence relations that can be derived are different in the social and in the normative context, the social structure and its effects are different from the dependence structure.

In any state s, the social structure is determined by all literals of the predicates *feas-dep*, *neg-dep*, and *pos-dep* that can be derived from a reactive co-ordination setting (R) augmented by the predicates *forbidden* (F) and *permitted* (P), given that the latter are deontically consistent $(D_1$ to $D_4)$ and based on our theory of agent and plan relations $(A_1$ to $A_8)$ as well as on the notion of preparedness in the normative context (C').

Definition 5.8. The social structure in a state s is determined by

$$A_1 - A_8, C', D_1 - D_4 \models_{R,F,P} feas-dep_s(\alpha, \pi, \gamma) \wedge neg-dep_s(\alpha', \pi', \gamma') \wedge pos-dep_s(\alpha'', \pi'', \gamma'')$$

Social structure compiles the dependence structure, which is a projection of objective relations between potential plans onto agents, and the normative structure, which can be seen as an instantiation of ideal behaviour, as specified by norms, individualised to agents and groups. From the point of view of structural co-operation, the normative structure modifies the "natural" dependence structure that plan relations and agent capabilities imply, so that the global functionality of the overall social structure emerges from the self-interested choice of autonomous agents.

5.4 Related Work

Conte and Castelfranchi (1995) have been among the first to present a rigorous model of the role of normative structures within societies of (potentially artificial) agents. In particular, they consider norms as an external source of behaviour modification, so as to reconcile autonomous agenthood and external control. However, Conte and Castelfranchi aim at a general theory of autonomous agent behaviour: the frame of discourse is not constrained to some type of domains or some specific types of agents. In consequence, their models have a rather general character and are biased towards social simulation. No attempt is made to build societies of autonomous agents that actually solve problems.

Sichman (1995) and Sichman et al. (1994) seek a notion of self-interested behaviour within heterogeneous groups of autonomous agents that incorporates a stronger bias towards engineering. For this purpose, they introduce the notion of plans into Conte and Castelfranchi's theory and express the resulting framework in first-order predicate logic. Plans are modelled as sequences of actions, which make use of resources in order to attain goals. An agent needs to "know" about a certain plan in order to enact it, and is additionally required to be endowed with the necessary resources and action capabilities. On this basis, a notion of social dependence between agents is defined: an agent may help an acquaintance by providing actions, resources or plans that the latter lacks in order to attain its goals. The theory does not comprise a notion of "resource limitation", i.e. an agent does not incur in any "cost" when providing resources or actions to others.

The approach presented in this chapter, in contrast, does not explicitly model the "origin" of plan interrelations, but sees them as basic notions which directly imply social dependence relations between the agents that are prepared to enact them. So, as our model accounts for different types of plan interrelations (including negative ones), it also comprises different types and degrees of dependence relations between agents. In part, this divergence between the approach of Sichman et al. and ours goes back to their different objectives: the former aims at open systems, where synergistic potentials due to complementary agent knowledge and capabilities are common, the overall attainment of goals prevails over efficiency considerations, and it is hard to establish a generally agreed taxonomy of plan interrelations. By contrast, we are concerned with the co-ordination of societies of agents for the purpose of efficient problem-solving, where knowledge about the different types of interrelated action can be "built into" the agents and negative interaction due to the scarcity of resources is rather the rule but the exception.

From this perspective, the aim of work by Jennings and Campos (1997) is quite similar to ours: they seek guidelines to support the design of groups of autonomous *problem-solving* agents. Still, they prefer to modify directly the concept of rationality, by assuming agents to be *socially rational*: an agent just selects a certain behaviour if it is either beneficial for itself or for society. Still, this concept does not say anything about what happens if both are in conflict.

Some game theoretic approaches are also searching for behaviour guidelines that lie between self-interest and benevolence. Brainov's notion of *altruism* (1996) is an example of these intents. However, they usually do not provide an instrumentation by means of a computational mechanism.

The idea of constraining agent behaviour by coercive entities is also present in the social laws approach of Shoham and Tennenholz (1992, 1995). In this framework, the designer proclaims a set of behaviour guidelines, called social laws. Agents are assumed a priori to abide to these laws, so they directly constrain the agents' action possibilities. The motivation for designing social laws is to exclude certain undesired global states "off-line", i.e. to prescribe agent behaviour that avoids potential negative interferences or to prescribe a certain standard way of coping with them (recall the coherence problems described in Chapter 2). Reasoning and communication costs are reduced that way.

Our notion of normative structures also restricts the action options (or: plan enactment options) of norm abiding agent. Still, contrary to the social laws approach, within structural co-operation normative prescriptions not just exclude certain alternatives, but also influence the *choice mechanism* of an agent that selects one of the "legal" options. By issuing prescriptions and prohibitions the social position of an agent is modified, which leads to different social interactions among agents. Therefore, they do not primarily constrain actions or plans, but rather influence social exchanges. This difference is also reflected in the *function* of normative prescriptions within structural co-operation: they are not intended to directly rule out certain global states a priori as social laws do, as this would be too complex and overly restricting for the real-world scenarios that we aim at. Instead, they are meant to bias social interaction and its outcome, in order that the resulting action at the society-level be instrumental for problem-solving purposes.

The same differential argument applies to *flexible* social laws that Briggs and Cook present (1995). As social laws have shown to be too constraining in many settings, sets of laws of increasing weakness are designed. So, in an overconstrained situation an agent just switches to the next liable social law. However, although the constraints imposed by flexible social laws are "weak", they do not have the same biasing character as the normative prescriptions of structural co-operation. They are exclusively used to rule out certain actions, in order to avoid undesired global states that can be characterised a priori by the designer.

5.5 Bottom Line

This chapter has been concerned with the notion of the functionality of social structure. Social structure shapes the social interaction between autonomous agents, so as to give an external observer the impression that the society deliberately pursues some collective goal. Reactive co-ordination settings have been presented. They have been illustrated by a specific problem instance in the synchronous blocks domain. By applying the notion of the functionality of social structure to reactive co-ordination settings, we have obtained the mechanism of structural co-operation, which models the self-interested behaviour of autonomous agents within a given social structure. It has been argued that an adequate normative structure can induce self-interested behaviour to become instrumental for a desired collective functionality.

Structural co-operation combines deliberate and emergent effects in one mechanism. The underlying social metaphor of the functionality of social structure provides a terminological framework for the description of multi-agent co-ordination processes. Furthermore, it propitiates an intuitive understanding the dynamics of the agent system. As agent behaviour is not determined by some "pre-programmed" co-operativeness, but by the result of self-interest in a multi-agent context, it can be rationalised more easily by an outside observer.

From the technical point of view, structural co-operation has the advantage of providing a certain basic co-ordination of agents, which corresponds to the equilibrium among the individual interests of autonomous agents as determined by their social strengths. By this, the knowledge necessary for co-ordination in reactive co-ordination settings becomes less complex, given that the amount of normative prescriptions is limited. Furthermore, if the problem-solving society is scaled-up by additional agents (or if certain agents break down), the co-ordination part of the multi-agent system does not fail or need not be rebuilt. Instead, the equilibrium among the agents' interests is shifted. Eventually, this needs to be compensated by adaptations in the normative structure. We will crosscheck these claims within the case study presented in the third part of this book.

Still, structural co-operation does impose some restrictions on the underlying multi-agent setting. While it is true that structural co-operation supports different classes of problem-solving agent societies (ranging from societies of completely self-sufficient agents to societies of fully complementary agents), the above advantages are conditioned to an underlying assumption: the "natural equilibrium" of the system needs to be "close" to the desired functionality. On the one hand, this means that co-operation between agents must be encouraged by situations of reciprocal dependence. By this, social exchanges are triggered that determine some equilibrium. On the other hand, it requires that the agents' social strength as implied by the dependence structure coincide with the relative importance that an agent plays in the generation of a desired solution. The globally most important agent must also be socially most important.

However, these conditions are often met in multi-agent problem-solving systems. This is especially true, when systems are based on *quantitative* problem decomposition. In these approaches, a complex global task is decomposed into smaller sub-tasks of the same type, which usually leads to agents with balanced social strengths and equal global importance.

Still, the mechanism of structural co-operation is far from being operational. We have outlined some desirable properties and connected problems for sequences of social exchanges. The "heart" of the mechanism – a precise model of self-interested behaviour in the social and the normative context – is still to be given.

A possible way to proceed in this book is to try to build such a model entirely based on qualitative notions. However, we have pointed out that this creates considerable difficulties, as it requires endowing each agent with a strategy that decides which exchanges to accept based on the dependence structure. One problem lies in the quantification of the exchanged commitments, i.e. in the determination of the exchange value. Another source of complexity lies in the transitivity of the effects of exchanges in general resource-bounded multi-agent societies comprising n agents. Although it is challenging to tackle the above problem, in this book we will proceed with a more practical objective in mind. In the following chapters, we will rely on quantitative measures to determine the outcome of self-interested behaviour in social and normative contexts, so as to analyse the resulting mechanism by means of a complex real-world application.

6 Structural Co-operation and Bargaining

It is a long way from the description of the mechanism of structural co-operation, based on findings in social sciences and transferred to artificial agent systems by means of the society metaphor, to an implemented problem-solving society that actually "runs" on a computer. Especially the dynamics of the mechanism needs to be specified more precisely, in order to come up with an operational model of structural co-operation.

Two issues are most important in that respect. On the one hand, we need to give a definition of self-interested action in the social and in the normative context that captures the essence of the corresponding sequences of social exchanges. On the other hand, based on this model it is necessary to provide an instrumentation of autonomous agent behaviour in these contexts. We will tackle the first issue in the sequel, thereby laying the ground for an approach to the second, which will be discussed in Chapter 7.

The basic idea of this chapter is to relate the qualitative, structural model of the last chapter to a quantitative model based on bargaining theory, and to make use of findings in bargaining theory to determine the outcome of structural co-operation among autonomous problem-solving agents. Section 6.1 illustrates how structural co-operation can be mapped onto a bargaining problem. Subsequently, in Section 6.2, different bargaining solutions are examined with respect to their adequacy to characterise the outcome of social interaction in the social and normative context of structural co-operation. Section 6.3 shows how the different contexts influence the result of social exchanges by relating them to the role of the disagreement point in bargaining solutions. Finally, Section 6.4 compares our model to related work, and Section 6.5 discusses advantages and drawbacks of modelling structural co-operation within the framework of bargaining theory.

6.1 Structural Co-operation as a Bargaining Scenario

In order to co-ordinate their actions in a reactive co-ordination scenario, the agents involved in structural co-operation exchange commitments respecting the characteristics of the individual plans that they will enact. For an external observer, the result of this social interaction process is an "agreement" on the multi-plan that will be enacted. From this perspective, the problem of self-interested action of norm-compliant agents in the social and normative contexts is essentially the same as the bargaining problem in game theory: agents can make mutually beneficial agreements, but have a conflict of interest regarding which agreement to make. No agreement is possible without the support of any one agent. In the sequel, we will develop and justify a procedure to associate a bargaining scenario to a reactive co-ordination problem.

6.1.1   Modelling Co-operation

The objective of this section is to develop a quantitative model of the agents' preferences over agreements, i.e. over the multi-plans that will be enacted.

In the previous chapter we have shown how the distance measure between a state and an ideal state, that the reactive co-ordination scenario provides, can be used to define a preference relation over states. We will now "re-formulate" it in quantitative terms. For this purpose, the "absolute value" of a state is introduced, which expresses the strength of an agent's preference for it. It is defined as the minimum distance between the state and some ideal state:

$$\left| s \right|_{\alpha} = min \left\{ d_{\alpha}\left(s, \bar{s}\right) \mid ideal\left(\alpha, \bar{s}\right) \right\} .$$

The bigger the absolute value of a state, the less is an agent's preference for it. Consequently, a state s is weakly preferred to s', if its absolute value is equal or less than the absolute value of s'.

In a next step, we will extend this notion to individual plans. In the individual context, an agent is only interested in plans that are executable, so will make use of the absolute value of a state in order to *quantify* an agent's preference over executable plans. In a particular state s, such an individual plan is the more preferred the closer the state that results from its execution is to an ideal state. When this notion of the reduction of distance that the plan brings about is quantified numerically, it expresses its utility for the agent.

Definition 6.1. In a state s, the *utility* of an executable individual plan π for an agent α_i is

$$U_i(\pi) = \left| s \right|_{\alpha_i} - \left| res(\pi, s) \right|_{\alpha_i} .$$

Note that the above definition assigns a negative utility to those plans that further separate an agent from its desired states. Analogous to our model in Chapter 5, in the individual context a self-interested agent will choose one of the individual plans that it can enact and that maximise its utility.

It is important to point out that the *strength* of preference between two individual plans is given by the difference of their utilities. Consider, for instance, the plans π_1 and π_7 in our example from the synchronous blocks domain. Although only agent α_1 is prepared to execute π_1, α_2 can assign utility to π_1 in accordance with Definition 6.1 and thus may also establish a quantitative comparison.

It is easy to check that the absolute value of the current situation s_0 is 3 utility units in the scale of α_1 and 4 utility units in the eyes of α_2 (recall that α_2 needs to free Block 4 before it can start to build its stack). The result of executing π_1 is that Block 3 is located on top of Block 2 while Block 1 is clear: there is just one operation missing in the eyes of α_1, while α_2 would have to unstack both blocks, so that it is still 4 operations away from its ideal state, i.e.

$$U_1(\pi_1) = 3-1 = 2 \quad \text{and} \quad U_2(\pi_1) = 4-4 = 0 .$$

The result of executing π_7 is that all blocks are clear on the table. So, there are two operations missing for both agents in order to end up in an ideal state:

$$U_1(\pi_7) = 3-2 = 1 \quad \text{and} \quad U_2(\pi_7) = 4-2 = 2 .$$

So, agent α_1 prefers π_1 to π_7 by one utility local unit. By contrast, α_2 favours π_7 over π_1 by two utility units in its personal scale.

In a next step, we will extend the notion of utility to multi-plans. As before, we are only interested in those multi-plans, that represent *possible* agreements in the social and normative contexts. Therefore, we introduce the set X of *legally enactable* multi-plans in a situation s. It comprises all plans that are executable in s and for which there is a group of agents prepared to do so:

$$X = \left\{ \mu \in M \mid exec(\mu,s) \wedge \exists \gamma \in \Gamma . \, prep_s(\gamma,\mu) \right\} .$$

The remaining interrelations between the component plans of a multi-plan are compiled in the function *res*, which determines the state that is expected to result from the simultaneous execution of the component plans. Therefore, we will again make use of the absolute value of a state in order to quantify an agent's preference over legally enactable plans, and define the utility of a multi-plan for an agent as the reduction of distance to some of that agent's ideal states.

Definition 6.2. In a state s, the *utility* of a legally enactable multi-plan $\mu \in X$ for an agent α_i is

$$U_i(\mu) = \left| s \right|_{\alpha_i} - \left| res(\mu,s) \right|_{\alpha_i} .$$

The utilities that each of the n agents obtain from an agreement on a multi-plan can be comprised in a n-dimensional utility vector. The set of utility vectors that are realisable over X is denoted by $U(X)$.

Recall that the agents usually have different preferences respecting which multi-plan to enact, and consequently assign different utilities to a multi-plan. Therefore, a multi-plan that maximises the utility of one agent will most probably result in a poor utility for some of its acquaintances.

In our synchronous blocks world example, where only two agents are involved, we actually get utility-pairs for each legally enactable multi-plan. The utility of all multi-plans can be summarised in a *scenario matrix*. Table 6.1 shows a scenario matrix that comprises the individual plans presented in Chapter 5. Rows indicate the individual plans of agent α_1, columns the plans of α_2, and each cell the utility vectors of the corresponding multi-plans. Cells that denote incompatible plans, and that consequently have no associated utility vector, are marked by $\perp$.

A two-agent scenario matrix can be represented graphically in a plane, such that the axis of ordinates represents α_1's utility and the abscissa α_2's utility. Each

Table 6.1. Scenario matrix

	π_1	π_2	π_3	π_4	π_5	π_6	π_7	π_8	π_9	π_{10}	π_{11}	π_{12}	π_ε
π_1	⊥	⊥	⊥	2,1	⊥	2,1	⊥	⊥	⊥	⊥	⊥	⊥	2,0
π_2	⊥	⊥	2,1	⊥	⊥	⊥	⊥	2,1	⊥	⊥	⊥	⊥	⊥
π_3	⊥	2,1	⊥	1,2	1,1	1,2	1,2	⊥	⊥	⊥	⊥	⊥	1,1
π_4	2,1	⊥	1,2	⊥	1,2	0,1	⊥	1,2	0,3	⊥	⊥	⊥	0,1
π_5	⊥	⊥	1,1	1,2	⊥	1,2	⊥	1,2	⊥	⊥	⊥	⊥	1,1
π_6	2,1	⊥	1,2	0,1	1,2	⊥	1,2	⊥	⊥	⊥	⊥	0,1	0,1
π_7	⊥	⊥	1,2	⊥	⊥	1,2	⊥	1,2	⊥	⊥	⊥	⊥	1,2
π_8	⊥	2,1	⊥	1,2	1,2	⊥	1,2	⊥	⊥	⊥	⊥	⊥	1,2
π_9	⊥	⊥	⊥	0,3	⊥	⊥	⊥	⊥	⊥	⊥	⊥	⊥	⊥
π_{10}	⊥	⊥	⊥	⊥	⊥	⊥	⊥	⊥	⊥	⊥	⊥	⊥	-2,-1
π_{11}	⊥	⊥	⊥	⊥	⊥	⊥	⊥	⊥	⊥	⊥	⊥	⊥	-1,-1
π_{12}	⊥	⊥	⊥	⊥	⊥	0,1	⊥	⊥	⊥	⊥	⊥	⊥	-1,0
π_ε	2,0	⊥	1,1	0,1	1,1	0,1	1,2	1,2	⊥	-2,-1	-1,-1	-1,0	0,0

utility vector out of $U(X)$, which results from an agreement on a certain legally enactable multi-plan, corresponds to a point in the plane. The remaining multi-plans are not considered. The graphical representation of the above scenario matrix is shown in Figure 6.1.

So far, we are capable of modelling the outcome of sequences of social exchanges, as long as the agents find a "real" compromise and agree on enacting individual plans that correspond to a particular multi-plan. Still, usually reactive co-ordination settings are only partially co-operative in the sense that the agents can benefit from an agreement, but have different points of view respecting which deal it should be. In the blocks example, agent α_1's most preferred agreement achieves a utility of $(2,1)$, while α_2 would select the agreement of utility $(0,3)$ if it could. A way to solve this conflict is to make the agents "flip a coin" in order to choose between alternative agreements: the agents "gamble" on who can execute its preferred alternative and who has to cede.

We will account for this possibility by permitting lotteries over multi-plans. A certain probability distribution over the set of compatible multi-plans is called a *mixed multi-plan*. Let m be the cardinality of X. A mixed multi-plan is a m-dimensional vector

$$\sigma = (p_1,...,p_m), 0 \leq p_i \leq 1, \sum_{i=1}^{m} p_i = 1 .$$

The set of mixed multi-plans is denoted by Σ. To illustrate the notion of mixed multi-plans, let us set out from a set of three "efficient" legally enactable multi-plans and their corresponding utility pairs:

$$\mu_1 = (\pi_1 \circ \pi_4), \mu_2 = (\pi_3 \circ \pi_4), \mu_3 = (\pi_4 \circ \pi_9)$$
$$U(\mu_1) = (2,1), U(\mu_2) = (1,2), U(\mu_3) = (0,3) .$$

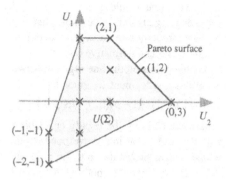

Figure 6.1. Graphical representation of the example scenario

An example of a mixed multi-plan is to have the agents agree on each of the above plans with equal probability, i.e.

$$\sigma_{(\mu_1,\mu_2,\mu_3)} = \left(\tfrac{1}{3},\tfrac{1}{3},\tfrac{1}{3}\right) .$$

In order to extend the notion of utility to mixed multi-plans, we have to define our conception of the expected utility of lotteries. We assume that the *expected* utility of a mixed multi-plan is given by the sum of each legally enactable multi-plan's utility weighed by its probability[1]:

Definition 6.3. The expected utility of a mixed multi-plan $\sigma \in \Sigma$ is defined as

$$U_i(\sigma) = \sum_{k=1}^{m} p_k U_i(\mu_k) .$$

The set of expected utility vectors that are realisable over Σ is denoted by $U(\Sigma)$. According to the above definition, the vector of expected utilities for the afore-mentioned mixed multi-plan is

$$U\left(\sigma_{(\mu_1,\mu_2,\mu_3)}\right) = \left(\tfrac{3}{3},\tfrac{6}{3}\right) = (1,2) .$$

There are several issues to notice respecting the above definitions. When agents agree on a particular *mixed* multi-plan, they implicitly state their conformity with the outcome of the corresponding lottery, i.e. with the execution of the winning multi-plan. So, our agents gamble on *multi-plans* instead of randomising over *individual plans*. We have favoured this option, being aware that it introduces an additional aspect of centralisation into the model: *one* agent must generate a random event that affects the actions that *everybody* in society will take. Still, this is the price to pay in order to obtain two important advantages.

Firstly, it is possible to explicitly exclude multi-plans that are not legally enactable. If agents could agree on randomising independently over individual plans, a

---

[1] The definition assumes that the agents have a neutral attitude towards risk. Of course, other positions might as well be taken.

considerable amount of restrictions would be necessary in order to assure that the outcome always constitutes a legally enactable multi-plan. Secondly, it allows the set $U(\Sigma)$ to be *convex*. This property will allow us to determine a unique outcome of social interaction in the social and normative context.

Consider, for instance, the points on the line segment between (2,1) and (1,2) in Figure 6.1. The points of this line segment are given by

$$L = \left\{ p(2,1) + (1-p)(1,2) \mid 0 \le p \le 1 \right\}.$$

Assume that the agents reach (2,1) by the legally enactable multi-plan $(\pi_1 \circ \pi_4)$ and (1,2) by $(\pi_5 \circ \pi_6)$. So, each point in L corresponds to the expected utility of the mixed multi-plan that assigns probability p to $(\pi_1 \circ \pi_4)$ and an inverse proportional probability of $1-p$ to $(\pi_5 \circ \pi_6)$. So, both agents need to refer to the same random event.

Moreover, some simple mathematics prove that $U(\Sigma)$ is not only a convex set. In fact, the definition of $U(\Sigma)$ suggests that $U(\Sigma)$ is a (bounded) convex polytope in $\mathfrak{R}^n$, whose extreme points are given by the set $U(X)$ of utility vectors reachable by legally enactable multi-plans $\mu \in X$. This convex polytope constitutes the convex and comprehensive hull (cch) of its extreme points (e.g. Jones 1980): it is the smallest convex and comprehensive set in $\mathfrak{R}^n$ that contains all utility vectors out of $U(X)$, i.e.

$$U(\Sigma) = cch(U(X)).$$

As Figure 6.1 suggests, in $\mathfrak{R}^2$ (the two agent case) this convex and comprehensive hull of $U(X)$ is a convex polygon, with the vertices corresponding to utilities of some legally enactable multi-plans. Note that not all utility vectors of legally enactable multi-plans, not even those of *undominated* compatible multi-plans, need to be vertices.

6.1.2   Modelling Conflict

So far, a quantitative notion of preference for different kinds of agreements on multi-plans has been modelled for each agent. When agents co-ordinate their strategies and agree on some mixed multi-plan, the corresponding vector of utilities is what each agent expects to obtain. Still, agents are autonomous and not forced to co-operate. They can decide to take a chance alone, without limiting their freedom of choice by some binding agreement. So, it remains to model what happens if agents do not converge on an agreement.

Therefore, the utilities that the agents obtain in case of conflict need to be defined. A common way to choose these parameters is to take the agents' "security levels" as a model of conflict utility. The security level is the maximum utility that an agent can achieve anyway, regardless of what its acquaintances do[2].

---

[2]   Other models prefer "levels of threat" to determine the conflict utility. Each agent threatens the other with what the latter will lose if the former denies agreement.

We will apply a similar idea to the reactive co-ordination settings. In a conflict situation, we define the *response* of the acquaintances of a single agent α to its individual plan π as the multi-plan μ that they are prepared to execute and that *minimises* α's utility from $(\pi \circ \mu)$.

$$response_s(\pi,\alpha_i,\mu) \quad \Leftrightarrow$$

$$U_i(\pi \circ \mu) = min\left\{U_i(\pi \circ \mu') \mid \pi \in FEAS_s(\alpha_i) \wedge \exists \gamma \in \Gamma, \alpha \notin \gamma. prep_s(\gamma,\mu')\right\}$$

This models that in case of disagreement an agent must account for the unpleasant situation that all its acquaintances jointly try to harm it. Note that the above definition requires an agent α's individual plan π to be feasible (i.e. $\pi \in FEAS_s(\alpha)$). This assumption excludes the existence of worst responses γ that lead to multi-plans $\pi \circ \mu$ which are not legally enactable. Recall that a feasible plan π of agent α can be executed together with any multi-plan μ of a group γ of acquaintances, $\alpha \notin \gamma$, given that γ is prepared enact μ. An agent's set of feasible plans is never empty, as at least the empty plan π_ε is contained in $FEAS_s(\alpha)$. So, in the above definition the utility function is defined for all multi-plans that cope with the condition stated and the existence of the minimum can be assured.

The above assumption is not constraining, as in conflict situation a self-interested agent α involved in structural co-operation is always *interested* in choosing a feasible plan. In fact, it will select a plan π that, when combined with the response from its acquaintances, results in a multi-plan *maximising* its individual utility value. This is called the *conflict utility* of the agent α.

Definition 6.4. In a state s, the *conflict utility* of an agent α_i is given by

$$U_i^d = max\left\{U_i(\pi \circ \mu) \mid response_s(\pi,\alpha_i,\mu)\right\}.$$

Note that in case there are autonomous plans of agent α in situation s (i.e. if the set $AUT_s(\alpha)$ is not empty), the agent's conflict utility is at least the stand-alone utility of its best autonomous plan. In this case, the most "malicious" response of its acquaintances is to jointly do nothing, so that an autonomous plan brings about the same state as in the individual context.

In our example, the only plan that α_1 can execute and which is guaranteed not to become incompatible is π_ε, which α_2 counters by π_{10}, resulting in a conflict utility of -2 for α_1. Agent α_2 also needs choose π_ε in case of disagreement, to which α_1's most malicious response is to enact π_{11}, giving rise to a conflict utility of -1 for α_2. So, the overall conflict utility is $(-2,-1)$.

Self-motivated agents will only converge on an agreement respecting a multi-plan, if it achieves *at least* the conflict utility for any of them. Note that in the blocks world example the conflict utility occasionally coincides with the worst legally enactable agreement. So, all points in the polygon of Figure 6.1 are individually rational agreements for the agents.

6.1.3   The Associated Bargaining Scenario

In this section we outline how a bargaining scenario can be defined on the basis of the above notions. For this purpose, we define the overall conflict utility within a society of agents in a certain situation as the vector $\vec{d}$ that comprises the individual conflict utility of every agent:

$$\vec{d} = \left(U_1^d, ..., U_n^d \right).$$

Furthermore, we will treat the conflict utility vector as an effectively reachable agreement, defining a set S to be the convex and comprehensive hull (*cch*) of the legally enactable multi-plans plus the conflict utility vector

$$S = cch\left(U(X) \cup \{\vec{d}\} \right).$$

The set S usually equals $U(\Sigma)$, but may also be a (convex) superset of the latter.

Definition 6.5. The *bargaining scenario* B associated with a reactive co-ordination setting is a pair $B = (S, \vec{d})$.

S is called the *bargaining set* and $\vec{d}$ the *disagreement point* of B. A vector $\vec{x} \in S$ is often referred to as a feasible outcome of B. For reactive co-ordination settings, we assume that there is always a possibility for the agents to "win" from co-ordination, i.e. that there is a multi-plan in S whose utility strictly dominates the disagreement point. So, a bargaining scenario B associated with a reactive co-ordination setting actually complies with the properties that bargaining theory assumes (Thomson 1994). In consequence, the whole mathematical apparatus of bargaining theory is applicable.

Still, it is necessary to observe as to how far the associated bargaining scenario comprises the notions of social dependence and social strength, which are essential in order to model self-interested behaviour in the social and normative contexts of structural co-operation.

First, and maybe surprisingly, it has to be noticed that the shape of the bargaining set is free of any reference to *social* relations between agents. A point in the bargaining set is not endowed with any "contextual attachment" that states which agents can actually decide whether it is reached or not. For instance, a utility vector $U(\pi \circ \pi') \in S$ may be a result of both, an *enables* or an *indifferent* relation between π and π'.

Still, social relations *do* have influence on the choice of the disagreement point. The conflict utility d_i for an agent α_i is affected as follows by the different types of social dependence:

- *feas-dep$_s(\alpha_i, \pi, \gamma)$*: $U_i(\pi)$ cannot be used as conflict utility.
- *neg-dep$_s(\alpha_i, \pi, \gamma)$*: only $U_i(\pi \circ \mu) < U_i(\pi)$ can be used as conflict utility.
- *pos-dep$_s(\alpha_i, \pi, \gamma)$*: $U_i(\pi)$ can be used as conflict utility.

So, the potential conflict utility of a plan reflects the degree of social dependence as depicted in Figure 5.4. In the sequel, we will see how these facts influence the result of agent interaction within the associated bargaining scenario.

6.2 Solutions to the Associated Bargaining Scenario

We have mapped the original problem to a bargaining scenario $(S, \vec{d}\,)$. Now, we endeavour to find a solution to the scenario: a vector $\bar{\varphi} \in S$ needs to be singled out upon which a bargaining process, and the process of social interaction that it models, is supposed to converge. The question is to model how much an agent is willing to give its acquaintances in order to reach a final agreement, or how little it is willing to accept as the "price" of co-operation.

Bargaining theory provides answers to this question. Usually, in line with the different stances from which this question can be affronted, it is divided in two areas: *strategic* and *axiomatic* models of bargaining[3].

The former takes a procedural approach to the problem of finding a solution to a bargaining scenario. It usually adheres to a sequential setting where agents alternate in making offers to each other in a pre-specified order, eventually converging on an agreement. The bargaining situation in which such sequences of offers are made is modelled as a game and decisions are analysed on the basis of strategies in equilibrium. As time goes by, the benefit that an agent gets from a potential agreement decreases, so they are interested in coming to an arrangement as fast as possible.

Instead of addressing the problem of a solution concept for bargaining problems based on some notion of equilibrium among the agents' strategies, axiomatic bargaining theory takes a declarative approach. It postulates *axioms*, desirable properties of a bargaining solution, and then seeks the solution concept that satisfies them.

In the sequel, we take the latter tack towards the problem. A series of reasonable conditions are presented that a feasible vector $\bar{\varphi} \in S$ (corresponding to the utility of a legally enactable multi-plan) should comply with, in order to constitute a solution to the bargaining scenario associated with a reactive co-ordination setting. These conditions are intended to characterise self-interested action of norm-abiding agents in a reactive co-ordination setting.

6.2.1 The Nash Solution

First of all, the agents' self-interest is to be modelled. Any such model requires that agents only choose to co-operate with others and make an agreement, when they can get more out of it than acting without any commitment between each other (but in the presence of others).

So, the first axiom captures *individual rationality* of agent behaviour: it requires that the utility that every agent obtains from a solution is at least its utility

---

[3] Game theoretic literature also employs the label *non-cooperative* for strategic models of bargaining, while axiomatic models are often called *co-operative*.

from disagreement. Otherwise, some agent(s) would not join an agreement on the solution, making it unfeasible[4]:

$$\vec{d} \leq \vec{\varphi} \ . \tag{N_1}$$

The grey region in Figure 6.1 shows the set of feasible individually rational outcomes. All legally enactable mixed multi-plans that achieve a utility to the "top-right" of the disagreement point are individually rational.

In settings with a high degree of interdependence between agents, most agreements will be individually rational. This is certainly true for any bargaining scenario associated with a reactive co-ordination problem, as in case of disagreement an agent has to suppose the worst case, i.e. that all its acquaintances jointly try to separate it further from its desired state. So, the only individually *irrational* agreement would be to join in and move the world away from its ideal. The situation changes when an agent is given rights, that allow it to execute some beneficial individual plan even in case of disagreement. Under these conditions, in order to be individually rational, the utility that the agent receives from agreement must be greater than the utility obtained from employing its rights alone.

Secondly, we require a solution to be *Pareto-optimal*. Using the above concepts, it states that a solution $\vec{\varphi}$ cannot be dominated by any other feasible outcome $\vec{x}$:

$$\neg \exists \vec{x} \in S, \vec{x} \neq \vec{\varphi}. \ \ \vec{\varphi} \leq \vec{x} \ . \tag{N_2}$$

This seems reasonable as, if such an $\vec{x}$ existed, at least one agent could benefit from switching to it without the veto of others. This is equivalent to requiring that no agent can be better off without some other agent being worse off. Graphically the set of Pareto-optimal outcomes, also called *Pareto-surface*, is given by the undominated boundary of S. As Figure 6.1 depicts, the Pareto-surface of the example scenario is the line segment that joins the utility pairs $(2,1)$ and $(0,3)$:

$$\partial S = \left\{ x \in S \mid \exists p \in \Re, 0 \leq p \leq 1. \ \vec{x} = p(2,1) + (1-p)(0,3) \right\} .$$

In the synchronous blocks world, the requirement of Pareto-optimality can be illustrated as follows: imagine that there is a clear yellow block on the table and that it is just mentioned in the ideal state of agent α_1 but not of α_2. Agent α_1 is provided with two individual plans. The plan π_1 does not touch the yellow block, while the plan π_1', in addition to the result of π_1, puts the yellow block in its place, i.e. π_1' is preferred over π_1 by α_1. Suppose that an agent α_2 aims to execute a plan π_2, which is compatible with both individual plans of α_1. Then, given that the use of the yellow block in π_1' does not interfere with α_2's plan π_2, Pareto-optimality states that the multi-plan $\pi_1 \circ \pi_2$ will *not* constitute a possible agreement of the autonomous agents α_1 and α_2: by agreeing on $\pi_1' \circ \pi_2$, α_1 would be better off without α_2 being worse. Note that this does not cover the case when π_1''s use of the yellow block accidentally obstructs a block that α_2's plan π_2 intended to use, as in this case α_2 prefers $\pi_1 \circ \pi_2$ over $\pi_1' \circ \pi_2$.

---

[4] Here, and in the following, $\leq$ expresses vector domination, i.e. $x \leq x' \Leftrightarrow \forall i \in \{1,...n\} \ x_i \leq x_i'$.

Furthermore, it is worthwhile pointing out that the above argument does *not* imply that the yellow block is irrelevant for α_2's bargaining, as long as it does not interfere with its "good" individual plans. Autonomous agents will certainly be given the opportunity to *pressure* with their ability to obstruct the others' plans. So, in case of disagreement, α_1 needs to take into account that its acquaintance might impede the use of the yellow block. So, as Figure 6.1 suggests, the disagreement point will not be located on the Pareto-surface.

Thirdly, a solution should be *symmetric*. No agent should have an a priori bargaining advantage besides its bargaining position specified within $(S, \vec{d})$. If the agents cannot be differentiated on the basis of the information contained in $(S, \vec{d})$, i.e. their utility function and their fallback payoff, then the solution should treat them alike, i.e. in this case holds:

$$\varphi_i = \varphi_j . \tag{N_3}$$

This requirement is quite intuitive in the synchronous blocks domain. If agent α_1 were agent α_2, i.e. if it had the same capabilities, ideal states, distance measures etc. (and vice versa), the result of bargaining would simply switch outcomes between both. No agent has more authority than another for "being somebody": our agents live in a world of equal opportunities. Still, it is the specific situation of each agent (its part in the social structure) that introduces inequality.

The fourth requirement is termed *scale invariance*. It captures the intuition that certain types of modification of the agents' numeric utilities should not influence the bargaining outcome. Scale invariance requires that if utility functions – and consequently the bargaining setting $(S, \vec{d})$ – are subject to positive linear transformations, then the solution does not change. Let λ be a positive linear transformation and $\vec{\varphi}_\lambda$ a solution to the bargaining scenario $(\lambda S, \lambda \vec{d})$, then

$$\lambda \vec{\varphi} = \vec{\varphi}_\lambda . \tag{N_4}$$

Scale invariance is necessary to capture the fact that in reactive co-ordination settings utilities constitute quantitative measures of an agent's preferences. Suppose, that in the blocks domain example setting agent α_1 adheres to a notion of distance as described in Chapter 5 (the minimum number of operations necessary to change between states). By contrast, agent α_2 multiplies the minimum number of operations by two and adds three, in order to define its distance measure. It appears reasonable that the resulting modified utility function of agent α_2 does not provide it with a bargaining advantage compared to the original scenario.

Finally, we would like to assure *contraction independence*. This requirement is also called "independence of irrelevant alternatives", as it states that if S' is a subset of the bargaining set that contains the disagreement point, and S' contains the solution to the original bargaining problem, then the solutions of the original and of the "smaller" bargaining problem are the same. Expressed formally: let $S' \subset S$, $\vec{d} \in S'$ and $\vec{\varphi}'$ be a solution to $(S', \vec{d})$, then

$$\vec{\varphi} \in S' \Rightarrow \vec{\varphi}' = \vec{\varphi} . \tag{N_5}$$

To put it another way: if new feasible outcomes are added to the bargaining problem but the disagreement point remains unchanged, then either the original solution does not change or it becomes one of the new feasible outcomes. So, in case only a subset of the bargaining set has been developed, but it can be assured that the remaining outcomes are no solutions, it is clear that the solution to this subset constitutes the overall solution.

Suppose that in the synchronous blocks domain agent α is suddenly given the capability of lifting two blocks in one operation, but only if others do not move at that tick. This certainly makes new agreements possible and α will probably benefit from them. Still, its acquaintances will definitely dislike these new agreements, as they are condemned to keep still. In such a setting, contraction independence states that the new capability of α does *not* strengthen its bargaining position and does *not* affect the bargaining outcome.

It is a remarkable fact that, given the axioms N_1 to N_5, there exists a unique solution for every bargaining setting $(S, \vec{d})$. As first shown by the Nobel Laureate economist and mathematician John Nash, the compromise is obtained by the utility vector $\vec{\varphi}$ that maximises the *product* of gains from the disagreement point.

Theorem 6.1. Let $(S, \vec{d})$ describe the *bargaining scenario* associated with a reactive co-ordination setting R. The only vector $\vec{\varphi}$ that complies with the axioms N_1 to N_5 maximises the function

$$N(\vec{x}) = \prod_{i=1}^{n} (x_i - d_i) .$$

The solution vector $\vec{\varphi}$ always exists and is unique. The proof of this theorem, and all the following, can be found in Appendix A.

Due to its characteristics, the Nash solution is also called *product-maximising* solution. It can be graphically depicted by means of curves ξ of the shape

$$\prod_{i=1}^{n} (x_i - d_i) = k .$$

As Figure 6.2 shows, the Nash solution is given by the point $\vec{\varphi} \in S$ which lies on the curve ξ with highest k. Note that it need not be located on the line segment that joins the utilities of legally enactable multi-plans with biggest value for N. In the example of Figure 6.2, the best "pure" alternative is P_1 which lies on ξ_b. The curve with maximum k, touches the line segment that joints P_2 and P_3, which actually have a smaller value of N than P_1. This is due to the fact that when constructing the convex hull of the set $U(X)$, the presumably best alternatives (like P_1 in Figure 6.2) may actually become "interior" points and do not constitute vertices[5].

The Nash solution for the synchronous blocks domain example can be found as follows. As the solution is Pareto-optimal (by N_2), the product-maximising agreement must be on the Pareto surface. So, in the example, the solution is within the following set:

$$\vec{\varphi} \in \left\{ (x_1, x_2) \in S \mid \exists 0 \leq p \leq 1. \ \vec{x} = (2p, 3 - 2p) \right\} .$$

---

[5] This has undesirable (but inevitable) consequences for algorithms to compute the Nash solution: it cannot be determined directly based on the utilities of a few "best" multi-plans.

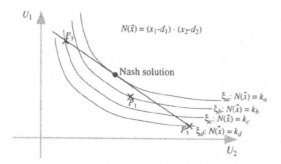

Figure 6.2. Mixed multi-plans and the Nash solution

Keeping in mind this constraint and the fact that conflict utility vector is $(-2,-1)$, the following function needs to be maximised.

$$N(\vec{x}) = (x_1 + 2)(x_2 + 1)$$
$$\Leftrightarrow \quad N(p) = (2p + 2)(-2p + 4)$$
$$\Leftrightarrow \quad N(p) = -4p^2 + 4p + 8$$

The function N is maximised for $p = \frac{1}{2}$. Therefore, the Nash solution to the synchronous blocks domain example is

$$\vec{\varphi} = (1,2) \ .$$

Consequently, the outcome of the bargaining process is to go for the "compromise" state in which all blocks are on the table. It can be reached by different multi-plans, from which the agents can choose randomly. Alternatively, agents can flip an equally weighed coin to choose between multi-plans that achieve the utility of $(2,1)$ and $(0,3)$.

6.2.2   Alternative Solutions

No axiom is universally applicable. This is certainly the case of Nash's axioms, and each of them has been subject to criticism. Especially, by dropping the requirement of contraction independence some interesting new solutions become possible. The argument is that if the set of alternatives is skewed, why should the compromise be prevented from moving against it. In the sequel, we depict two solutions that substitute contraction independence by a notion of individual monotonicity: an expansion of the bargaining set in direction favourable to a particular agent always benefits it.

The *Kalai-Smorodinsky solution* sets utility gains from the disagreement point proportional to the agents' most optimistic expectations. These expectations are given by the highest utility ω_i that an agent α_i can get from the bargaining set

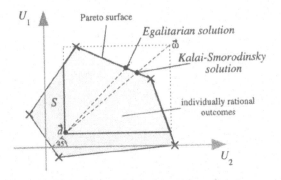

Figure 6.3. Alternative bargaining solutions

given that no acquaintance receives less than its utility from disagreement. This value is given by

$$\omega_i = max\left\{ x_i \in \Re \mid \exists \vec{x} \in S. \ \vec{x} \geq \vec{d} \right\}.$$

The Kalai-Smorodinsky solution is the maximal vector in S on the segment connecting $\vec{d}$ and $\vec{\omega}$. Figure 6.3 illustrates this fact graphically for a fictitious bargaining scenario.

In many approaches, such as social choice or welfare economics, it is believed that a solution to the bargaining problems should provide equal gains to the participants. The *Egalitarian solution* formalises this idea: it considers utility vectors of equal component utilities and picks out the biggest of them from the bargaining set. Figure 6.3 indicates that this solution obeys the following formula

$$\vec{\varphi} = max\left\{ \vec{x} \in S \mid \forall i, j \in \{1,...,n\}. \ x_i - d_i = x_j - d_j \right\}.$$

6.2.3 Analysis

The previous section showed that there are many different reasonable solutions to a bargaining scenario. So, the question arises whether any of the alternative approaches is more adequate to model self-interested social exchange in the frame of structural co-operation than the Nash solution. The answer is that neither the Kalai-Smorodinsky solution nor the Egalitarian solution to the bargaining problem have the same "nice" properties as Nash's approach.

First of all, the Egalitarian solution does not comply with the requirement of scale invariance. It obviously requires "direct" comparisons between the agents' utilities, thus violating the idea that utilities are local quantitative reflections of an agent's preference structure. Furthermore, although in the Egalitarian solution an improvement of an agent's bargaining position is reflected in an increase of that agent's utility, it does not translate such a personal advantage into a larger relative compensation for that agent: all utility gains are immediately and equally collectivised, regardless of which agent achieved them. So, using the Egalitarian solution it is impossible to use the bargaining strengths in order to modify the relative importance of one agent in the society.

The Kalai-Smorodinsky solution does not exhibit these problems. Still, technical difficulties arise when it is applied to the n-agent case (Thomson 1994). Furthermore, in Chapter 7 we will show that contraction independence facilitates the design of algorithms for computing the outcome of the bargaining scenario associated with our initial problem.

So, although for specific domains it might be advantageous to choose alternative bargaining solutions for an instrumentation of structural co-operation, the Nash solution seems to be most adequate in general. Therefore, throughout this book we take the Nash solution for the outcome of the bargaining scenario associated with a reactive co-ordination setting.

6.3 The Role of the Disagreement Point

Up to this point, a model of self-interested action in the social and normative context of structural co-operation has been developed. It has been mentioned that the designer needs to be given the opportunity to influence the outcome of the mechanism by adequately designing the normative structures within the normative context. It remains to model how this happens, i.e. to discuss what possibilities the designer has to bias the result of structural co-operation.

From the facts presented in the previous sections it becomes clear that there are essentially two ways of affecting the outcome of a bargaining scenario:

- The shape of the bargaining set S can be modified. As we are concerned with the Nash solution that requires contraction independence, this has to be done in a specific way: we have to introduce a new solution, or to exclude an existing solution.
- The disagreement point $\bar{d}$ can be modified.

Throughout this book, we have argued that the primary function of the normative structure is *not* to oblige agents directly to enact certain plans or refrain from others. This would not just be very complex, but often also too constraining. Instead, normative prescriptions are a means to modify the agents' social strengths. In terms of the associated bargaining scenario, this comes down to the fact that we are *not* interested in excluding (and re-including) certain regions from the bargaining set S. We are rather concerned with the second of the aforementioned options and focus on the possibilities of changing the disagreement point.

In Section 6.1.3, we have seen that the relations comprised in the dependence structure do not affect the bargaining set, but do modify the disagreement point.

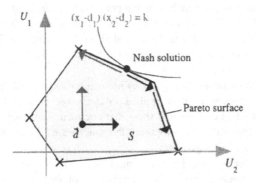

Figure 6.4. Disagreement point monotonicity

The stronger a dependence relation due to which an agent α depends on a group γ for a plan π, the less the conflict utility that the plan π potentially implies for α. Moreover, the more dependence relations relate to the agent and its plans, the bigger is the chance to suffer a decrease of conflict utility. In much the same way, if an agent becomes less dependent on its acquaintances, its conflict utility may increase. In line with our mechanism, in such a case we would like the agent to potentially improve its individual utility from the solution to the associated bargaining scenario.

In the normative context, a similar argument applies. A permission makes an agent less vulnerable and increases its social strength. In the associated bargaining scenario, its conflict utility may increase, and the disagreement point possibly moves towards it. In this case, the agent should expect a larger bribe in a potential compromise. A prohibition limits a group's freedom of choice, potentially making some other agent less dependent on them. In consequence, the social strength of the latter can be improved and its conflict utility potentially increases. Again, it should obtain a larger share in a potential agreement.

Fortunately, our associated bargaining model complies with the above requirements: when the disagreement point "moves" in the direction of a certain agent, the bargaining outcome "moves towards" it. This is described by the property of *disagreement point monotonicity*. It can be formally expressed as follows: let $\bar{d}$ and $\bar{d}'$ be two arbitrary disagreement points for the same bargaining set S, and let $\bar{\varphi}$ and $\bar{\varphi}'$ denote the solutions to the corresponding bargaining scenarios, then

$$d'_i \geq d_i \wedge \forall j \neq i . d'_j = d_j \quad \Rightarrow \quad \varphi'_i \geq \varphi_i .$$

The Nash solution satisfies this property (Thomson 1994). As Figure 6.4 indicates, it makes the bargaining solution move on the Pareto surface in the direction of the agent that strengthens its position in the case of disagreement. This fact facilitates the design of normative structures within societies of problem-solving agents that apply structural co-operation. It helps the designer to "foresee" the effect of issuing permissions or prohibitions pertaining to certain agents or groups.

Let us illustrate this for the example from the synchronous blocks domain. Suppose that all plans manipulate light grey blocks are *forbidden* for agent α_2. As a result, agent α_2 is no longer prepared to execute plan π_{10}, as it intends to move the light grey block 4 in the second step. So, α_1's bargaining position is strengthened, as it cannot be harmed by π_{10} any more. Now, the worst situation that α_2 can bring about in the eyes of α_1 is to put the dark grey block 1 on top of Block 2 by means of π_{12}. The conflict utility of α_2 remains unchanged, so that the disagreement point changes in favour of α_1 to

$$\vec{d} = (-1,-1).$$

It can be easily proved that the above function N is maximised for $p = \frac{3}{4}$, which gives rise to a solution utility vector of

$$\vec{\varphi} = \left(1\tfrac{1}{2}, 1\tfrac{1}{2}\right).$$

This can be reached by randomising equally between (1,2) and (2,1), which means that in 50% of all cases the agents reach a compromise agreement, while with the same probability agent α_1 can expect to achieve its most preferred possible state.

Imagine another normative structure in which it is *forbidden* for agent α_1 to enact plans that alter the left stack at the first tick. Therefore, α_1 is not prepared to enact π_{11} any more, and the plan π_4, which puts Block 1 on the table in the first step, becomes feasible for α_2. Consequently, the worst response of α_1 to the plan π_4 of α_2 is to obstruct Block 2. This can be achieved by putting Block 2 on the table in the first step and subsequently stacking Block 3 on top of it. The resulting situation is as good as the initial situation for α_2: it needs an additional action to clear Block 2, but Block 4 need not be freed any more. So, α_2's bargaining position is strengthened, as the new conflict utility vector changes in favour of α_2 to

$$\vec{d} = (-2,0).$$

The function N is maximised for $p = \frac{1}{4}$, so that the solution utility vector becomes

$$\vec{\varphi} = \left(\tfrac{1}{2}, 2\tfrac{1}{2}\right).$$

This can be reached by randomising equally between (1,2) and (0,3). So, in 50% of all cases the agents reach a compromise agreement, but this time agent α_2 is given the chance to achieve its most preferred state with the same probability.

6.4 Related Work

A variety of approaches set out from a quantitative, utility-based approach to model self-interested behaviour in a multi-agent world. The scenarios that they are concerned with often share some properties with our approach, but also show some important differences that limit their applicability to reactive co-ordination settings. For instance, just like structural co-operation the market-oriented programming approach (Wellman 1995) is concerned with n-agent settings. However, it also makes assumptions about the existence of a monetary unit and explicit side-payments that we do not have.

The work by Rosenschein and Zlotkin (1994) shows most similarities to our formalisation of structural co-operation as a bargaining scenario. So, we will have a closer look at the relation of both. Either approach sets out from a multi-agent setting, where self-interested agents can benefit from co-operation, but have diverging preferences respecting the agreement to be made. In particular, both models share the following properties and assumptions:

- Perfectly rational agenthood is assumed and modelled as the maximisation of expected utility.
- Only isolated scenarios are considered. Agents cannot commit themselves to certain behaviour in future negotiations or in future world states.
- Agents make public binding agreements. The compliance to agreements is enforced.
- There is no commonly accepted monetary unit. No explicit transfer of local utility through side-payments is possible. However, the agents' utilities can be implicitly transferred through "gambling".
- The Nash solution is accepted as a reasonable bargaining outcome.

These similarities are not surprising as the roots of both approaches can be found in traditional bargaining theory. Still, additional domain characteristics and different research agendas have led to quite different frameworks. Let us first contrast the objectives.

Rosenschein and Zlotkin are concerned with *heterogeneous* agent societies. Agents are assumed to be self-interested, but also to comply with certain conventions. They are supposed to behave in accordance with specific negotiation protocols. Agents reveal their preferences at the beginning of negotiation. Based on this information the complete "negotiation set" can be determined, which comprises the individual rational and Pareto-optimal joint plans as well as the different roles that the agents can play in them. The Nash solution is used to model an agreement on joint plans.

Rosenschein and Zlotkin's primary interest refers to the properties of the behaviour of *individual* agents and, in particular, to their behaviour towards their acquaintances. For instance, they *analyse* when and how agents are liable to cheating when declaring their preferences (with the effect of modifying the negotiation set) and how different kinds of agreements influence such incentives. Their approach comprises a *descriptive* component, as it is assumed to constitute a reasonably adequate model of *heterogeneous* agent societies in the outside world. However, it prevails the *constructive* aim of designing mechanisms that induce the members of heterogeneous agent societies to adopt certain types of *individual strategies*.

We are concerned with structural co-operation within *homogeneous* societies of problem-solving agents. As such, our approach is only "descriptive" in as far as we try to model self-interested behaviour as long as this is appropriate for our problem-solving mechanism. Our objective is essentially *constructive*. Still, we can assume certain agent properties[6] in order to "construct" instrumental *society behaviour*. In structural co-operation, the designer establishes a set of norms, so as to make agent interactions instrumental for a global functionality. The result is *not* a provably instilled property of the agents' strategies (stability, sincerity etc.). Instead, the designer needs to incrementally adjust the normative structure in order to create a global functionality of sufficient quality.

In addition, the bargaining model presented in this chapter aims at formalising the mechanism of structural co-operation, so as to come up with an *operational* co-ordination model in societies of problem-solving agents. The Nash solution is not just an assumption, based on which agent and society properties can be *analysed*. As we will see in the next chapter, it allows us to *compute* the outcome of self-interested interaction within structural co-operation.

It is also worthwhile pointing to some differences in the characteristics of the domains under investigation. The most obvious is given by the fact that Rosenschein and Zlotkin focus on two-agent interaction, while we are concerned with the *n*-agent case. Still, there are some more subtle differences.

Firstly, Rosenschein and Zlotkin's agents assign a fixed cost to actions and plans, which expresses a certain "laziness": acting is *always* bad, as long as this is not compensated by the utility achieved. Therefore, an agent prefers a plan with shared activities to a plan that it performs alone, although they both end up in the same world state. The cost measures of actions may be due to resource limitations within the domain, but as there is no upper limit on the cost that agents *can* incur (which is independent of whether they *want* to or not), the domain imposes soft (preference) but no hard constraints on the agents' actions.

Our agents, by contrast, have a neutral attitude towards action: they hold no genuine "cost" measure over plans. So, in principle, executing an action is "free". Resource-limitation is modelled by the fact that some individual plan might be incompatible with one another (e.g. because one "consumed" the resources that the other needed). So one might think of "opportunity costs" to be assigned to plans[7]. Still, these opportunity costs are a *function* of utility and do not influence it. Furthermore, they vary with the situation and with the agents: some plan might be free to one agent while being expensive for another, because the former has no alternative plan to perform whilst the latter is prevented from performing other plans that it is interested in.

Secondly, Rosenschein and Zlotkin require agents to have symmetric abilities: *everything* that can be done by a joint plan can be done by one agent alone; the existence of the other may only make it *cheaper* to do so (in co-operative encounters). So, no "hard" dependencies can arise between agents. In our scenario, hard dependencies are expressed by *invalidates* relations: the existence of others

---

[6] For instance, we just *program* our agents not to lie.

[7] Microeconomic theory defines opportunity costs as follows: given two mutually exclusive options *A* and *B*, the opportunity cost of *A* is equal to the gain of *B*, i.e. the cost of not being able to realise *B* when choosing *A* (e.g. Wöhe 1986).

might make it *possible* or *impossible* to execute some plan. This has important consequences respecting the class of encounters that can come up.

Finally, Rosenschein and Zlotkin use stand-alone costs as baseline for their concept of utility. In our approach, this is similar to define the disagreement point in terms of the utility of individual plans. In Rosenschein and Zlotkin's domain, such a definition makes sense, as in the worst case an agent will have to execute its plan all alone. The outcome of encounters is influenced by different parameters, e.g. by assuming conventions respecting certain types of deals or certain shapes of utility functions.

Again, our agents are not concerned with reducing cost, but to come as close as possible to an ideal state. As resources are not just expensive but limited, the worst thing that can happen to an agent is that all its acquaintances execute plans that take it further away from its ideal, while with the remaining resources the agent cannot do anything beneficial for it. This leads to our notion of conflict utility, that is not just conditioned by the agent it refers to, but also by its acquaintances. So, our definition of the disagreement point is far more liable to manipulation by the designer. It allows influencing the bargaining scenario by means of indirect normative modifications of the disagreement point.

6.5 Bottom Line

In this chapter, we have shown how structural co-operation is expressed within a precise formal framework. The advantages have already been pinpointed: we have obtained a prescription of how structural co-operation should behave in order to constitute a *justified* model of self-interested action in societies of autonomous problem-solving agents. Still, the "price" of choosing axiomatic bargaining theory as a vehicle for the formalisation of structural co-operation is that the applicability of the mechanism becomes sensitive to certain society characteristics.

A basic implication of modelling structural co-operation as a bargaining problem is that agreements within the agent society are *binding*. Otherwise, an agent might agree on an exchange, wait for the other party to deliver its share and then vanish without fulfilling its part. In fact, if agreements are not binding, an autonomous agent will prematurely terminate an exchange in this fashion whenever it considers it beneficial to do so[8]. Thus, heterogeneous agent societies will usually include some *enforcement* mechanism that "binds" agents to their commitments and keeps them from defecting (e.g. Sandholm 1996, Brainov 1996 or Krogh 1996). For instance, the expectation of a potential retaliation by an authority or by their acquaintances might keep agents from breaking their agreements.

In particular, in reactive co-ordination settings it is crucial for the mechanism of structural co-operation that the agents' final agreements are binding. When an

---

[8] Recall the Prisoners' Dilemma, where both agents ended up playing "Defection" as there was no justified reason to believe that the other would choose "Co-operation".

agreement on a multi-plan has been reached, the involved agents start executing their corresponding individual plans. Still, in doing so, every agent actually relies on its acquaintances to keep their promise and not to switch to plans that result incompatible when executed together. Furthermore, structural co-operation is based on the implicit "agreement" that agents abide to normative prescriptions. The agents' behaviour has to be influenced notably by the imperatives of the normative structure, as their biasing effect would vanish otherwise and they would be rendered useless. However, these requirements do not constitute an important limitation for the application of structural co-operation to problem-solving societies, as in centrally designed agent systems, such behaviour can simply be "built into" the agents.

Another requirement has not become directly obvious in the previous discourse, as our illustrative examples have dealt only with two-agent interactions. In such settings, agents can either both agree or both disagree. If one agent refuses co-operation, the other cannot help but take a chance alone, as it makes no sense to make agreements with itself. Still, things change when groups of n agents are taken into account. Agents may form *coalitions*, within which they co-operate by agreeing on some "small" multi-plan, while they are in disagreement with their remaining acquaintances. There can be as many coalitions, as there are groups in our model. One extreme is the degenerate case when every agent constitutes its own coalitions, which corresponds to our notion of disagreement. The grand coalition, in which all agents join in, maps to our notion of agreement. Still, a whole lot of coalitional configurations are possible in between.

Our model of structural co-operation considers "coalitions" only with respect to an agent's conflict utility, i.e. for the determination of the disagreement point. In this case, it is supposed that all acquaintances "co-operate" in order to harm the agent. However, total disagreement is never actually reached, as in reactive co-ordination settings agents can always "win" from co-operation. Instead, our model assumes that in the end *all* agents reach an agreement. In general, it does not account for the formation of coalitions.

This is problematic for heterogeneous societies, where each designer would like to endow his or her agent with the opportunity to maximise its benefit by co-operating just with some acquaintances, while risking conflict with others. The same argument holds for agent systems that support groups of humans involved in a bargaining process. Still, for centrally designed agent societies this is not a severe problem. In fact, when mapping the reactive co-ordination problem to a bargaining scenario, we never really *want* agents to end up in any form of disagreement. This is because for problem-solving purposes, the option of (unresolved) conflict is no good choice. We suppose that this is not only true for total, but also for partial conflict as reflected by coalitions. Therefore, in our model the possibility of disagreement (i.e. of reaching conflict) is just a fictitious but effective "threat": what agents *might* lose from disagreement shapes the kind of agreement they *actually* reach.

It can be argued that by not supporting the possibility of coalition formation between agents the above approach loses *plausibility* as a model of self-interested choice. This is undoubtedly true, although examples of all-or-nothing agreement situation are also frequent in the real world. Still, concerning *efficiency* the absence of partial agreements appears to be an advantage. For instance, as Figure 6.4 illustrates, in our model the designer can use the property of disagreement point monotonicity to predict the effect of changes in the normative structure. It is not clear, as to how far such properties can be assured when coalitions are considered. A similar argument respecting the complexity of computational models will be provided in the next chapter.

Another criticism goes back to the fact that traditional bargaining models assume an ideal setting where agents behave *perfectly* rational. It supposes that an agent is always endowed with the necessary information and is always given enough time to determine its "best" choice. Obviously, this is seldom the case in real-world situations.

The very nature of open, heterogeneous systems of computational agents suggests that agent interaction relies on a strategic bargaining mechanism, so that negotiations evolve through various stages of offers and counter-offers. An agent acts under time pressure, and it cannot spend an unlimited amount of computation power in computing its best choice. Furthermore, it needs to take into account that the decisions of its acquaintances will also be based on some model of *bounded rationality*. Consequently, neither the process nor the outcome of the negotiation process usually coincide with the strategies and outcomes that traditional bargaining theory suggests. Again, the same argument holds for agent systems that support groups of humans involved in a bargaining process. In both types of scenarios, the lack of descriptive adequacy discourages the use of traditional bargaining theory as a model of self-interested action.

Still, the situation changes when problem-solving societies are considered. In principle, in such centrally designed societies the outcome of agent interaction need not be determined by means of an extensive simulation of a real negotiation process. The result of self-interested interaction in the contexts of structural co-operation can be *directly* computed, given that a declarative specification of the outcome exists. The question, then, comes down to whether it is easier to compute a bargaining outcome that complies with axioms modelling perfectly rational agents, or if the solution of boundedly rational bargaining scenario can be computed more efficiently. Besides the fact that a general agreement respecting an axiomatic model of the latter is still to come, there is no reason to suppose that the former is harder to compute – or, in general, that it constitutes a less adequate model – than the latter.

In short: classical bargaining theory as a model of self-interested behaviour in heterogeneous societies is problematic, but it constitutes an adequate foundation for modelling structural co-operation among autonomous agents within centrally-designed societies of problem-solving agents.

7 An Instrumentation of Structural Co-operation

This chapter aims at building an operational model of the mechanism of structural co-operation. Given knowledge about a specific domain, this model shall be *executable* on a computer network. Consequently, an agent architecture needs to be devised that generates the corresponding individual behaviours.

Once such a framework is given, it must be assured that the desired outcome emerges from the interplay of the individual behaviours. The basic idea underlying our model has already been alluded to in previous sections: the Nash solution is taken as the intended outcome of specific contexts of structural co-operation. Still, instead of "simulating" strategic negotiations between agents, we develop agent interaction strategies that give rise to a "direct" search for this solution.

This chapter first describes an agent architecture that supports structural co-operation. Subsequently, an agent interaction strategy is developed, and its characteristics are analysed. Finally, related work is sketched and the potentials and drawbacks of our approach to the instrumentation of structural co-operation are discussed.

7.1 The ProsA$_2$ Agent Architecture

The foundation of the instrumentation of any distributed mechanism within artificial agent societies is an appropriate agent architecture. This section introduces the ProsA$_2$ (Problem-solving Autonomous Agent) architecture, that has been devised to make structural co-operation operational. We first give an overview of our design guidelines, and outline how they have been realised in the different components of the ProsA$_2$ agent architecture. The subsequent sections are dedicated to particular components of ProsA$_2$ agents, describing in detail their structure and functionality.

7.1.1 Overview

The ProsA$_2$ architecture relies on a model-based approach: agent design is seen primarily as a modelling activity. The agent architecture has been developed on the basis of the following design principles:

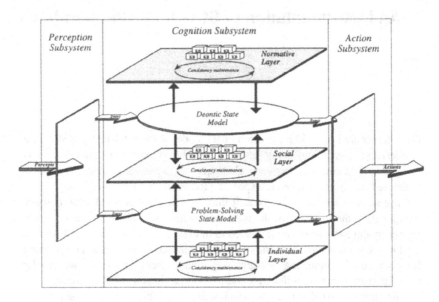

Figure 7.1. ProsA$_2$ agent architecture

- layered control model
  The process that relates agent perception and action emerges from the interplay of different control layers. The layering principle reflects the different perspectives and contexts from which a situation is framed within structural co-operation.

- structured knowledge model
  Agent knowledge is not centralised in one monolithic knowledge base, but it is structured in line with its use within the agent architecture. In consequence, the structuring principle of knowledge bases also reflects the contexts of structural co-operation.

- structured but shared information model
  The dynamically generated information of the agent (its "beliefs") is also stored within structured models in the ProsA$_2$ architecture. The underlying principle assures that every reasoning component can access the information it needs[1].

The general architecture of ProsA$_2$ agents is depicted in Figure 7.1. It comprises three subsystems.

The *perception subsystem* is in charge of detecting features of the world that the agent acts in. It is endowed with perceptors that capture stimuli of the outside world. *Sensors* monitor *objects*, i.e. the agent's physical environment. A *commu-*

---

[1] So, in terms of Chapter 3, there is no *information model mismatch* within ProsA$_2$ agents.

nicator is in charge of perceiving messages from the surrounding *subjects*, i.e. the agent's acquaintances.

The result of the perception process is passed to the *cognition subsystem*, where the information model is updated. Among other possible classifications (see Section 7.1.2) two parts of the information model can be distinguished: deontic and problem-solving state models. They constitute the agent's symbolic representation of the state of the world. New information provided by perceptors can bring them into an "inconsistent" state. The cognition subsystem comprises three layers, in charge of reacting to these changes. They use their layer knowledge to determine the adequate model updates. The *normative* layer applies normative knowledge to achieve consistency respecting deontic imperatives. The *individual* layer relies on local domain knowledge so as to keep local problem-solving information up-to-date. The *social* layer makes use of social knowledge in order to achieve consistency among the agent's beliefs about itself and its acquaintances.

Finally, the *action subsystem* checks for relevant changes in the information model and forwards them to the corresponding *actors*, i.e. to the devices by means of which the agent influences the outside world. The physical environment is manipulated by *effectors*, while the *communicator* "acts upon" the subjects of the agent's environment by sending messages.

In the following we will centre on the cognition subsystem. The structure of the information model is presented and the respective notions of model consistency are outlined. Subsequently, the different layers are described, paying special attention to their reasoning cycles.

7.1.2 Information Model

The information model constitutes a shared data space that comprises the totality of an agent's dynamic beliefs about its environment. For instance, in the blocks world example, the information model of a robotic agent based on the ProsA$_2$ architecture will contain *sensory data* concerning the position of blocks, *diagnostic* information concerning the difference between the current and ideal world states, as well as *repair* information concerning the plans (sequences of *move* and *NOP* operations) by means of which the agent can reduce that difference. In addition, it comprises the *current individual plan* of the agent itself and of its acquaintances. Finally, *normative* information concerning the blocks that are permitted or prohibited to access for the agent as well as for its acquaintances are present.

As Figure 7.2 indicates, the information model can be subdivided by several criteria. Each criteria partitions it in disjointed parts, but the sub-models that result from a classification on the basis of different criteria overlap. In the following, the different separations of the information model are outlined and illustrated within the synchronous blocks domain. They provide the basis for the notion of consistency that characterises the different layers described in Section 7.1.3.

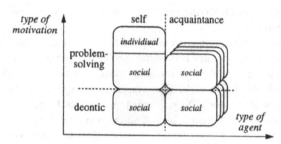

Figure 7.2. ProsA₂ information model

7.1.2.1 Self and Acquaintance Models

The information model can be separated into *self* and *acquaintance* models. The criterion for this separation is, obviously, the agent whose state the respective model describes. A ProsA₂ agent maintains one model for each acquaintance that is of interest to it. All these models follow the same arrangement, i.e. the beliefs about others are always expressed in the same terms. The self model, by contrast, refers to an agent's beliefs about itself. Besides the information types contained in the acquaintance model, the self model contains *additional* private information.

In the synchronous blocks world example mentioned above, a minimal configuration of an acquaintance model comprises information about the current individual plan of the modelled agent, as well as normative information concerning its prohibitions and permissions. In addition to this, the self model contains the sensory data that an agent locally perceives as well as diagnostic and repair information.

The self and acquaintance models can be mutually inconsistent. If we assume normative prescriptions to be issued in a deontically consistent way, this is essentially due to the interrelation of the individual plans that agents are executing or pretend to enact. As outlined in the previous chapters, this interrelation between the agents' plans can either make their concurrent execution impossible or influence in their outcome.

7.1.2.2 Problem-Solving and Deontic Models

By distinguishing between *deontic* and *problem-solving* models, the criterion of "motivation" is applied. This separation is based on the different interests that these models refer to. The problem-solving model contains an analysis of the state of the world from a self-interested point of view. An agent frames a situation in a multi-agent world with respect to its individual motivation. By contrast, the deontic model contains information concerning what ideally should (not) be done.

It can be conceived as a description of what the problem-solving society (i.e. the designer) "wants" to be the case.

In the blocks world example, sensory data, diagnosed problems and the potential repair plans of the agent, as well as the current individual plans of itself and acquaintances pertain to the problem-solving state model. The deontic model comprises prohibitions or permissions to execute certain plans or to use certain blocks.

Both sub-models are obviously interrelated. The problem-solving model may contain plans that bring the world closer to some ideal state, and that are thus beneficial from the point of view of the agent's individual motivation. Still, there is a conflict if the deontic model contains prescriptions that directly declare this plan to be forbidden, or that deny the agent to use a resource that the plan requires. As outlined in the previous chapters, our norm-abiding agents have to resolve those conflicts by letting the deontic model prevail.

7.1.2.3 Individual and Social Models

Finally, a separation of sub-models can be made by the criterion of privacy. The *individual* model contains information that is just available locally to the agent. No other agent that follows the ProsA$_2$ architecture maintains a model of it. The *social* model, by contrast, contains characteristics that an agent represents for itself as well as concerning all others. Ideally, the individual model contains only information *relevant* to the agent itself. No other agent is interested in it. So, everything that might be relevant with respect to the relation of the agent and its acquaintances (i.e. the beliefs of the agent "directed towards" its acquaintances or vice versa) is stored in the social parts of the information model. Still, in order to limit the amount of communication, the size of the individual part of the information model may be augmented.

The distinction between characteristics that belong to the individual and those that pertain to the social part of the information model depends on the design chosen for a specific problem instance. In our synchronous blocks world example, we will most probably consider the sensory data that an agent locally perceives, as well as the results of its local diagnosis, to be part of the individual model. The agent's current individual plan, the normative prescriptions pertaining to it, as well as all information respecting the acquaintances should be stored in the social part of the information model.

Consistency between individual and social sub-models is not conceived as a genuine conflict as before, but as a lack of "coherence" between the different parts. For instance, the perceived sensory data, as well as the problems that have been diagnosed on the basis on this data, may no longer be coherent with the set of individual plans of the agent. They no longer constitute an adequate "repair" for the detected problems. In this case, restoring consistency means to update the set of individual plans.

7.1.3   Layer Models

The purpose of each layer of the ProsA$_2$ architecture is to maintain consistency between certain parts of the information model. Layers differ with respect to the notion of consistency that they assure, and regarding the knowledge that they use to achieve this. A layer becomes active, when these parts of the information model have been modified by the perception subsystem or by other layers.

Each layer runs the same basic control cycle, which can be summarised in three steps. The *model revision* step determines whether the changes in the information model are relevant to the layer and, if appropriate, related information is derived. The *diagnosis* step detects potential consistency problems in the current state of the information model. Finally, the *repair* step updates the information model in order to overcome the previously detected problems[2]. In the following, the different ProsA$_2$ layers are characterised by these specific differences.

7.1.3.1 Individual Layer

The individual layer operates on the self model of the agent. Its purpose is to keep the individual part of the information model consistent with the social part. In particular, when perceptors provide new data, the individual layer is in charge of updating the set of potential individual plans. The following steps are performed:

- *Model revision*: any change in the sensory data is considered relevant to the individual layer. If data from the robot's perceptors in the blocks domain or its derived magnitudes change, a cycle of the individual layer begins. Knowledge concerning data processing etc. is needed for model revision. If we suppose that the robots in the synchronous blocks domain perceive their environment by means of cameras, they need to be endowed with knowledge concerning how to filter out noisy data, to determine shapes etc.

- *Diagnosis*: the difference between the current state and some ideal state is determined by the diagnosis step. In the blocks domain, this comes down to the evaluation of the distance between current and ideal states. Knowledge is needed to abstract from augmented sensory data to a representation that refers to blocks and their relative position. Furthermore, it must be known how to determine differences between this representation and ideal states.

- *Repair*: the repair step determines the set of potential individual plans to restore model consistency by performing the corresponding updates. Concerning the synchronous blocks domain, a ranking of individual plans that reduce the distance between current and ideal states is generated. Planning knowledge is necessary as well as the capability of estimating the outcome of these plans. In the blocks domain, the potential outcome of individual plans determines their ranking.

---

[2] From a knowledge and software engineering point of view, the above considerations allow an elegant realisation of the particular ProsA$_2$ layers as specialisations of a generic layer.

7.1.3.2 Social Layer

The social layer has to keep the acquaintance part of the information model consistent with the self model. The notion of consistency used here determines directly the outcome of agent interaction and its adequacy with respect to the mechanism of structural co-operation. It will be discussed in detail in Section 7.2. The layer control cycle has the following shape:

- *Model revision*: acquaintance models are updated in accordance with incoming messages. Knowledge about consistency is used to check whether the self model, and the agent's current individual plan in particular, is still consistent with the current plans of the other agents as cached in the acquaintance models. If this is not the case, the cycle of the social layer continues.
- *Diagnosis*: the plan interrelations that cause the inconsistency between self and acquaintance models are diagnosed. Again, this is done on the basis of knowledge concerning the consistency of plans.
- *Repair*: the repair step selects an individual plan based on the result of the diagnosis step. The current individual plan in the self model is updated and interested acquaintances informed about the change. Knowledge about the possibility of influencing acquaintances (and being influenced by them) is necessary in order to determine their interests.

7.1.3.3 Normative Layer

The purpose of the normative layer is to keep the deontic part of the information model consistent with the problem-solving part. Consistency is given when all expressions of the current situation correspond to deontically ideal situations, i.e. no permission and no prohibition is violated. So, in particular, the normative layer needs to be capable of *identifying* the currently valid normative situation based on the pertinent environment characteristics. The deontic layer's control cycle comprises the following steps:

- *Model revision*: changes in the information model are analysed as to whether they concern features that might imply a change in the normative situation. For instance, if in the synchronous blocks domain example the normative situation depends on the current world state s, and a change in s is conditioned to a movement of blocks, then this step checks whether the position of some blocks has been altered. If so, the cycle of the normative layer proceeds.
- *Diagnosis*: in the diagnosis step the currently valid prescriptions are deduced. Knowledge about norms is necessary in order to realise this deduction. In our example, the permissions and prohibition pertinent to the current world state s are deduced. For instance, a prohibition might require the agent not to access light grey blocks in a state s.
- *Repair*: finally, normative prescriptions are stored in the deontic model, invalidating certain individual plans that violate some of them. For this purpose,

knowledge relating the concepts used by prescriptions (e.g. actions or resources) to individual plans is needed. In the blocks world example, if a prescription states that it is forbidden for the agent to access light grey blocks, all
plans that do access these blocks are forbidden, which potentially makes certain
individual plans illegal.

7.2 Social Interaction Strategy

This section describes the social interaction strategy that ProsA$_2$ agents use, giving
rise to a social interaction process that converges on the outcome of structural co-
operation. We first motivate the specific characteristics and requirements for our
social interaction strategy. Subsequently, a brief overview of the proposed method
is given, followed by a more detailed description of the different stages of the
strategy. We end this section by proving some interesting properties of our proposal.

7.2.1   Motivation

In centrally designed agent systems, the agents can be endowed with whatever
strategy the designer prefers. Structural co-operation limits this freedom of choice
by requiring that the outcome of agent interaction corresponds to "self-interest".
Still, as we assume total control over all agents and are also provided with a
characterisation of the bargaining outcome among self-interested agents, there is
no need to explicitly simulate the bargaining process. Instead, the solution can be
computed directly by a distributed algorithm. Within this algorithm agents may
act even in a "selfless fashion", such as taking over the burden of performing steps
that do not directly benefit them, and entrusting the responsibility to perform
certain crucial actions to another agent. Both behaviours do not appear rational at
first glance. Still, as long as the algorithm computes a plausible bargaining outcome, they provide an adequate instrumentation of structural co-operation. This
procedure is a compromise, a trade-off between *simplicity* (due to co-operative
search) and ideal *social plausibility* (based on the axiomatically determined
bargaining solution).

   In the sequel, we will determine the outcome of structural co-operation directly
by means of such a distributed algorithm. The social interaction strategy that we
will develop for ProsA$_2$ agents is the essential part of this algorithm. If followed
by all agents, it gives rise to social interaction processes that converge on the
solution to the bargaining scenario associated with a reactive co-ordination setting.

   Ideally, the distributed algorithm that the social interaction strategies build up
should be *sound* and *complete*. As the Nash bargaining solution always exists, we

would like the algorithm to determine this solution always *precisely*. Obviously, this implies that social interaction needs to be guaranteed to terminate eventually. As we will see, determining the precise solution is often rather difficult, so we sometimes need to accept approximately correct outcomes.

In practice, our algorithm is to be used to co-ordinate groups of cognitive software agents acting in the framework of real applications. So, besides direct computation of the bargaining outcome, the following requirements can be stated:

- parallel asynchronous execution
  It is not unusual that simultaneous action within artificial agent societies is simulated sequentially in a computational testbed environment. This is legitimate, if the interest concerns high-level issues of a distributed intelligence ("emergent properties"), and consequently problems respecting parallel asynchronous execution are of minor importance. Still, our approach is intended to co-ordinate autonomous agents within *problem-solving* societies, so these problems cannot be excluded beforehand.

- limited communication load
  The approach shall take advantage of distribution. The agents should *not* broadcast *all* local knowledge and information to the acquaintances. For instance, we would like the overall shape of the individual utility functions to remain local. By this, the load of the communication channels is limited.

- anytime property
  Determining the exact bargaining outcome usually implies an elevated computational cost, which might be prohibitive in certain real-world scenarios. Therefore, the social interaction process is to show anytime properties: whenever an outcome is required, a time-out signal can be sent to the agent society, which responds immediately by returning an approximate solution of reasonable quality. This *approximate* solution gradually improves the more time is given to the algorithm.

- incrementality
  In asynchronous settings, it is usual that at a specific instant the individual plans or preferences of just one agent are altered, while the situation of its acquaintances remains unchanged. In this case, the bargaining outcome need not be computed from the scratch, but the current multi-plan might just be "adapted". Therefore, social interaction should make use of previously found solutions. It should set out from the current multi-plan and try to adapt it, trusting that the amount of changes required is limited.

7.2.2 Multi-Stage Co-ordination Process

Setting out from the above comments, we have developed a social interaction strategy for ProsA$_2$ agents. If followed by all agents, it gives rise to a multi-stage

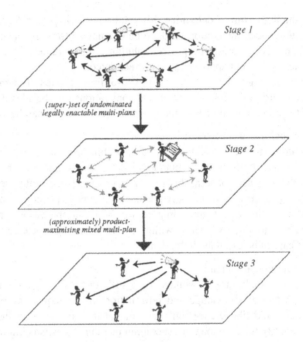

Figure 7.3. Overview of the social interaction process

algorithm that converges on the solution to the bargaining scenario associated with a reactive co-ordination setting, while complying with the aforementioned requirements. As Figure 7.3 depicts, according to this algorithm the co-ordination process is a sequence of three stages.

- Stage 1: asynchronous search for Pareto-optimality
  Setting out from the alternative individual plans that an agent is prepared to enact, messages are exchanged repeatedly in order to determine (a superset of) the undominated, legally enactable multi-plans. This is done in an asynchronous distributed fashion, which allows for local and temporarily incompatible views of the overall state.

- Stage 2: determination of the Nash bargaining outcome
  The agent that detects the termination of Stage 1 plays the role of the leader in this stage. On the basis of the result of Stage 1, it computes the (approximate) product-maximising solution in mixed multi-plans.

- Stage 3: probabilistic assignment of individual plans
  The leading agent generates a lottery in accordance with the outcome of Stage 2, and urges its acquaintances to execute the corresponding individual plans accordingly.

The graphical delineation of the social interaction process might give the reader the impression of a mainly centralised computation. Still, the stages two and three just constitute a common numerical optimisation and a probabilistic selection of results. The core of the "intelligent" computation is done in Stage 1. In the next section, we will describe in detail the different aspects of this stage.

7.2.3   Asynchronous Search for Pareto-Optimality

In the general case, Stage 1 aims at finding undominated (i.e. Pareto-optimal) legally enactable multi-plans in *reactive co-ordination settings*. However, as our case study in Chapter 9 will be of that type, we will pay particular attention to *detached* reactive co-ordination settings, where the executability of the agents' individual plans can be turned down by the multi-plans of the acquaintances, but the utility that an agent obtains from its plan is *independent* of what others do. Obviously, they are special cases of reactive co-ordination settings, where no *interferent* relations are present. Another special kind of setting is given when plan relations remain stable and do not vary with the situation *s*. In this case, a reactive co-ordination setting is said to be *stable*. Again, this is the case for our case study in Chapter 9.

The method that we use for computing Pareto-optimal multi-plans in any of these settings relies on asynchronous search in the space of multi-plans that the agents are prepared to enact. It belongs to the class of "dependency-directed backtracking" algorithms, which have recently been transferred to *distributed constraint satisfaction* problems. They are different from parallel/distributed methods for constraint satisfaction, in that there is an *a priori* distribution of problem knowledge among asynchronously acting agents, while the latter aim to *design* a distributed architecture in order to generate solutions more *efficiently* through parallelism (Yokoo et al. 1992).

Still, the problem that we face is actually a special instance of a distributed constraint *optimisation* problem. Each agent has control over a decision variable to which it can assign *values* from its local *domain*. There are *hard constraints* (often referred to as "genuine constraints" or just "constraints") defined over the agents' variables, determining whether sets of assignments of values to the agents' variables are consistent or inconsistent. In addition, *weak constraints* imply a preference ordering over value assignments. We call a set of value assignments *consistent*, if it complies with all hard constraints. It is a *solution*, if it is consistent and also "optimal" with respect to the preference ordering.

In the sequel, we first outline how the problem of finding legally enactable, undominated multi-plans can be modelled as a distributed constraint optimisation problem and sketch the essential ideas of our solution. The remaining sections are dedicated to a detailed discussion of the different aspects of this stage of our distributed algorithm and the corresponding agent behaviours.

7.2.3.1 Overview

Our original problem of finding legally enactable, undominated multi-plans in a reactive co-ordination setting can be mapped onto a distributed constraint optimisation problem without mayor problems. An agent's decision variable corresponds to the choice of the individual plans that it is going to enact. We consider the domain to be given by the set of individual plans that the agent is *prepared* to enact. The genuine hard constraints between variables express multi-plan *executability*. If a set of value assignments complies with the constraint, the corresponding individual plans can be executed together. Due to the "coherence" properties of preparedness discussed in Chapter 5, the value assignments of a group of agents constitute a multi-plan that the group is prepared to enact. In consequence, consistent sets of value assignments are a synonym for legally enactable multi-plans.

The weak constraints in our model are given by the *interferes* relations and their quantitative counterparts, i.e. the local utility functions. Setting out from the subsequent notion of local preference, the preference ordering over legally enactable multi-plans is given by multi-plan domination. So, a *solution* to our distributed constraint optimisation problem corresponds to an undominated legally enactable multi-plan. Note that in detached reactive co-ordination settings the notion of multi-plan domination is based on local utility functions that are "detached" from the choices of others. In these particular class of reactive co-ordination settings, the executability but not the utility of an individual plan is subject to the plans that others enact.

Our approach to the computation of such solutions requires all agents to behave in accordance with the same behaviour strategy. An agent keeps track of the *current multi-plan*, i.e. the individual plans that its (relevant) acquaintances intend to enact and its individual plan (its current *value*). The basic idea of the individual behaviour strategies is simple: an agent chooses a current value, which results in a current multi-plan that is "locally consistent" and most preferred by it. The agents' attempts to achieve local consistency produce a chain reaction, which eventually leads to a stable state. The definition of local consistency in conjunction with the strategy of choosing always the locally most preferred option assures that in stable states, when all agents are quiescent, the agents' values constitute a legally enactable and hopefully undominated multi-plan.

A major difficulty in an asynchronously acting agent society is to avoid cycles, i.e. to prevent infinite processing. This is achieved by dynamically generating *nogoods*. Nogoods are multi-plans that cannot be extended to a legally enactable multi-plan involving all agents. As such, they describe new, *dynamic constraints*: all multi-plans that constitute a *superset* of a nogood are *not* legally enactable. For instance, if a multi-set of individual plans is not executable for a group of agents, and if it cannot become executable regardless what plans the remaining agents enact, then this multi-set of individual plans will constitute a nogood.

We are interested in finding not just one but all undominated legally enactable multi-plans. Therefore, once a solution has been found, the search process must be restarted until no further solutions are present. For this purpose, previously found solutions are recorded as another type of dynamic constraint. These *solution constraints* assure that the same legally enactable solutions cannot be encountered twice. In the sequel, we describe the key aspects of the agents' behaviour strategy.

7.2.3.2 Local Choice

The distributed search process within our agent society is guided by the notion of *authority levels*. An agent has a higher authority level than another, if the authority value of the former is higher than the one of the latter. If authority values are the same, the agent with a bigger identifier respecting the lexicographic order possesses the higher authority level.

Local consistency is defined with relation to an agent's authority level. An individual plan of an agent α is called *locally consistent*, if the resulting multi-plan fulfils all static and dynamic (hard) constraints that involve only *higher* authority agents. Therefore, for the value π of agent α to be locally consistent, the current multi-plan $\pi \circ \mu$ must obey the following conditions:

- It complies with all genuine hard constraints, in which the agent α has lowest authority.
- It is not a superset of a nogood, in which α has lowest authority.
- It does *not* coincide with a solution, in which α has lowest authority.

In detached reactive co-ordination settings, an agent can easily check whether a multi-plan $\pi \circ \mu$ is dominated by a solution $\overline{\pi} \circ \mu$, because in this case it prefers its plan $\overline{\pi}$ to π. So, for a value π to be locally consistent in detached settings, we also require the corresponding multi-plan plan not to be *dominated* by a solution constraint in the above manner.

A locally consistent value is called an *option* of the agent. Our behaviour strategy requires an agent to choose always the most preferred option. Therefore, in order to perform local choice and determine its current value in every situation, in reactive co-ordination settings an agent needs to be informed about the current values of the agents that it shares some constraint with. In addition, it needs to be aware of the values of all agents that might influence the utility of its individual plans, so as to assure that its current individual plan constitutes the most preferred option.

As we will show later, the authority levels do not affect the *result* of the distributed search process. They just influence the order in which undominated and legally enactable multi-plans are found. So, they do *not* favour some agents and harm others, but are part of a mechanism that agents use to efficiently compute the bargaining outcome.

7.2.3.3 Knowledge and Information Requirements

The above discussion highlights the need to have a closer look at the agents' knowledge and information endowments. In order to apply the social interaction strategy, an agent needs to be provided with three "types" of knowledge:

- problem-solving knowledge
  An agent needs to be endowed with knowledge to determine the individual plans that it *can* enact. In addition, in every situation, it is capable of determining their *executability* as well as the *utility* that they are expected to achieve individually.

- social knowledge
  The agent needs to be capable of deriving the hard and weak constraints that concern it in a specific situation. By this, it can determine how potential plans of its acquaintances influence the *executability* and the *utility* of its individual plans. We assume that the constraints can be used to "generate" the information contained in them (e.g. the set of individual plans that can be influenced by others). In particular, this means that the agent has implicit knowledge of the groups of agents that can (directly) influence it.

- normative knowledge
  An agent is capable of deducing the normative prescriptions referring to it in a specific situation, as well as the prescriptions pertaining to the agents that might influence it (i.e. that it shares constraints with).

The beliefs contained in the agents' information models go back to two different sources. On the one hand, they may have been deduced based on the above knowledge. On the other hand, they may be adopted due to messages of the acquaintances and are thus generated dynamically during the distributed search process.

An agent's *acquaintance models* comprise the modelled partner's current individual plan (its current "value"), its current authority and the normative prescriptions pertaining to it. As outlined previously, the *self model* is a specialisation of the acquaintance models. Therefore, it contains the *additional* information that is summarised in the sequel. With the help of its local problem-solving knowledge, an agent keeps track of the plans that it can enact as well as their local utility. The prescriptions deduced from the normative knowledge are used to exclude plans that the agent is not prepared to enact, thereby defining the domain out of which it chooses its current value. Besides this current value, the self model also contains its utility within the current multi-plan. In addition, the dynamic constraints (i.e. nogoods and solution constraints) that the agent is involved in are stored.

Note that a great amount of information remains local. For instance, neither does an agent possess knowledge about the *executable* local plans of its acquaintances in the current situation, nor is it informed about them during the search process. As we will indicate in interaction strategy, the agents' current local plans (individual plans that they are *prepared* to enact) are just sent selectively, i.e. when there is a chance to integrate them into legally enactable multi-plans. A similar argument holds for the shape of the utility function. An agent is not aware at all of the preferences of its partners, as the local search strategies do not rely on this information. Utility values are just exchanged when a potential solution has been found.

Still, we do assume the existence of common and consistent knowledge. In particular, the prescriptions derived from normative knowledge are supposed to be deontically consistent. Obviously, we also require agents that share some constraints in certain situations to deduce these constraints consistently by means of their social knowledge.

7.2.3.4 Message Types

Our approach is based on homogeneous societies of agents. Agents behave according to a fixed strategy. When an agent receives a message, it reacts according to this strategy. Neither does the sender have an explicit "intention" when sending the message, nor does the receiver ascribe an intention to it. The chain of actions and reactions is "hard-coded" into the agents' laws of behaviour.

Still, different message types are used within the algorithm and these can be considered as speech acts in the tradition of Searle (1969). Seen from the outside, it is possible to ascribe intentions to the sender of a message as a function of their types. In general, the messages that agents exchange are *assertive acts*, as the receiver is supposed to update its social models according to the message content. No specific reaction is intended[3]. *Directive acts* are also present, as some messages imply a change in the receiver's behaviour guidelines. For instance, it might perform terminating actions whilst ignoring any other types of received messages.

In the following, we list the messages used in the distributed search phase that have informative character.

- *value* messages: the receiver is informed that the sender changes its current value. The receiver is supposed to update its acquaintance models accordingly.
- *nogood* messages: the receiver is informed that its current value is part of a nogood. It is supposed to update its self model accordingly.
- *authority* messages: the receiver is informed that the sender changes its current authority. The receiver is to update its acquaintance models accordingly.
- *utility* messages: the receiver is informed about the sender's multi-plan utility or its disagreement utility. It updates its acquaintance models accordingly.
- *solution* messages: the receiver is informed that the sender has detected a solution state. The receiver is supposed to record the current multi-plan in its self model as a new solution constraint.

---

[3] However, the *indirect* reactions to messages, implied by the corresponding model updates and the agents' desire to maintain local consistency, constitute an essential part of our distributed algorithm.

```
Method reviseModels(Event)
    IF mesg(α_j, α, value(π))∈ MesgBuffer THEN
        AcqModel[α_j].Value ← π ;
    IF mesg(α_j, α, nogood(χ))∈ MesgBuffer THEN
        SelfModel.Nogoods ← SelfModel.Nogoods ∪ {χ} ;
    IF mesg(α_j, α, authority(ϑ))∈ MesgBuffer THEN
        AcqModel[α_j].Authority ← ϑ ;
    IF mesg(α_j, α, utility(μ, υ))∈ MesgBuffer THEN
        AcqModel[α_j].Utility ← U_j(μ) = υ ;
    IF mesg(α_j, α, solution)∈ MesgBuffer THEN
        SelfModel.Solutions ← SelfModel.Solutions ∪ {currentMP};
```

Figure 7.4. Some model revisions in Stage 1

- *new* messages: the receiver is informed that the sender's set of plans has changed. The receiver is supposed to reinitialise its information model accordingly. In a stable reactive co-ordination setting, the receiver only deletes those nogoods from its self model, that have been created due to the sender.

Figure 7.4 summarises the effects of these messages on the revision of an agent's information model. Some of the above messages are "pure" assertive actions, as they just induce the receiver to update its information model. Still, as we will see, *solution* and *new* messages also have side-effects, that direct the receiver to perform certain actions. In general, the following three message types share this characteristic:

- *time-out* messages: Stage 1 is to be terminated immediately. The receiver shall directly enter a consistent state and ignore all further messages pertinent to Stage 1.
- *new* messages: the receiver shall send its disagreement utility to the leader.
- *solution* messages: the receiver shall send its current multi-plan and its utility from it to the leader.

7.2.3.5 Local Behaviour Strategy

We are now provided with all ingredients to describe the agents' behaviour strategy. The agent that initiates the social interaction process, the *leader* agent, plays a special role. It is in charge of detecting solutions, as well as of composing and collecting the corresponding legally enactable multi-plans. So, it hosts the result of the asynchronous search when Stage 1 terminates. Apart from that, it behaves like all other agents (the *followers*) in line with the "intention" of the different message types, and driven by the desire to maintain their information

```
Method socialLayer.deliberate(Options)
    IF Options ≠ ∅ THEN
        π̄ ← arg max{U,(π) | π ∈Options };
        updateModels(value, π̄);
    IF Options = ∅ THEN
        FOR EACH{ χ ∈ X | isNogood(χ) }DO
            updateModels(nogood, χ)   ;
        determineAuthority(Options, ϑ̄);
        IF selfModel.authority ≠ ϑ̄ THEN
            updateModels(authority, ϑ̄);
            NewOptions ← calcOptions(ϑ̄)   ;
            socialLayer.deliberate(NewOptions);
    IF checkQuiescence(α) AND leader(α) THEN
        updateModels(solution).
```

Figure 7.5. Asynchronous search for Pareto-optimality

models locally consistent. Note that every agent can initiate the interaction process, i.e. every agent can play the role of the leader.

After receiving an initial *new* message and initialising their information model accordingly, the agents calculate their disagreement utility. This is done by determining the set of feasible plans and the response of the acquaintances to it, given the set of normative prescriptions that is currently in force. The plan with highest resulting utility for the agent is chosen, and this information is sent to the leader. Subsequently, agents update their information models in line with the received messages and try to maintain local consistency.

Suppose that an agent has determined its information model to be currently in a *locally inconsistent* state in the sense of Section 7.2.3.2. In consequence, the agent generates the set of its options, i.e. the set of individual plans that are locally consistent with the acquaintance models. Subsequently, it behaves according to the strategy shown in Figure 7.5.

If the set of options is not empty, the interaction strategy determines the locally most preferred option $\bar{\pi}$ of the agent and updates its self model accordingly. This implies storing the chosen option as the current plan and informing all interested agents about the value change. Messages are sent to all acquaintances with which the agent shares some type of constraint.

The second alternative that the interaction strategy considers, is the case when the agent has no option left. Asynchronous search has come to a dead-end and backtracking needs to be done. For each subset of the current multi-plan that makes it impossible to restore local consistency, i.e. for each combination of values of higher authority agents that leaves no options to the agent, a nogood is generated and models are updated accordingly. As the agent itself is not mentioned in the nogood, just the involved acquaintances need to be informed[4].

Subsequent to this, the agent checks if it should change its authority level to overcome this situation. If so, it stores the new authority value in the self model, informs all related agents about the authority change and restarts deliberation with the new authority level. Note that the associated method *determineAuthority* settles the kind of search to be performed. If an agent does not change its authority level, the interaction process constitutes a distributed "chronological" backtracking. If it gives itself highest authority, or the smallest consistent authority level, "dependency-directed" backtracking is done.

Finally, the agent checks for quiescence thereby consuming and sending signals in accordance with the solution detection scheme described in the next section. If the leader detects quiescence, a solution has been found and the models are updated accordingly. The leader stores its current multi-plan as a new solution constraint, and sends *solution* messages to *all* acquaintances. Upon the reception of these messages, the acquaintances also convert their current multi-plans into a new solution constraint and store it in their self models. Still, as a "side-effect" of the reception of the solution messages, the acquaintances also calculate their local utility from the current (solution) multi-plan and send it together with the corresponding *utility* messages to the leader. Based on these messages, the leader constructs a global multi-plan and stores it, together with the utility that each agent expects from it, as an outcome of the asynchronous distributed search process of Stage 1[5].

Still, by converting their current multi-plans into solution constraints, some agents have come into a locally inconsistent state. So, the distributed search process recommences, but with a search space of reduced size. Stage 1 concludes when no more legally enactable multi-plans can be found. This is detected when an empty nogood is generated and the method *updateModels* tries to store it in the self model.

7.2.3.6 Solution Detection

The above strategy makes use of a method that, despite its modest appearance, raises substantial implementation problems. When *checkQuiescence* is true for the leader agent, *all* agents are in a locally consistent state.

In order to implement this method, let us reformulate the problem in terms of the underlying agent processes. We say that an agent is *quiescent* when it is waiting for messages from its acquaintances. It is called *engaged* when it has received messages and has not yet become quiescent. Agents with non-empty message buffer are assumed to be engaged. Expressed in these terms, *checkQuiescence* has to evaluate to true for the leader, if *all* agent processes are quiescent.

---

[4] An agent actually keeps track of the nogoods it has transmitted and avoids sending them twice.
[5] In certain situations, several solution multi-plans can be constructed by the leader.

Our implementation of the method goes back to techniques for termination detection in distributed computing theory. When all agents are quiescent, one step of our asynchronous distributed search has "terminated"[6].

In a centralised implementation of our agent society, termination would be easy to detect, as the queue of ready processes would have to be empty. However, in a distributed implementation some mechanism must provide a "snapshot" of the global state of the system. A signalling scheme, to be superimposed of the message passing mechanism, provides us with such a snapshot. This scheme runs concurrently with, but does not alter, the underlying computation[7].

We assume that our agent processes communicate by means of directed error-free communication channels, which deliver messages in the order in which they are sent. By representing agent processes as nodes and channels as edges, a directed *process graph* is implied. When the process graph is a tree, termination detection is easy: leave processes send signals to their predecessors when they become quiescent. Interior nodes inform the ancestors when they have terminated and the signals corresponding to all their sons have arrived. By this, the root of the tree, i.e. the source process that initiated computation, eventually detects termination. Things become more difficult if the process graph can be of any shape. There may be cycles that make an agent recommence its computation after having become quiescent, i.e. there are no "leaf nodes" any more that such a detection process may set out from.

Our termination detection mechanism, shown in Figure 7.6, is actually an instance of the algorithm published by Dijkstra and Scholten[8] (1980). It relies on the fact that there is a partial ordering of agents. Dijkstra and Scholten achieve this by dynamically generating a spanning tree on the basis of the messages that are sent first. We just consider the leader agent (called the *parent* node $\overline{\alpha}$) to be of higher order than all remaining agents. Each agent keeps track of the total number of messages that have been sent in a variable *outstandingSignals* and of the amount of messages that it received on each incoming channel in an array *deficit[]*. As Figure 7.6 indicates, these variables are updated accordingly during message processing.

---

[6] Although we will use the terms *termination detection* and *deadlock detection*, which are commonly used in distributed computing theory, as synonyms to *solution detection*, in the context of our distributed algorithm the latter appears most suitable. On the one hand, it does not really *terminate* when a solution has been found. On the other hand, a *deadlock* is usually associated with an undesirable situation, while we would like agents to converge on states of global quiescence as fast as possible.

[7] In the realisation described below, we actually subdivide the solution detection mechanism into several "methods", that have to be "scheduled" adequately into the agents' genuine behaviour strategies.

[8] Chandy and Lamport (1985) present a termination detection algorithm that comprises the method used by Dijkstra and Scholten. Still, for the purpose of solution detection within our algorithm the simpler Dijkstra/Scholten variant is sufficient.

```
Method sendMessage(α,α',η)
        send(mesg(α,α',η));
        outstandingSignals ← outstandingSignals +1.

Method receiveMessage(α',α,η)
        receive(mesg(α',α,η));
        deficit[α'] ← deficit[α']+1.

Method checkQuiescence(α)
        FOR EACH {α' ∈ A \ ᾱ | deficit[α'] ≠ 0 } DO
                send(signal(α',deficit[α']));
        WHILE receive(signal(α,n)) DO
                outstandingSignals ← outstandingSignals − n ;
        IF outstandingSignals = 0 THEN
                send(signal(ᾱ,deficit[ᾱ]));
                return(true);
        ELSE    return(false).
```

Figure 7.6. The solution detection algorithm

Before an agent becomes quiescent, it should check for termination by means of the method *checkQuiescence*. It reduces its deficits on each channel by sending signals to the corresponding agents except the parent agent $\bar{\alpha}$. Subsequently, it reads all signals destined to itself, thereby reducing the number of outstanding signals. If there are no outstanding signals left, the agent reduces its deficit with its parent agent and becomes quiescent, having (locally) detected termination. Global termination is determined when the outstanding signals of the *parent* node (i.e. the leader agent) have been reduced to zero. Note that the methods for sending and receiving messages are non-blocking, as the agent continuously needs to check for termination, thereby sending and receiving signals.

7.2.4 Applying the Nash Solution

The leader agent, which detects the termination of Stage 1, becomes the active agent in Stage 2. It faces a continuous optimisation problem: given the set of m pure multi-plans μ_k computed in Stage 1, the corresponding utilities $U_i(\mu_k)$ for all n agents as well as the corresponding disagreement utilities, the following non-linear function needs to be maximised:

$$f(a_1,...,a_m) = \prod_{i=1}^{n} \left(\sum_{k=1}^{m} a_k U_i(\mu_k) \right) - d_i, \quad 0 \le a_j \le 1, \ \sum_{j=1}^{m} a_j = 1 .$$

Method $stage2(UndominatedMPs)$

    $SolutionProbabilities \leftarrow optimisation(f, UndominatedMPs)$

Method $stage3(UndominatedMPs, SolutionProbabilities)$

    $SelectedMP \leftarrow lottery(UndominatedMPs, SolutionProbabilities);$

    $\forall \alpha_j \in A \quad mesg(\alpha, \alpha_j, perform(SelectedMP_j)).$

Figure 7.7. The stages two and three

This function is equivalent to a polynomial of m variables and degree n. Some fundamental mathematics tell us that it is impossible to determine the maximum of such a polynomial analytically even for small numbers n of agents. Findings from the area of non-linear optimisation with restrictions imply that the constraints on the coefficients a_k do not improve this unpleasant situation. We have no chance to apply analytical methods to determine the exact maximum of the function f in the general case.

So, the maximum of f must be approximated, which can be achieved by means of standard numerical optimisation methods. For instance, iterative improvement methods such as simulated annealing or evolutionary programming methods are appropriate to maximise the function. They appear to be particularly well suited, as they preserve the anytime property of the overall algorithm.

As Figure 7.7 indicates, we just require the existence of some function *optimisation*, that maximises f in the space of *mixed* multi-plans based on the outcome of Stage 1. The result of the numerical optimisation algorithm is a vector *SolutionProbabilities* that represents the probabilities with which each (undominated) legally enactable multi-plan will be chosen in the (approximate) Nash solution to the bargaining problem.

Figure 7.7 also illustrates Stage 3 of our distributed algorithm. The leading agent performs a lottery among the set of undominated multi-plans in accordance with the probabilities calculated in Stage 2. The winning alternative contains the multi-plan that will be executed. The leading agent is in charge of informing the followers about the individual plans that have been assigned to them in accordance with the winning alternative. Upon receiving the corresponding message, each agent is determined to execute its individual plan, i.e. to perform its part in the multi-plan that has been chosen.

In standard situations, the algorithm performs successively stages one, two and three. It remains to specify its behaviour in the exceptional cases. If a time-out message is sent to the algorithm during Stage 1, the "best" legally enactable multi-plan found so far is chosen and sent to the agents. The same procedure is applied if a time-out signal arrives in Stage 2 and the method *optimisation* does not show anytime properties. Otherwise, the present tentative result of Stage 2 is taken and passed to Stage 3. The latter is not influenced by time-out signals, as its execution time is minimal.

7.2.5   Analysis

In this section we will show that the above algorithm complies with the desired properties as outlined previously. Some characteristics can easily be shown.

The different agent processes are executed in *parallel*. They may be hosted by different machines and can be run on the same or on different processors. Although nogood messages only imply the reaction of one agent (the one with the lowest priority in the nogood), messages informing about value changes cause simultaneous activity: the related agents check in parallel whether they are still in a locally consistent state. Furthermore, the execution sequences of agent processes are *asynchronous*. As message transmission is done on buffered channels with non-blocking primitives, communication cannot be used for *rendezvous*.

The *communication load* is limited by selective addressing. *Value* messages are only sent to those agents that are "interested" in them, as they share some weak or hard constraints. *Nogood* messages are sent only to those agents that are involved in them. Note that at the time sending nogoods it would suffice to direct them just to the lowest priority agent involved in the nogood. Still, authority levels are changing and our policy of routing nogood messages anticipates potential future communication. Furthermore, the search space is pruned on the basis of nogoods, as all multi-plans that comprise a nogood are not explored. In addition, in detached reactive co-ordination settings, all multi-plans that an agent detects to be dominated by a solution constraint are discarded. These facts imply an additional reduction of message traffic.

The time-out handling mechanism implements the *anytime property* of our algorithm. By sending *time-out* messages in Stage 1, it is always possible to access the set of legally enactable multi-plans that have been found so far. The implementation of Step 2 cannot detriment this property, as it only selects between different legally enactable alternatives.

The fact that the algorithm always sets out from the "present" solution, which corresponds to the assignment of individual plans immediately prior to initiation, contributes to *incrementality*. But, most important, in *stable* reactive co-ordination settings previously found nogoods are reused. In such scenarios, a *new* message indicates that the situation of just one agent (the sender of the message) has changed. So, its acquaintances only remove those nogoods from their information models that have been created due to that agent.

The characteristics of our algorithm with regard to soundness and completeness are not evident, especially because of the distributed asynchronous computation in Stage 1. The following theorems present our results respecting the adequacy of our algorithm and its stages. The first states that if all agents employ the social interaction strategy, Stage 1 does its job and comes up with (a superset of) all undominated, legally enactable multi-plans.

Theorem 7.1. Suppose a reactive co-ordination setting, where all agents apply the social interaction strategy. The following holds: after finite time Stage 1 terminates and the leader is endowed with a superset of all undominated, legally enactable multi-plans.

Corollary. Given that the agents set out from an undominated multi-plan, in a *detached* reactive co-ordination setting the leader hosts precisely the set of undominated, legally enactable multi-plans.

The corresponding proofs – as well as all the following – can be found in Appendix A. Our next theorem states that the social interaction process, i.e. the process that the application of the interaction strategy by all agents implies, can actually calculate the Nash solution to the bargaining problem.

Theorem 7.2. Suppose a reactive co-ordination setting, where all agents apply the social interaction strategy. The following holds: if Stage 2 is sound and complete, then the social interaction process is sound and complete with respect to the Nash solution.

Another interesting question concerns the complexity of the algorithm. Suppose the algorithm is applied to a setting of n agents, where the cardinality of the sets of individual plans is bounded by m. As the whole search space needs to be traversed in order to guarantee completeness, the algorithm's time complexity is exponential in n in the worst case. This is inevitable as the problem of finding legally enactable multi-plans can be mapped onto a generic constraint satisfaction problem, which is known to be NP-complete. Time complexity of Stage 2 depends on the optimisation method used and on the required solution quality, but will not be worse than the above. Stage 3 obviously performs in constant time.

Given these findings, in some settings it will be necessary to rely on the anytime properties of the algorithm (or to limit in advance the number of solutions to be searched for). In this context, the question of the solution quality in case of time-outs arises. In a *detached* reactive co-ordination setting and given that Stage 1 has found at least one solution, our time-out handling mechanism guarantees that an undominated, legally enactable multi-plan is returned, regardless of when the *time-out* message has been sent. Under these conditions, even though the algorithm cannot compute all undominated multi-plans, no utility is wasted due to time-outs. A *globally efficient* (though not socially plausible) outcome is assured. In the general case, we can only assure the existence of a legally enactable multi-plan based on the above assumption. Still, making agents choose the locally most preferred individual plan from their set of options is a good heuristics in order to find undominated multi-plans as soon as possible.

The worst case space complexity of Stage 1 for each agent is determined by the number of recorded nogoods. So, it may also grow exponentially in the number of agents. This "unpleasant" result seems inevitable as both completeness and a dynamic traversal of the space of multi-plans have to be assured. Space complexity of Stage 2 depends on the optimisation algorithm used and can be kept constant, and so does Stage 3.

7.3 Related Work

An overwhelming diversity of different agent architectures has come up in recent years. In the first part of this book, we have pointed to only some of them. Many architectures allege to be generic, applicable to a seemingly infinite range of applications. Still, as Wooldridge and Jennings (1998) point out, "such claims are often unsubstantiated and based on flimsy evidence". Just a few architectures, usually based on the BDI paradigm (Haddadi and Sundermeyer 1996), have been applied successfully to fundamentally different domains.

By contrast, the ProsA$_2$ agent architecture has been developed for the clearly defined purpose of making structural co-operation operational in reactive co-ordination settings. In particular, this implies that we are concerned with *short-term* plans, which are executed *en bloc* and thus need *not* be reconsidered in the face of contingencies. Using BDI-based general-purpose architectures in such reactive settings means to break a butterfly with a wheel. Many features of generic architectures appear as an overhead, introducing complexity that is not really needed. In addition, we argue that, for the class of settings that we are concerned with in this book, the ProsA$_2$ agent architecture does not only provide an adequate reflection of structural co-operation on a conceptual level, but also helps to structure the process of agent *design* in line with our mechanism. We *do* believe that certain aspects of our architecture, such as the distinguished role of normative knowledge and information, are also crucial for generic architectures. However, in this book we only provide evidence for this with respect to the aforementioned class of settings.

In the *research* field of agent architectures, layered agent architectures are ultimately receiving much interest. Often, the principle by means of which an agent's layers are designed is of *functional* nature. In the MECCA architecture (Steiner 1996), for instance, a layer corresponds to different functionalities of the agent and is concerned with particular aspects of the outside world. In other approaches, the layering principle is *conceptual*. For example, in the InterRap architecture (J. Müller 1996) each layer deals with the entire world state. Still, this is done based on conceptual frameworks that correspond to different levels of abstraction. The essential characteristic that distinguishes ProsA$_2$ agents from those architecture approaches is the layering principle. Rather than functional or conceptual, we conceive the ProsA$_2$ layering principle as "contextual": each layer frames relevant parts of the world state from a standpoint of one of the different contexts that structural co-operation considers. The information model is interpreted in the light of individual motivation, of social interaction and of collective functionality. This layering principle is the result of the purpose of the ProsA$_2$ architecture: it is intended to support the instrumentation of social co-ordination among autonomous problem-solving agents based on structural co-operation.

Distributed constraint satisfaction is being investigated from practical (e.g. Sycara et al. 1991) as well as from theoretical (e.g. Collin et al. 1991, Montanari and Rossi 1996) points of view. Work on distributed constraint *optimisation*, by contrast, is scarce (but see Yokoo 1991). We model the particular problem of determining negotiation sets (or, more specifically, sets of undominated multi-plans) in different types of reactive co-ordination settings as a constraint optimisation problem. The specific characteristics of this problem have shaped our approach to distributed constraint optimisation. In much the same way, the notion of multi-stage algorithms has already been introduced to the distributed problem-solving community (e.g. Conry et al. 1991). However, its application as an asynchronous distributed algorithm to compute bargaining outcomes is a contribution of this work. The approach of Ephrati and Rosenschein (1993) is related to ours, in so far as they make a group of agents search jointly for the maximum of a generic social welfare function. Still, rather than distributed constraint satisfaction, they use a distributed hill-climbing algorithm based on voting schemes.

The social interaction strategy presented in this chapter is related to the *asynchronous backtracking* (Yokoo et al. 1992) and the *asynchronous weak commitment search* (Yokoo 1995) algorithms for distributed constraint *satisfaction*. In essence, they share the idea of guiding asynchronous search by authority levels. Still, our approach is different in a variety of aspects. Most important, the notion of local consistency has been extended in order to account for the specific characteristics in our domain. In addition, the *variable ordering heuristics* of the afore-mentioned algorithms have been changed to deal with the quantitative measure of utility that the "weak constraints" imply. By this, we try to find *undominated*, legally enacted multi-plans first. Furthermore, the social interaction strategy described in this chapter allows guiding the distributed search by means of flexible changes of authorities. Different types of dynamically generated constraints and new message types have been introduced in order to accommodate asynchronous search to our multi-stage algorithm.

In short: the "basic ingredients" of the social interaction strategy presented in this chapter draw on paradigms that have been developed in different areas. Our contribution consists in integrating these techniques and adapting them to our class of problems, so as to present an operational model of structural co-operation.

7.4 Bottom Line

In this chapter the ProsA$_2$ agent architecture has been developed that provides the foundation for an instrumentation of structural co-operation in specific application domains. The different layers of the ProsA$_2$ architecture reflect the different contexts in which structural co-operation unfolds. A social interaction strategy has been devised, that allows for an asynchronous distributed computation of the outcome of structural co-operation in reactive co-ordination settings and the associated bargaining scenarios.

The ProsA$_2$ agent architecture constitutes an adequate vehicle for the instrumentation of structural co-operation. Stating this, we do not claim that the architecture presented here is beneficial *per se*, nor that it is the only feasible frame-work to make the mechanism of structural co-operation operational. Rather, we would like to highlight that, besides the benefits usually associated with layered architectures (J. Müller 1996), it presents two additional advantages.

From a *design* stance, it allows structuring agent design and implementation. Each layer can be designed and implemented separately and successively. First, the problem of individual problem solving can be approached in the design of the individual layer. In a next step, the adequacy of co-ordination based on the agents' social strengths is evaluated by means of the social layer. Finally, successive adjustments of the collective behaviour of the agent society are introduced by tuning the agents' normative layers. From a *conceptual* point of view, the different contexts of the mechanism of structural co-operation are reflected in the layers. The explicit analysis of consistency of the information model from individual, social and normative perspectives provides a model of the different expressions of self-interested behaviour in the contexts of structural co-operation.

The social interaction strategy presented in this chapter gives rise to a collective behaviour in line with the solution to the associated bargaining scenario. As this solution is calculated directly, we lose social plausibility. This might have pro-hibitive consequences if the algorithm was to be used in heterogeneous agent societies. Still, from the perspective of the centralised design of societies of autonomous problem-solving agents, it appears less severe. After all, we gain an intuitive, transparent way of making structural co-operation operational.

A problematic aspect of the above approach is its high space and time com-plexity. Still, these results need to be put into perspective by recalling the charac-teristics of the problems that we face. Contrary to "connectionist" settings, which usually rely on a great amount of simple agents, the number n of cognitive agents in our problem-solving societies is rather small. Furthermore, plans are usually complex, structured objects whose generation consumes a remarkable amount of resources, so the number m of alternative individual plans will also be quite small. This advocates in favour of the adequacy of the algorithm within the envisioned class of problems. In the next part of the book, we will underline the suitability of the ProsA$_2$ agent architecture and our social interaction strategy by means of a case study.

In this part of the book, a novel perspective on co-ordination in multi-agent problem-solving systems has been developed. It has been presented in the order of its genesis: from the abstract metaphor of the emergence of co-ordination from social structure, based on the transfer of theories from social science to artificial agent societies, to a rigorous model of the corresponding mechanism of structural co-operation within bargaining theory, and finally down to its implementation by means of an agent architecture that supports asynchronous distributed agent interaction within societies of problem-solving agents. The following part aims at demonstrating the feasibility of structural co-operation by applying it to the domain of intelligent road traffic management.

8 Road Traffic Management

In this third part of the book, we will validate the mechanisms presented previously: societies of autonomous traffic management agents are co-ordinated in a decentralised manner, in order to solve traffic problems. A case study will be presented that concerns intelligent road traffic management.

This chapter introduces the road traffic management domain. It is organised as follows: first, the traffic control problem is described and the evolution of the role of computer systems for traffic control is depicted. Section 8.2 describes the TRYS family of intelligent traffic management systems. Finally the key ideas of multi-agent TRYS are introduced: it extends the TRYS local problem-solving model by embedding it into the ProsA$_2$ agent architecture, so as to augment the agents' degree of autonomy and to achieve decentralised co-ordination.

8.1 Urban Traffic Management

The increasing popularity of road transport and the incessant rise of the number of vehicles have caused a tremendous growth of the magnitude of traffic flows on public roads. Especially in urban areas, where the road network is dense and the traffic volume in peak situations is enormous, significant economic losses are produced by enduring and recurrent congestions. Still, it is precisely in these urban areas where there are severe obstacles to the expansion of traditional infrastructure, due to the scarcity of space and resources as well as for environmental reasons. In consequence, urban road traffic management has become an increasingly important task: strategies to guide traffic flows are essential in order to avoid collapses of individual transport and the corresponding losses for the local economy.

8.1.1 Traffic Control Infrastructure

In big cities, traffic control centres (TCC) are in charge of managing urban transport. A TCC's responsibilities cover a wide range of different tasks. In particular, traffic engineers within a TCC are to supervise the current road traffic situation, detect problems and take actions to overcome them, so as to maintain and restore "smooth" flows of vehicles. Information about the current traffic state is obtained from many different sources, the most important of which include:

- observers
  Messages transmitted from human observers constitute the classical source of information for traffic control centres. In most cases, such information is provided by the urban police or members of related public organisms.

- TV cameras
  Visual control of certain problematic areas is possible by means of TV cameras. They are especially useful to assess unusual and emergency situations, such as the gravity of accidents etc.

- sensors
  Sensors are installed in strategic parts of the network and generate a continuous flow of numerical data about traffic conditions at a certain point. There are different types of sensors with different costs and capabilities. One of the classical sensors are *loop detectors* that usually provide information about *speed* (mean velocity of the vehicles detected by the sensor), *flow* (average number of vehicles that pass through a certain road section per time unit) and *occupancy* (the average time that vehicles are spotted by the sensor).

On the basis of such heterogeneous traffic information – informal, visual and numeric data – a traffic control engineer identifies potential problems and decides upon *signal plans* to overcome them. Such signal plans comprise a coherent set of uses of control devices that the TCC can act upon. The most popular devices for urban road traffic management are the following:

- variable message signs (VMS)
  VMS allow influencing traffic behaviour by dynamically setting, modifying or deleting traffic signals. The most advanced VMS are panels that are installed above the road. They allow displaying arbitrary messages that inform drivers about the network situation downstream. In addition to this, they can show pictograms and traffic signs, thereby announcing warnings, speed limits, prohibitions to overtake etc. Older types of VMS support just a small collection of different traffic signs or constrain the set of messages that can be displayed due to technical limitations.

- traffic lights
  The access of vehicles to certain parts of a road network, especially to junctions, is controlled by traffic lights. It is possible to modify different features of traffic light signalling: the relative amount of green time may be increased or decreased, the overall length of a cycle can be changed, or the time offset between different cycles may be altered. Ramp meters are special traffic lights that are positioned on the entry ramps of motorways. They enable the traffic controller to regulate the amount of vehicles entering the motorway.

Figure 8.1 depicts a typical traffic management installation. The task of traffic management performed in the TCC is to generate signal plans for control devices in order to alleviate traffic problems that have been identified based on the col-

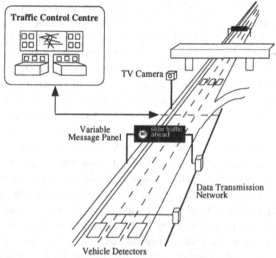

Figure 8.1. Traffic control infrastructure

lected traffic information. Obviously, the quality of control decisions depends strongly on the timeliness, accuracy and relevance of traffic information. Furthermore, the responsible person must not just be familiar with the dynamics of traffic networks in general, but is also required to be an expert in the behaviour of the specific problem area under discourse: only by making adequate short-term prediction of traffic behaviour on the basis of the present data, and by good estimations of the effects of potential control actions, satisfactory signal plans can be enacted.

8.1.2   Decision Support for Real-Time Traffic Management

The last decade has shown an important upsurge of investigation in the area of traffic management. As a result, new technologies are being introduced, leading to rapid and significant changes in work context of TCCs. The task of traffic engineers becomes increasingly complex. For a variety of reasons, they are facing a qualitatively new situation:

- Huge amounts of unstructured data arrive continuously within short time periods.
- The number and complexity of control devices that can be acted upon increases constantly.
- The number of simultaneous traffic problems increases, while the time frame for elaborating signal plans becomes shorter.
- The co-ordination of local management strategies becomes more complex.

So, it does not surprise that information technology is being used to assist the work in TCCs. Telematics systems have been installed, that allow the operators to receive traffic information *on-line* from sensors and to issue remote commands for control devices. Still, besides the support of the transmission and presentation of information, there are also attempts to assist the *decision-making process* of the control engineers in TCCs, which obviously needs to be accomplished in real-time. Of course, *real-time decision support systems* of this type must be reactive to the various states of traffic flow in the controlled area (see Cuena and Ossowski 1998).

Early traffic control systems have been endowed with a library of static signal plans. By applying time-based criteria (fixed-time systems) or sensor data patterns (traffic-actuated systems) to a certain traffic situation, one of these plans is chosen for enactment. Still, the pre-calculated plan approach lacks the conceptual granularity necessary to adapt signal plans to specific problems: it cannot cope adequately with the immense variety of traffic situations that usually arise within traffic networks. Experience has shown that continuous operator intervention is necessary in problem situations to "mould" the system's control proposal, so as to accommodate it to the specific problem case (Cuena et al. 1995).

A qualitative change in the design of traffic management applications has been introduced by the SCOOT system (Bretherton et al. 1981, Bretherton and Bowen 1990). SCOOT receives its traffic data from sensors in an urban street network, and acts upon the cycle times of traffic lights at the junctions. It is endowed with an "on-line intelligence" to analyse the problem at one junction in isolation. This local evaluation step is performed within time-slices of a few seconds. Adaptive aspects of the integration of local signal plans are of minor importance in SCOOT's domain. A whole bunch of traffic control systems follows this philosophy (e.g. Lowrie 1982, Gartner 1983, Mauro and di Taranto 1989).

SCOOT has proved to perform well in situations of moderate saturation of the street network. However, the experience with the SCOOT philosophy has shown deficiencies in severe problem situations, and operator intervention is frequent in most installations (Cuena et al. 1995). This has given rise to the development of systems that consider *strategic* aspects of traffic management. The TRYS approach, described in the following sections, is a major representative of this class.

8.2 The TRYS Approach

The section introduces the TRYS family of traffic control systems[1]. We first motivate the TRYS approach to traffic control by highlighting the needs for

---

[1] All TRYS systems have been developed within the Intelligent Systems group (ISYS) at the Artificial Intelligence Department of the Technical University of Madrid since the early nineties.

knowledge-based models for an intelligent management of traffic flows. Subsequently, the TRYS system architecture and some of its basic characteristics are described.

8.2.1 Motivation

Practical experience with systems following the SCOOT philosophy suggests good performance of the generated signal plans in traffic scenarios with sporadic problems, in which congestions generally last a limited amount of time. However, in persistently congested situations operator intervention is usually required. Cuena et al. (1995) point to two major reasons for this:

- shallow problem diagnosis
  The identification of problem situations based only on sensor data may be insufficient to determine the correct control actions. On the one hand, unusual and extreme situations might lead to erroneous interpretations, for instance when the length of a queue at a stop line exceeds the position of queue detection sensors. On the other, deeper contextual information may be crucial for taking the right control decisions. Consider two events: the end of a soccer game, and a usual evening peak situation. Although the data profile in terms of speed, flow, occupancy etc. is the same in both cases, it is undoubtedly beneficial to approach them by different control actions.

- incremental adjustment policy
  Systems following the SCOOT philosophy show a high degree of reactivity, i.e. their decision cycles last less than a minute. So, in each cycle only minor, incremental adjustments are made to the current signal plan, in order to assure stability within the network. Still, in heavy congestion situations this approach does not converge fast enough (if at all) on the drastic changes that the situation requires.

The above findings suggest complementing existing traffic control systems with an additional *strategic layer*. This layer needs to be endowed with background knowledge concerning the dynamics of specific problem areas. With the help of this knowledge, it can analyse the reasons and the potential evolution of congestions in terms of the underlying traffic flow processes. As the decisions taken are of strategic character, the cycle time of such a system needs to be situated in the frame of a few minutes, so as to be able to evaluate the effectiveness of a certain proposal.

It is acknowledged that signal plans resulting from such strategic decisions are subject to the supervision of human operators that might introduce modifications. Hence, this type of application must be conceived as a decision support system.

8.2.2   The Centralised TRYS Architecture

The above remarks suggest designing traffic management architectures based on *knowledge-based* systems technology. The knowledge and reasoning processes of an expert, the operator, and his or her understanding of particular situations need to be explicitly modelled to overcome the above drawbacks.

Human operators usually analyse the traffic flows on urban motorways in terms of *problem areas*. The decomposition of the city into problem areas allows a better understanding of the causes and evolution of traffic problems than a global analysis. The decomposition criteria usually reflect special characteristics of the network topology, but also comprise empirical behaviour rules for certain parts of the network. In some cases, the creation of a problem area is induced by pre-existing (conventional) traffic management installations (Cuena et al. 1995). The components of the TRYS architecture that are knowledgeable of the traffic management for a certain problem area are called *traffic agents*. Traffic agents receive traffic information, detect traffic problems in their problem area, diagnose their causes and generate signal plans to overcome them. Due to their deep problem knowledge, within the terminology used in this book they fall in the class of *cognitive agents*.

The nature of the reasoning cycles of traffic control agents is another specific characteristic of the TRYS approach. As signal plans are generated at the strategic level, their effectiveness can only be evaluated after a couple of minutes. One alternative is to conceive them as long-term "composite" plans, specifying a temporal sequence of different states for the involved control devices. However, even within a certain problem area, traffic flows are highly dynamic and the complexity of making effective predictions is high. So, TRYS systems just generate short-term signal plans, which remain valid for a couple of minutes. Afterwards, the situation is re-evaluated. In consequence, the system may switch to another signal plan that is better suited for the newly assessed situation. This behaviour strategy underlines the *reactive* property of the "planning" behaviour of TRYS traffic agents.

Still, the subdivision of an urban road network into problem areas is made on the basis of *logical* criteria (e.g. in order to obtain zones, within which the dynamics of traffic behaviour and the effects control actions can be easily conceived). So, the *spatial* division of the road network implied by problem areas is not perfect. Problem areas are not disjointed, but rather constitute a collection of mutually *overlapping* zones. Therefore, they share resources such as sensors and control devices.

In consequence, traffic agents generating signal plans for overlapping problem areas may try to employ the same resource in different ways. In this case, there is potential interference between local signal plan proposals: while sensor data may be easily shared among agents, it is just impossible to use traffic lights with two different cycle times or, in general, to display different messages on the same VMS. Another source of interference between local signal plans is given by the

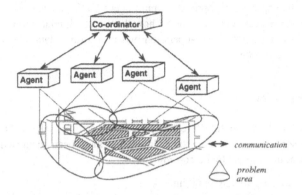

Figure 8.2. Centralised TRYS architecture

fact that the *effects* of local control actions need not be restricted to the corresponding problem area. When an agent deviates traffic out of its problem area, these flows do not vanish (as a purely local perspective might imply), but enter neighbouring areas, where they may aggravate existing problems. Therefore, TRYS systems comprise a special agent that is endowed with knowledge on how to integrate local control proposals into a coherent global signal plan. This agent is called *co-ordinator* in TRYS.

Cuena et al. (1995, 1996) have developed different traffic management systems based on the TRYS architecture systems for various Spanish towns: applications for Seville (TRYS Giralda), Madrid (TRYS) and Barcelona (InTRYS) have been presented. Despite minor modifications due to the improvement of performance in the course of the evolution of the TRYS approach, all systems share the basic architecture shown in Figure 8.2. The co-ordinator sequentially instructs each traffic agent to produce a local signal plan. The traffic agents do what they are told and send the results of their local reasoning back to the co-ordinator. When the local signal plan from the last agent has arrived, the co-ordinator integrates the control proposals for individual problem areas into a consistent global signal plan.

8.3 Multi-Agent TRYS

The multi-agent TRYS approach joins our model of emergent co-ordination of autonomous problem-solving agents with the TRYS paradigm described above. The functionality of the co-ordinator is achieved by endowing local traffic agents with additional social and normative knowledge, substituting the authority of the co-ordinator by the socially bounded autonomy that agents enjoy within structural co-operation.

After motivating the development of multi-agent TRYS, its general traffic control architecture is presented. It is shown how this approach relates to the previous findings respecting structural co-operation and its instrumentation based on the ProsA$_2$ agent architecture.

8.3.1 Motivation

The centralised TRYS architecture has proved to perform well in the different application scenarios. However, some drawbacks have been identified. An important part of them refers to the co-ordinator:

- co-ordination knowledge requirements
  As the size of traffic management systems grows, the co-ordination task becomes increasingly important. The TRYS architecture does not provide a means for structuring the knowledge of interdependencies between problem areas. Furthermore, the complexity of elicitation and maintenance of knowledge concerning the priority of areas in case of conflicting signal plan proposals grows over-linearly with the amount of traffic agents.

- no exploitation of a priori distribution
  The TRYS architecture relies on the existence of a central co-ordinator as the essential component of the system. It does *not* account for any pre-existing distribution. For instance, organisational requirements such as the distribution of control decisions among traffic engineers with disparate responsibilities, or the existence of various low-level control rooms for different problem areas are outside the scope of the original TRYS approach. In addition, certain technical constraints, such as the limitation of communication load by processing data in the area in which it is generated, are not supported by the architecture.

Besides, some of the basic arguments that justify the development of distributed applications are especially pertinent for the domain of road traffic management:

- robustness
  As a central component of the TRYS system, the co-ordinator cannot be substituted by any other agent: it is the main part of the architecture that guides the activity of all other components. Therefore, the co-ordinator constitutes a bottleneck: in case of its breakdown the whole system immediately stops functioning. A multi-agent architecture, by contrast, allows the society to recover from the failure of any one of its members.

- performance
  Multi-agent architectures account for parallel problem solving in all problem areas. This suggests an increase in the overall performance, which may be employed to perform deeper analysis of the traffic situation. Furthermore, the asynchronous and incremental character of multi-agent problem solving allows taking advantage of previously calculated signal plans: when one agent decides

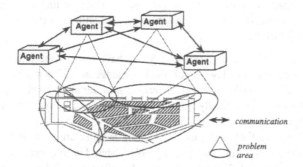

Figure 8.3. Multi-agent TRYS architecture

to generate a new local signal plan, co-ordination is achieved by incrementally integrating its new local proposals into the existing global signal plan.

The above considerations suggest applying distributed architectures to the road traffic management domain. The multi-agent TRYS approach has been developed as a step in this direction.

8.3.2 The Multi-Agent TRYS Architecture

The multi-agent TRYS architecture is the result of mapping of the centralised TRYS design to a society of $ProsA_2$ traffic management agents, which co-ordinate in a decentralised manner by means of structural co-operation. Figure 8.3 sketches the corresponding architecture.

In order to demonstrate the viability of this approach, we first need to show that the traffic control agents actually face a reactive co-ordination problem. Still, the relation is straightforward:

- *Plans*: the individual plans of the reactive co-ordination problem correspond to signal plans. The resources that an individual plan uses are given by the control devices it refers to. The empty plan just consists of doing nothing.
- *Reactivity*: as described in Section 8.2.2, TRYS agents generate individual signal plans in a reactive fashion. Individual plans are executed *en bloc*; their effect is not evaluated before they have been executed entirely.
- *Ideal states*: obviously, states that do not show problems in an area are ideal for the responsible agent. In these ideal states, the capacity of any of the sections in a problem area exceeds the corresponding traffic demand.
- *Distance measure*: the gravity of a traffic situation is measured by TRYS agents in terms of the excess of traffic in certain sections, i.e. by the difference between the traffic demand and the capacity of the section. Hence, the "distance" between a certain state of a problem area and an ideal state is given by

the aggregate traffic excess in the problem area. Respecting signal plans, this implies that sets of control actions are compared with respect to their expected reduction of traffic excess.

So, ProsA$_2$ agents for multi-agent TRYS will have roughly the following shape: the individual layer is endowed with the knowledge of TRYS traffic agents. The social layer comprises knowledge concerning how certain individual plans interact. The deontic layer, finally, issues prohibitions and permissions for certain plans by regulating the access to control devices.

As indicated by Figure 8.3, in the resulting architecture a traffic management agent is still interested in exactly one problem area, but the centralised top-level component of Figure 8.2, the co-ordinator, has disappeared. Instead of receiving requests and sending signal plan proposals to the co-ordinator, agents now exchange messages, thereby mutually adapting their individual signal plans.

So far, we have argued in favour of the suitability of a multi-agent approach for strategic decision support in urban road traffic management. The adequacy of the ProsA$_2$ architecture and structural co-operation in particular has been depicted. In the next chapter we will underline these claims by means of a case study.

9 A Case Study

This chapter applies our previous findings respecting social co-ordination by structural co-operation to the domain of road traffic management. It presents a case study for a real-world problem: traffic management in the urban motorway network around Barcelona. We first describe some general characteristics of our distributed traffic management system. The subsequent chapters are dedicated to the agents' local problem-solving and social co-ordination based on structural co-operation. Finally, implementation issues are discussed and an evaluation of the case study is presented.

9.1 The Scenario

Pushed by the 1992 Olympic Games the traffic management infrastructure in the Barcelona area has become increasingly complex in the last couple of years. Nowadays, information about the traffic state of the urban motorway network, consisting of one ring road and five adjacent motorways, is provided by over 300 telemetered loop detectors. These devices are connected to the Barcelona Traffic Control Centre (JPT) by means of high-performance fibre-optics communication links, which allow for fast transmission of sensor data. From within the JPT, remote control actions can be taken by means of 52 variable message signs (VMS), three traffic lights for junction control, as well as by ramp metering on seven ring-road drives.

The InTRYS traffic management system has been developed to provide real-time decision support for traffic controllers at the JPT[1]. InTRYS belongs to the TRYS family of systems. On the basis of sensor data, operator notifications and contextual information, proposals of signal plans for the above control devices are generated. They are presented to the operators who finally decide whether to enact, modify or reject them. InTRYS is being installed and evaluated at the Barcelona test site (Cuena et al. 1996).

TRYSA$_2$ (TRYS Autonomous Agents) is an experimental multi-agent traffic control system for the Barcelona area, which has been developed based on the InTRYS approach. Still, it is essentially different from the above (and from all other systems of the TRYS family), as there is no central co-ordinator. TRYSA$_2$

---

[1] InTRYS has been developed within the Intelligent Systems group at the Artificial Intelligence Department of the Technical University of Madrid.

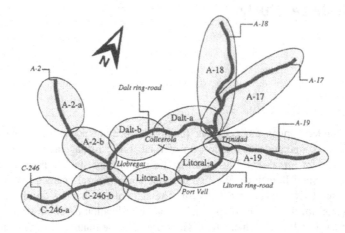

Figure 9.1. Autonomous traffic agents for Barcelona

traffic control agents co-ordinate socially, without the need to refer to a central authority, by means of structural co-operation. Two major modifications have been introduced in the InTRYS architecture:

- rearrangement of problem areas
  The InTRYS system originally subdivides the Barcelona test site into 22 problem areas, referring to "one-way" sub-networks: each direction of a motorway belongs to a different problem area. In the TRYSA$_2$ approach, these problem areas have been united. Despite their spatial vicinity, in- and outbound (or: north- and southbound, east- and westbound etc.) sections of the same motorway portion are not logically related in terms of traffic flows. So, this rearrangement does not create additional problems respecting coherence and consistency of local signal plans. However, a higher degree of mutual dependence among neighbouring agents has been achieved. In addition, the rearrangement of problem areas has led to a reduction of the number of agents that need to be co-ordinated.

- integration of InTRYS traffic control agents into the ProsA$_2$ architecture
  The functionality of the central co-ordinator has been distributed among the traffic control agents. In order to achieve this, the InTRYS traffic control agents have been integrated in the individual layer of the ProsA$_2$ architecture. The social and normative layers have been endowed with additional knowledge to perform structural co-operation, which has been partially reused from the knowledge bases of the InTRYS co-ordinator agent.

Figure 9.1 shows the resulting 11 traffic control agents for the Barcelona case study as well as their corresponding problem areas.

TRYSA$_2$ reuses a great part of the software and knowledge provision of the InTRYS system. In particular, the knowledge bases and the corresponding reasoning methods for local problem solving have been adopted without major modifications. In the following, we will first describe the local problem-solving process of the traffic control agents. Subsequently, the agents' social co-ordination by structural co-operation is exposed in detail.

9.2 Local Problem Solving

Local problem solving of TRYSA$_2$ agents consists in detecting problematic traffic situations, diagnosing their reasons, and generating a set of alternative local signal plans as well as an estimation of their impacts. In terms of our model of structural co-operation, during its local problem-solving process a traffic management agent α_i comes up with a set of plans π, that are executable in the current situation s ($exec(\pi,s)$) and that it is capable of enacting ($can(\alpha_i,\pi)$). In addition, the agent constructs a local utility function U_i, computing a utility value for each of the above plans π. In the sequel, we will describe the underlying process of local traffic management from three perspectives. First, the basic terminology, within which the process unfolds, is introduced. Subsequently, the agent's knowledge endowment is depicted. Finally, it is shown how the agent uses this knowledge to generate local signal plans.

9.2.1 Conceptual Model

An agent's local problem solving is based on an explicit symbolic model of its environment. This section introduces the basic ontology for such a model. We set out from concepts that describe the network topology. The following terms model "physical" aspects of the road network:

- nodes
  A node describes a part of the town whose structure is not explicitly represented by the local model, but which is relevant as an entry to or an exit from the modelled part of the road network. As such, it constitutes a source or a drain of traffic volume.

- sections
  The road network is subdivided into smaller pieces called sections. Sections support traffic flows in *one* direction. So, the result of performing transversal "cuts" on a motorway is usually a pair of sections, one for each direction. The number of lanes of the network fraction modelled by a section is not explicitly represented. However, it is included in the notion of capacity of a section, i.e. its ability to absorb a certain amount of vehicles per hour. Traffic problems manifest by an *excess* of vehicles in this section, which is the case when the

current traffic demand exceeds the capacity of a section. The partition of the road network into sections is usually made with relation to existing sensors.

- connections
  Several sections are related by a *connection*. In the simplest case, this connection is linear: one section is the successor of another. The confluence of different roads or motorways is expressed by a special class of connections called *ramps*: entry ramps, exit ramps and combinations of both can be modelled.

In the sequel, notions related to devices for the perception of and for the actuation on road traffic are presented:

- measurement points
  The road network is endowed with a series of sensors that measure traffic flow, speed and occupancy. One or various sensors are grouped into logical perceptive entities, called measurement points, in order to obtain semantically richer data. For instance, loop detector sensors are usually installed in groups, covering the whole width of the motorway at a certain location. Each of them gathers basic data for just one lane. These sensors are logically integrated into measurement points, whose "measurements" are a function of the data that the constituent sensors supply. By this, relevant information about magnitudes at certain kilometric points is available. In addition to this, the concept allows to obtain data at virtual points: if no physical sensors are present in a certain region, fictitious data can be calculated based on related upstream and downstream measurement points.

- control devices
  The traffic flow within a network is guided by control devices. In the case of the Barcelona experimental area, these are VMS and regulators. VMS influence the relative amount of traffic that chooses a certain itinerary between two nodes. By this, the traffic demand on sections located on itineraries with reduced service level decreases, while the number of vehicles per hour on sections included in more important itineraries augments. Regulators correspond to sets of traffic lights that are controlled in a co-ordinated fashion. By changing the duration of green cycles of these regulators the capacities of certain ramps or junctions can be influenced.

Finally, we introduce a conceptual framework for modelling network traffic flows and their modification:

- itineraries
  An itinerary is a way from one node to another that passes through connected sections. Usually, such an itinerary comprises a set of physical paths between two locations. Although origin and destination nodes belong to the modelled problem area, the entire length of the path need not be included in the local network model, i.e. respecting its spatial extension an itinerary can exit the problem area at one location and re-enter it at another.

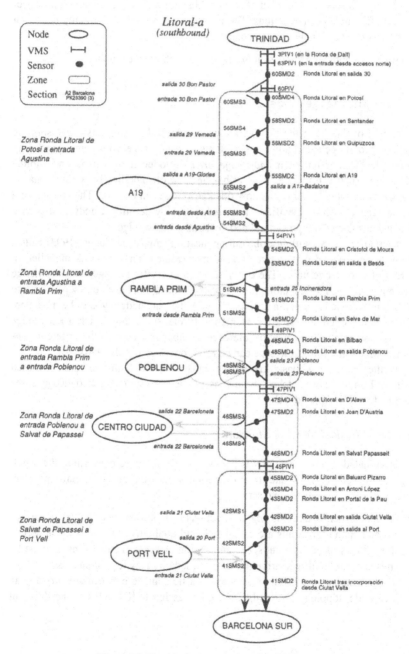

Figure 9.2. Graphical representation of a problem area

- control zones
  Control zones comprise a set of sections that are logically coherent with respect to traffic management actions. The target of control action is usually not given by a single section, but by the control zone.

Figure 9.2 graphically depicts an example of a problem area model.

9.2.2   Knowledge Model

The state of the art in the field of knowledge modelling suggests organising the expertise of large-sale knowledge systems in accordance with some structuring principle. The notion of a *knowledge area*, introduced by Cuena and Molina (1997), is such a principle. It describes an area of expertise by stating what is *known* of a particular topic and how this knowledge can be *used*. The concept of a *knowledge unit* (KU) specifies a knowledge area by defining a body of expertise that encapsulates both procedural and declarative knowledge.

In the sequel, we will describe our application from what Cuena (1993) calls a *knowledge-oriented* perspective. Traffic management knowledge is modelled in terms of knowledge units. The different areas of traffic management knowledge are not comprised in one monolithic knowledge base, but have been separated into different knowledge units in accordance with the knowledge type to be modelled. Each such KU comprises a representation formalism within which a knowledge base is constructed, and a set of inference methods that express the different lines of reasoning that this knowledge can be used for (Cuena et al. 1996).

In the sequel, four basic knowledge units of InTRYS that have been reused within TRYSA$_2$ are sketched. Examples of the corresponding knowledge bases can be found in Appendix B.

9.2.2.1 Physical Network Structure

This knowledge unit essentially is endowed with expertise concerning the topology of the road network and the traffic control infrastructure of specific problem areas. It offers essentially two services:

- *Data abstraction and filtering*: abstractions from the sensor data such as temporal and spatial gradients are calculated, and qualitative measures of numerical magnitudes of occupation, speed and saturation are computed. This is done by means of probability distribution tables based on fuzzy logic concepts.
- *Traffic assignment*: given an estimated traffic demand between an entry and an exit node, topology knowledge is used to assign traffic flows to the different paths.

9.2.2.2 Problem Scenarios

The second type of knowledge is modelled by the *problem scenario* KU. Its knowledge base uses frames as basic knowledge representation scheme upon which inference is made by means of pattern matching. Each frame describes a set of undesired network states within a problem area, which comprise a so-called *problem scenario*. Usually, traffic problems at a certain location of the problem area are expressed in terms of abstract sensor data. So, a problem scenario frame comprises three parts:

- The *where* section: the location of the problem as well as its characteristics in terms of basic qualitative traffic values are described.
- The *why* section: the causes and the severity of the problem are expressed. The causes are described by the different paths that send traffic flows to the critical section. The severity is given in terms of traffic excess, i.e. by the difference between the capacity of the critical section and its current traffic demand.
- The *how* section: different criteria to estimate the level of matching between real data and the situation represented in the frame are defined.

Two types of frames are considered. Specific problem frames are applied to well-defined recurrent problems whose location, evolution and causes are well known. Generic problem situations are not bound to a specific physical configuration, but correspond to general problem patterns. So, they are applicable to a variety of different traffic situations and in different parts of the road network.

Inference upon this knowledge base allows for problem identification and diagnosis. Traffic problems, as well as their causes and severity, are identified by matching abstracted traffic data against problem scenario frames.

9.2.2.3 Traffic Distribution Scenarios

The *traffic distribution* KU comprises expertise about the dispersion of traffic flows. The corresponding knowledge respecting signal plans and their effects is also expressed in terms of frames. A traffic distribution scenario expresses a relation between the state of the control devices in a certain situation, the traffic state and the use that drivers make of the different paths between nodes. This relation is reflected by three frame sections:

- The *state of control devices* section describes a signal plan associated with the frame.
- The *path use* section describes the impact of the enactment of the above control plan on the distribution of traffic flows within the problem area. This is done by specifying the relative traffic volume that each of the paths, connecting a certain origin and a destination node, will carry.
- The *traffic state* section specifies the set of traffic situations in which the control plan is appropriate.

Again, inference upon distribution scenario frames is done by pattern matching. Such inference can fulfil two purposes, depending on information provided in the pattern that is matched against the knowledge base:

- Determination of the *current traffic distribution*: given the current state of control devices and an abstract description of the current traffic situation, the distribution of traffic flows between two nodes is inferred.
- Determination of a *signal plan* to overcome problem situations: given the current state of control devices and the causes of traffic problems in terms of the paths contributing to it, an adequate signal plan is inferred.

9.2.2.4 Historic Traffic Demand

Finally, the *historic demand* KU provides information concerning the expected volume of traffic flows between network nodes in a specific situation. The underlying idea is to take advantage of the fact that traffic demand patterns are recurrent. Prototypic traffic demand situations are defined and associated with a specific temporal context.

Temporally qualified demand situations are represented by a knowledge base of patterns that contain two sections:

- *Temporal classification*: the current day and time is classified based on qualifications such as *working day*, *holiday* etc.
- *Demand pattern*: an exhaustive description of the traffic demand between all pairs of nodes associated with the problem area is given.

An inference method uses the knowledge base to deduce a set of traffic demand patterns given certain date and time.

9.2.3   Reasoning

The knowledge model described previously is put to use within the TRYSA$_2$ reasoning cycle. It neatly fits into the three-step control model of ProsA$_2$ layers: *model revision* is done by filtering and completing traffic data; traffic problem identification corresponds to the *diagnosis* phase; finally, the *repair* step generates control recommendations. We will illustrate this in the sequel.

Every couple of minutes, temporal series of magnitudes such as traffic speed, flow and occupancy are received from the road sensors. This raw data is initially pre-processed in order to filter out noisy and erroneous data. Subsequently, data abstraction is performed by calculating aggregate magnitudes such as temporal and spatial gradients for the different sections. Both tasks are performed by means of the physical network structure KU. The agent updates its problem-solving model with this completed traffic information.

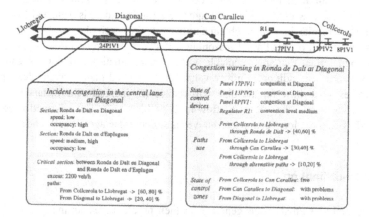

Figure 9.3. An example scenario

In the second step, problem identification is performed by matching the abstracted traffic data against the frames in the problem scenario KBs. Suppose that as a result of data abstraction low speed and high occupancy are identified in *Ronda de Dalt en Diagonal* and medium to high speed and low occupancy in *Ronda en d'Esplugues*. These facts match the frame shown in Figure 9.3. In consequence, an incident in the central lane of Diagonal road is identified, which manifests itself as a traffic excess of 2200 veh/h between *Diagonal* and *Llobregat* in the *Dalt* ring road. Traffic from *Collcerola* to *Llobregat* and, in a minor degree, from *Diagonal* heading towards *Llobregat* contributes to this excess.

Step 3, the plan formation phase, adheres to the following line of reasoning: first, the historic traffic demand between nodes is retrieved and the contribution of each path to the problem in the critical section calculated. This is done by matching the current abstract traffic state and the state of the control devices against the distribution scenario frames.

Coherent alternative signal plans are generated by using the distribution scenario KU again: every frame applicable to the current situation is pre-selected. Assume that this is the case for the frame shown in Figure 9.3. Its short-term effects are estimated by simulating its impact on the current traffic situation. This is done by using the physical network structure knowledge to assign traffic to the road network in accordance with the potential distribution of traffic volume among paths. The frame in the example suggests to display congestion warnings at *Diagonal* for panels *17PIV1*, *13PIV2* and *8PIV1*, while setting the contention level of regulator *R1* to medium. It specifies that about half of the traffic volume from *Collcerola* to *Llobregat* will pass through *Dalt* ring road, while a smaller amount chooses a path through *Can Caralleu* or other alternative paths, if the corresponding signal plan is set. For each signal plan contained in a pre-selected frame, the simulation process produces an estimation of its impact in terms of expected traffic excess. The current aggregate traffic excess is deducted from the simulation results, in order to obtain a utility value for each plan.

As the result of this line of reasoning, a $TRYSA_2$ traffic agent obtains a set of local signal plans that are executable in the current situation and that it is capable of executing. In addition, a utility value for each local plan is available, which expresses as to how far the plan will reduce (or increase) the distance to the agent's ideal state of swift traffic flow in its problem area. The information corresponding to these local action alternatives is stored in the agent's self model[2].

9.3 Co-ordination

The signal plans that agents generate for their problem areas in the course of the local problem-solving process are interrelated. Thus, they need to be co-ordinated. In this section, we describe how decentralised co-ordination of $TRYSA_2$ traffic agents is achieved by means of structural co-operation. We first introduce the conceptual framework upon which co-ordination is based. In the following, the knowledge types and the corresponding knowledge representation schemes are described, which are necessary to make structural co-operation operational in the application domain. Finally, the social interaction strategy and the interaction process in general are revisited in the light of the case study.

9.3.1   Conceptual Model

In principle, it is conceivable to apply to the co-ordination problem the same conceptual framework that has been used to describe local problem solving. The interrelation of local signal plans may be expressed in terms of the relations of data from measurement points, the traffic excess in the different road sections, the states of individual control devices etc. Such an approach, however, is rather knowledge intensive and promises to be of prohibitive complexity.

So, the ontology underlying our co-ordination model will rely on more coarse-grained concepts in order to reduce complexity. We will set out from local signal plan proposals and consider them primary entities with respect to the co-ordination problem. Co-ordination, then, is a function of the explicit and primitive interrelations between local signal plans. A classification of such interrelations will be developed in the sequel.

---

[2] As this section illustrates, the design of computational utility functions with a sufficient degree of accuracy for real-world applications is definitely *non-trivial* (and might sometimes even be impossible). It is important to notice this fact in the light of current trends in multi-agent system research, which tend to take the existence of precise utility functions for granted.

Before doing so, it is convenient to point to some characteristics that multi-agent TRYS has inherited from the TRYS philosophy. As in InTRYS, the agents of the TRYSA$_2$ system share the following characteristics:

- executability of local signal plans
  An agent generates a set of alternative local signal plans for its problem area. Each such plan is assured to be *internally consistent*. It is executable by itself and does not need to be "completed" by the enactment of any other plan. For instance, if traffic regulations require a certain control action to be performed in conjunction with others, then any local signal plan proposal that comprises this control action will also include the complementing actions.

- complete local expertise
  An agent is knowledgeable respecting all problems or classes of problems that may occur in its area, and knows about the possible signal plans to influence the traffic flows of this area. This includes plans using control devices that are located outside the agent's problem area.

The above points are design decisions that have been taken during the construction of InTRYS knowledge models, and that have proved to perform well so far. Of course, other approaches are also possible. For instance, agents may generate incomplete (non-executable) local signal plans, which need to be complemented by the signal plans of others before they can be enacted. Another design option is to accept knowledge dependencies between agents: a certain agent may not know how to deviate traffic from its local problem area, but a neighbouring acquaintance potentially does and can "help it out". Still, in the following we discard these options and stick to the above paradigm. It is to be pointed out, however, that structural co-operation as a generic co-ordination model does not require these design decisions.

Figure 9.4 classifies the interrelations between local signal plans according to different criteria. The first concerns their desirability. The above design decisions imply that there are no *mitigating* interrelations: agents never need the help of others to enact their signal plans. From the perspective of the individual context, an agent is a self-sufficient stand-alone problem solver. It never welcomes but often dislikes the existence of others.

Therefore, all interrelations between signal plans are *compounding*, i.e. one proposal hinders or even cancels the effectiveness of another. The latter is the case of *physical* dependencies, which are present when different local signal plans need to access the same non-sharable resource. For instance, two proposals may include different messages to be displayed on the same VMS, or may intend to establish different contention levels for the same regulator. In terms of the plan relations discussed in Chapter 5, an *inconsistent* relation is present.

The second type of undesirable interrelations is *logical*. In contrast to the physical dependencies described above, which arise due to resource conflicts, the cause of logical interrelations lies in the effects of plans. Based on the different

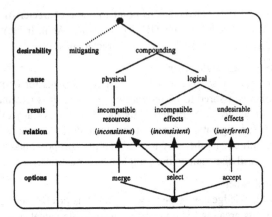

Figure 9.4. Relations between local signal plans

impacts or results, logical interrelations are classified in two groups: *incompatible effects* arise within a set of local signal plan proposals, when their joint effects are prohibitive, e.g. when some traffic regulation is violated. For example, it is not allowed to display contradictory messages concerning speed limits on neighbouring panels. As above, this constitutes an *inconsistent* relation.

Undesirable effects are present, when the outcome of a local signal plan undermines the effectiveness of another. For instance, consider an agent whose plan proposal deviates traffic flows, which originally contributed to the traffic demand in its local problem area, to a neighbouring area. This may aggravate a traffic problem in the neighbouring area, and thus have a negative impact on the effectiveness of the signal plan proposal of the responsible agent. In the terminology of Chapter 5, we are concerned with a *hinders* relation.

Figure 9.4 also depicts possible ways of dealing with plan interrelations. The most obvious option is to be *selective* with interrelated plans. This is equivalent to choosing one of them to be integrated in a global signal plan while discarding the other. Obviously, this co-ordination action is applicable to any of the above compounding plan relations.

The two other options are restricted to specific cases. If signal plans have undesirable effects, their coexistence is detrimental but not fatal. Thus, this type of plan relations can just be *accepted*. If physical conflicts refer to panel messages, there is the possibility of *merging* the conflicting messages. For instance, congestion warnings for the zones A and B, included in different local signal plans and to be displayed on the same VMS, can be merged into the message "Congestion at A and B" on that panel. The merged message will have the same local effect as the initial ones.

In the experimental TRYSA$_2$ system, just physical conflicts and logical conflicts due to incompatible effects are modelled explicitly. If applicable, the corresponding co-ordination actions *merge* and the *select* are considered in order to cope with the corresponding incompatibility between local signal plans.

Note that the reactive co-ordination setting of the TRYSA$_2$ is *stable* and *detached* in the sense of Chapter 7. On the one hand, the aforementioned determination to model explicitly only hard constraints (*inconsistent* relations) means that the *executability* of the agents' local signal plans can be influenced by the choices of the acquaintances. Still, the *utilities* of local signal plans *cannot* be affected by them, so the reactive co-ordination setting is detached. On the other hand, it is stable as the hard constraints are implied by general rules respecting the use of resources and thus do *not* change with the traffic situation.

9.3.2   Knowledge Model

This section describes the knowledge units used for co-ordination within TRYSA$_2$. In order to enact its social interaction strategy in the traffic control domain, a TRYSA$_2$ agent needs to be endowed with knowledge that provides the following services:

- *Normative* situation: the agent's normative layer requires a means of deducing the "legal status" of using control devices and enacting local signal plans.
- Signal plan *compatibility*: the agent's social layer needs to determine which individual signal plans are locally consistent with relevant portions of the current global signal plan.
- Interest in the *state of control devices*: the agent's social layer needs to know whom to inform about local plan changes.
- Degree of *social dependence* for local plans: the agent's social layer needs to determine the local disagreement plan.

The three knowledge units, that will be described in the sequel, fulfil this purpose. Examples of the corresponding knowledge bases can be found in Appendix B.

9.3.2.1 Plan Interrelations

The social layer is endowed with the *plan interrelation* KU, which expresses relationships between plans as well as possible ways of dealing with them. This knowledge is represented by rules, that obey to the following format:

$$[cdev_1, \dots, cdev_n] \quad \Rightarrow \quad [cdev_m, \dots, cdev_j] \qquad \text{or}$$
$$[cdev_1, \dots, cdev_n] \quad \Rightarrow \quad [nogood] \, .$$

The antecedent of such rules describes sets of states of control devices that imply an *incompatible* relation, if they are present together in a set of signal plans. The consequent expresses the result of co-ordination actions to overcome the undesirable plan relation. It can be either an alternative set of control device states, or the constant *nogood*.

The semantics of such a rule determines that the control device states of the antecedent can be substituted by those of consequent without important changes in the effectiveness of signal plans. There will be no significant change in the expected excess within the problem areas, if the control device states of the consequent are established instead of those of the antecedent. The constant *nogood* in the consequent indicates that there is no known way to overcome the inconsistent control device states of the antecedent.

The co-ordination action of merging divergent control device states into one is modelled easily. If the antecedent contains different states for the same device, then the consequent just needs to specify a new state for this device that corresponds to the "conjunction" of the states mentioned in the antecedent. Consider the case of VMS: a simple plan relation rule might determine that if a plan aims to set a message M on panel P and another intends to have P switched off, then these requirements can be synthesised by showing M at P without any repercussion in both plans' effectiveness. The selection co-ordination action needs to be applied when the *nogood* constant is present in the consequent. In this case, the result of applying the corresponding plan relation rule is that at least one of the signal plans involved must be withdrawn.

As mentioned above, in the experimental TRYSA$_2$ system we will not explicitly take care of logical plan interrelations that arise due to undesirable effects. Instead, in case of "severely" interfering plans, an additional rule is included in the plan interrelation KB. This rule deduces a *nogood*, and thus leads to the rejection of one of the interfering plans.

9.3.2.2 Agent Dependence

The above knowledge defines relations between *plans*. Still, the social layer lacks a possibility to account for social relations between *agents*, as there is no knowledge concerning which signal plans an acquaintance can enact or which sets of control devices it can use. Knowledge about such agent dependencies is crucial for the social interaction strategy: an agent needs to know with which acquaintances it can actually come into conflict, in order to guide its messages and to determine its bargaining position.

The *agent dependence* KU hosts this type of knowledge. It is represented by rules of the following format:

$$[cdev_1, \dots, cdev_n] \quad \Rightarrow \quad [\alpha_1, \dots, \alpha_m].$$

The above rule states that if the control device states $cdev_1$ to $cdev_n$ are established, then the agents α_1 to α_m are potentially affected by that fact. The agent that hosts the rule *depends on* any of the agents α_1 to α_m with respect to the control device states $cdev_1$ to $cdev_n$.

Note that these rules actually compile knowledge about the capabilities of an agent's acquaintances upon the background of potential plan interrelations. For instance, if agent α_i may set a message M_i on VMS P, and α_j is capable of establishing some incompatible control device state (say displaying a message M_j on the same panel which cannot be merged with M_i), then the knowledge base of α_i's dependence KU will contain a rule stating that setting M_i on VMS P concerns agent α_j. So, agent dependence rules do not explicitly state *what* plans others can enact, but that they are capable of doing *something* that might turn down the agent's local signal plans.

The KU serves two purposes, depending on whether it is used with forward or with backward inference:

- *Interest*: the dependence KB determines which acquaintances are interested in a change of the local signal plan. Setting out from the control device states of a new local signal plan as facts, these agents can be deduced by means of forward inference. Interested agents are informed about the corresponding changes in accordance with the social interaction strategy.

- *Dependence*: when using backward inference on the knowledge base, it is possible to determine the agents that can influence the possibility of enacting a local signal plan. If some acquaintance can be "proved" based on the control device states of a local signal plan by applying rules backwards, then the acquaintance is capable of turning down this local signal plan. As long as the agent is not permitted to enact that plan (which implies that the acquaintances are forbidden to influence it negatively), it cannot be used as local disagreement plan.

Note that the knowledge requirements of the agent dependence KU do not imply a knowledge acquisition overhead with respect to a centralised approach. The knowledge base of the agent dependence KU compiles expertise concerning the agents' action capabilities, which also needs to be present in a centralised system. The multi-agent TRYS approach just relies on a different and redundant representation of the same type of knowledge.

9.3.2.3 Norms

The normative layer requires expertise to determine the normative situation of the agent. The *norm* KU is in charge of hosting and enacting this knowledge.

In TRYSA$_2$, normative situations are rather stable over time, as they only need to be altered in case of important changes in the traffic situation. Such qualitative changes are reflected by variations of the traffic demand structure. So, normative situations are qualified temporally, in much the same way as historic traffic demands. In consequence, knowledge representation and reasoning of the *norm* KU are similar to the *historic demand* KU. The knowledge base of the norm KU is subdivided in two parts:

- temporal classification
  The current date and time is classified in terms of two categories: *type of day* and *type of season*. Values for the former are either *Working day, Sunday, Sat-*

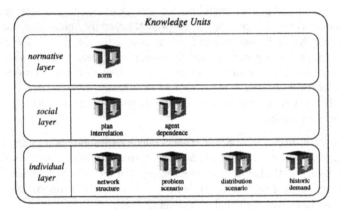

Figure 9.5. TRYSA$_2$ layer knowledge

urday or *Holiday*. Rules specify how the value *holiday* is derived. The category season may be instantiated to *Christmas*, *Easter*, *Summer*, or *Normal*. Again, the values are related to the current date and time by means of rules.

- normative structure
  As a function of the *type of day* and the *type of season*, a normative structure is defined by two categories: *prohibitions* and *permissions*. Each of these categories may be instantiated by a set of control device states.

Associated reasoning methods first classify the current date and time. Subsequently, the resulting temporal categories are matched against the normative patterns. Consequently, the historic demand KU enables the agent to infer its normative situation.

In the experimental TRYSA$_2$ system, normative imperatives are pertinent only to agents. Furthermore, agents are only aware of their own prohibitions and permissions. We assume the knowledge bases of the agents' norm KUs to be deontically consistent in the sense of Chapter 5. In particular, if one agent is allowed to establish certain control device states, all its acquaintances that might detriment their effectiveness are prohibited to enact the corresponding plans.

9.3.3 Reasoning

The reasoning process that TRYSA$_2$ agents perform with respect to co-ordination follows the lines that have been described for the ProsA$_2$ architecture in general in Chapter 7. Still, in this section we will revisit it in relation to the case study. Special emphasis is put on the role of the knowledge types, represented by KUs, which have been discussed above. Figure 9.5 resumes the knowledge that each layer of a TRYSA$_2$ agent is endowed with.

In Section 9.2.3 we have shown how the individual layer makes use of its KUs to deduce local signal plan proposals. The control loop of the normative layer operates as follows. First, the *norm* KU is activated to determine abstract temporal categories from the current date and time (e.g. working day, Sunday, holiday etc.). If the temporal context has changed, the set of current prohibitions and permissions is updated by matching the new temporal context against patterns of the norm KU. In a last step, the agent's information models are updated accordingly.

The social interaction strategy that the social layer supports employs its knowledge units as follows. In the first step, the information model is revised (in accordance with rules described in Chapter 7). For instance, if a *value* message from an agent has arrived, the corresponding acquaintance model is updated.

Subsequently, the set of local signal plans that are legal and consistent in the eyes of the social layer is determined. Within this process, the *plan relation* KU is used to determine if a local signal plan is compatible with the proposals of acquaintances with a higher "authority level" (see Chapter 7). If the constant *nogood* is deduced, the local signal plan is incompatible and does not constitute a local option. In case the *plan relation* KU comes up with a set of control device states, there is also a conflict with some high authority agent. Still, it can be overcome by updating the current local signal plan in accordance with the equivalent control device states that have been deduced.

In the last step of the control loop of the social layer, the agent restores model consistency. In line with the deliberation part of the social interaction strategy, the agent selects the local signal plan with highest utility value from its options. The self model is updated accordingly and the *agent dependence* KU is used to determine which agents should be informed about the change. If no alternative locally consistent signal plan has been found based on the current authority levels, *nogood* messages are sent to the involved agents and the pertinent model updates are performed as described in Chapter 7.

Finally, we will shortly illustrate how the control loops of the three layers of TRYSA$_2$ agents interact. Three classes of events may cause the activation of TRYSA$_2$ agents: the arrival of new traffic data, changes in the normative situation, or the reception of new messages from acquaintances. Each class typically gives rise to a certain sequence of activations of TRYSA$_2$ layers. These "typical" lines of reasoning of TRYSA$_2$ agents will be sketched in the sequel:

- arrival of new traffic data
  If new data about the current traffic state arrives, an agent's *individual* layer generates a set of local signal plans. The change in the problem-solving model triggers the social layer, which starts a social interaction process. Messages are sent and received in accordance with the social interaction strategy. In case the agent detects the end of this phase, it determines the solution to the associated bargaining scenario and informs its acquaintances about the outcome of the corresponding lottery.

- arrival of new messages

  If messages from an acquaintance have been received, the corresponding changes in the information model trigger the *social* layer. The layer reacts to this by restoring local consistency and sending the appropriate messages in line with the social interaction strategy. In case the agent receives a message from the "leading" agent informing it about the outcome of a lottery, the action subsystem is instructed to enact the corresponding local signal plan.

- change in the normative situation

  If the current temporal context has changed, the *normative* layer deduces the new normative situation. In case the social layer detects a change in the set of potential local signal plans or in the local disagreement plan, it initiates a social interaction process as above.

9.4 Implementation Issues

The TRYSA$_2$ system has been implemented experimentally on networked workstations. This section describes relevant aspects of this implementation. We first describe the way in which the traffic management knowledge of the InTRYS system has been reused. Subsequently, the arrangement of the processes that make up the TRYSA$_2$ environment is depicted. Finally, some issues concerning the object-oriented implementation of individual agents are outlined.

9.4.1   Knowledge Acquisition and Reuse

A fundamental design decision during the development of the TRYSA$_2$ system was to reuse the major part of the traffic management knowledge provided by InTRYS in order to limit design time and costs. This is justified by the fact that the main interest of applying ProsA$_2$ agents to traffic control lies in an evaluation of the mechanism of emergent co-ordination by structural co-operation, rather than in providing support for distributed knowledge acquisition.

The InTRYS traffic management system has been developed within the KSM (Knowledge Structure Manager) framework (Cuena and Molina 1997). KSM comprises a design methodology and a software tool for knowledge-based systems construction. As opposed to the traditional knowledge acquisition of prefixed representations, KSM understands the development of an application as a knowledge modelling activity. The KSM environment sees the specification of a knowledge system as a structured collection of knowledge areas, modelled by means of knowledge units (KU). As outlined above, KUs encapsulate knowledge representation schemes together with their inference procedures. Organised hierarchically, they constitute a structuring device for the knowledge of an expert system.

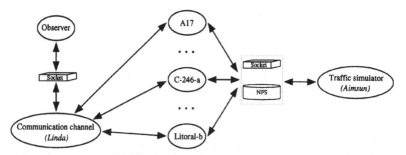

Figure 9.6. TRYSA$_2$ process arrangement

Due to technical reasons, it has been decided not to construct TRYSA$_2$ based on the KSM software environment, but to reuse knowledge bases and reasoning methods so as to integrate them in a separate system. The concept of knowledge units has greatly facilitated this reuse: neither the reasoning methods nor the knowledge bases have been modified significantly.

In addition, it has to be acknowledged that the acquisition and instrumentation of traffic control knowledge would have been far more difficult, if not impossible, without the use of methodologies and tools such as KSM. This is especially true for large-scale systems such as InTRYS.

9.4.2   Process Arrangement

The TRYSA$_2$ system has been implemented experimentally on a heterogeneous pool of UNIX workstations (Hewlett Packard, Sun), interconnected within a TCP/IP Local Area Network (LAN). It constitutes a distributed system, comprising a set of independently running processes. In particular, each TRYSA$_2$ agent constitutes a separate process. Ideally, all processes should run on different workstations for efficiency reasons, but limitations in the available hardware equipment may require that some of them share the same machine.

The TRYSA$_2$ agents have been implemented in an object-oriented extension of SICStus Prolog. This choice was driven by the fact that the relevant high-level functionalities of InTRYS traffic control agents as well as their KSM support were coded in that language. Despite an increased need for computational resources compared to procedural languages, logic programming in Prolog has greatly facilitated the implementation work. Figure 9.6 shows the distributed environment in which TRYSA$_2$ agents operate.

The Barcelona test site is simulated by the AIMSUN traffic simulator (Barceló et al. 1994)[3]. AIMSUN is endowed with a precise description of the traffic man-

---

[3] The AIMSUN traffic simulator has been developed within the Traffic Laboratory at the Statistics and Operations Research Department of the Technical University of Catalonia.

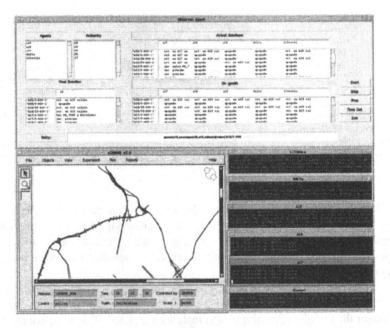

Figure 9.7. An example TRYSA₂ environment

agement infrastructure at the test site, including detailed models of the road network, the sensors and control devices etc. It performs microscopic ("car by car") simulation of traffic flows. AIMSUN constitutes a separate process within the environment. TRYSA₂ agents exchange information about traffic states and control actions with it by means of sockets and files within the network file system (NFS). The interface between TRYSA₂ agents and AIMSUN has partially been implemented in the C++ programming language.

Communication between agents is realised through the Linda tuple space (Carreiro and Gelernter 1989), which is supported by means of a dedicated *channel* process. Tuples of specific structure model a message queue for each agent on the Linda blackboard.

The standard Linda distribution of SICStus Prolog has been modified to notify each change on the blackboard to a specific socket. A special observer agent is connected to this socket, so as to keep track of the global system state. The observer agent is a separate process: it provides a Tcl/Tk-based graphical interface, showing global information such as the agents' presently chosen local signal plans, their current authority levels, active nogoods, tentative global signal plans etc. Figure 9.7 shows a snapshot of an example TRYSA₂ environment. The upper window corresponds to the observer agent.

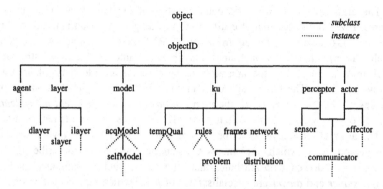

Figure 9.8. TRYSA₂ object diagram

9.4.3 Object Hierarchy

In the previous section, the implementation of the TRYSA₂ society of traffic agents and its environment has been outlined. A description of the components of the distributed system and their interaction has been given. We are now concerned with the internal implementation of TRYSA₂ agents.

TRYSA₂ agents are homogeneous not just in their architecture, but also in their implementation. About 90% of the code of each agent is written in Prolog, while the remaining part is given by C++ code. A huge portion of the software has been reused, especially the objects that implement the local problem-solving capabilities of the individual layer of TRYSA₂ agents, as well as the code that supports the knowledge units used at the remaining layers[4].

Figure 9.8 shows how the code of TRYSA₂ traffic agents is organised. It depicts the general class structure of ProsA₂ agents as well as the specific instances that TRYSA₂ traffic agents are made of. In the sequel, we will have a short look at the different classes, without going into details of coding.

The class *objectID* is a specialisation of the generic class *object*, which augments the original object system by some general-purpose features. It provides mechanisms for referencing objects through unique identifiers as well as specific methods for dynamically creating and deleting such objects.

Model is an abstract class that comprehends common features of the information models of ProsA₂ agents. An agent comprises several instances of the class *acqModel*, which hold information about the deontic and the problem-solving state. Just one instance of the class *selfModel*, a specialisation of *acqModel*, is present in each agent.

---

[4] The observer agent has been implemented from the scratch in Tcl/Tk.

The class *ku* contains generic characteristics of the knowledge units of the agents. Five knowledge units for different knowledge representation and reasoning methods have been reused from the InTRYS system: *tempQual* (temporal qualification), *rules*, *problem* frames, *distribution* frames and *network* structure. Each instance of such a specialisation of the class *ku* is endowed with its own knowledge base. The knowledge units in charge of social co-ordination are instances of *rules* and *tempQual*: the *plan relation* KU and the *agent dependence* KU are based on the former, while the *norm* KU is an instance of the latter class.

The abstract class *layer* describes common features of ProsA$_2$ layers. Besides the method *cycle*, which implements the generic control loop described previously, it is endowed with attributes that refer to self and acquaintance models. *Ilayer*, *slayer* and *dlayer* are specialisations of *layer* which represent the individual, deontic and social layer respectively: they redefine the methods that the generic control cycle activates in accordance with the knowledge units that the particular layer uses.

Perceptor and *actor* are abstract classes comprising basic characteristics of the action and perception capabilities of ProsA$_2$ agents, such as their names as well as enabling and disabling actions. *Sensor* and *effector* constitute specialisations of the above classes, which implement the interoperation with the AIMSUN traffic simulator. A *sensor* object notifies a relevant event when a corresponding AIMSUN message arrives at the socket. It acquires the corresponding percepts by reading simulation results from a file. An *effector* object acts upon the (simulated) environment by writing control device states into a file and informing AIMSUN about the modifications by means of socket messages.

The class *communicator* inherits the properties from both, *perceptor* and *actor*, as it allows for two-way communication with the agents' acquaintances: messages can both be sent and received. As mentioned in the previous section, communication channels are supported by the Linda tuple space. A *communicator* object notifies a relevant communication event, if a tuple of type "*queue(id, message)*" is present on the Linda blackboard (*id* is the agent's unique identifier). When *message* is read, the corresponding tuple is deleted. Messages are sent by asserting the corresponding *queue*-facts, instantiating the first element with the receiver's id.

9.5 Evaluation

The previous sections have outlined how structural co-operation has become operational for our real-world traffic management case. We have shown how the ProsA$_2$ agent architecture has been instantiated to this domain, so as to give rise to the experimental TRYSA$_2$ traffic management system, which is based on decentralised emergent co-ordination.

TRYSA$_2$ has been run with simulated data from the Barcelona test site. For this purpose, it has been connected to the AIMSUN simulator. Using scenarios based

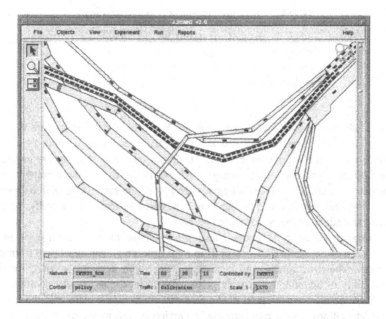

Figure 9.9. A simulated traffic problem

on a set of standard traffic demand patterns for simulation, the TRYSA$_2$ traffic agents co-ordinate adequately. Figure 9.9 shows a simulated traffic problem.

We conclude this chapter by contrasting centralised and distributed approaches to the design of traffic control systems. In particular, we will evaluate TRYSA$_2$ by comparing it to InTRYS, as both systems provide a similar functionality in the same application domain. We will first approach the topic with respect to the particular co-ordination policies of InTRYS and TRYSA$_2$. Subsequently, we focus on the knowledge requirements of both approaches. Finally, the co-ordination architectures of the systems are compared.

9.5.1   Co-ordination Policy

This section examines the co-ordination *methods* that InTRYS and TRYSA$_2$ use. The decentralised co-ordination method of TRYSA$_2$ based on the mechanism of structural co-operation has been discussed extensively throughout this book. The centralised policy of the InTRYS co-ordinator has been sketched in Chapter 8.

The first important difference between the co-ordination policies of both systems concerns *synchronisation* issues. The InTRYS co-ordinator enforces a synchronisation of agent activity during the co-ordination process. Every couple of minutes, it activates the InTRYS traffic agents by instructing them to produce

Table 9.1. Comparison concerning co-ordination policy

	InTRYS	TRYSA₂
synchronisation	−	+
incrementality	−	+
method complexity	+	−

sets of alternative local signal plans. The InTRYS co-ordinator waits until the last set of local proposals has arrived and then starts generating a coherent global signal plan. $TRYSA_2$ agents, by contrast, do not rely on a strict synchronisation mechanism. Synchronisation is easy to achieve in the case of the current implementation of InTRYS, where all agents are part of the same computational process. However, it will cause problems to centralised systems whose traffic agents are independent, spatially distributed processes.

Strongly related to the above question is the topic of *incrementality*. In each activation cycle, the InTRYS co-ordinator constructs a global signal plan from the scratch. The synchronous and centralised conception does not account for the possibility of *adapting* an existing global plan to local changes. By contrast, the $TRYSA_2$ policy "reuses" parts of the previous global signal plan: only the necessary adaptations are made incrementally. Obviously, this may considerably reduce the co-ordination overhead.

Concerning the *complexity* of the co-ordination policy, the InTRYS approach defeats the decentralised solution of $TRYSA_2$. In our case study, this is largely due to the fact that both methods apply different search paradigms. The InTRYS co-ordinator combines the locally most preferred signal plan from the set of each traffic agent's control proposals into a tentative global signal plan. The possibility of solving conflicts within this plan by merging control devices states is exploited exhaustively. If some conflict persists, the global plan is rejected and a new one is constructed by choosing alternative local signal plans for certain problem areas based on agent priority knowledge. Otherwise, the global signal plan constitutes the co-ordination outcome. Thus, InTRYS sticks to the first globally coherent solution it finds. By contrast, the social interaction strategy of structural co-operation implies an "exhaustive" search for Pareto-optimal signal plans (given that no time-out signals are sent and the number of signal plans to be searched for is not limited a priori). Although the search space is pruned by every solution that has been found, it is obviously more complex than the InTRYS policy.

In addition, it has to be acknowledged that even though both architectures used the same search method, a centralised algorithm would result less complex: all activities concerning termination detection and the coherent update of several redundant information models are not necessary in centralised implementations.

Table 9.1 recompiles the findings with respect to the co-ordination policy. A comment is necessary in order to avoid misinterpretations. It has to be pointed out that the positive results of the distributed $TRYSA_2$ approach concerning synchronisation and incrementality could also have been achieved in a centralised setting:

Table 9.2. Comparison concerning knowledge requirements

	authority (InTRYS)	autonomy (TRYSA₂)
plan relation	o	o
agent relation	–	o
scalability	–	+

there is no technical impediment for implementing an asynchronous incremental co-ordination regime within the frame of a central co-ordinator. Still, on a conceptual basis a distributed approach "calls for" an asynchronous incremental computation, while from a centralised perspective the InTRYS co-ordination approach appears more "natural".

9.5.2 Knowledge Requirements

From the standpoint taken in this book, one of the most interesting dimensions of comparison concerns the knowledge requirements of both systems. From a knowledge-oriented perspective, the complexity of knowledge acquisition for structural co-operation becomes the decisive factor of analysis. The criteria and the results of our analysis respecting knowledge requirements are compiled in Table 9.2.

Both co-ordination approaches rely on the same type of knowledge respecting signal *plan interrelations*. This is not surprising as these relations are implied by objective domain characteristics. Every system of cognitive agents has to consider them.

In the same way, both approaches are endowed with knowledge respecting *agent relations*, specifying how conflicts, that have been detected based on plan interrelation knowledge, should be managed. Still, the way of doing this is quite different. The "authoritarian" InTRYS approach relies on a knowledge base that deduces a priority ordering among agents for each specific situation. This priority knowledge may not be available (e.g. in the case study it could not be elicited from the experts) and thus needs to be constructed *ad hoc* at design time. The autonomous solution presented in this book, by contrast, lets conflict resolution emerge from agent interactions. The final decision about conflict resolution is given by the solution to the associated bargaining scenario and can be biased by the normative structure. So, the complexity of designing a priority ordering is to be related to the effort of designing adequate normative structures for TRYSA₂ agents. It is hard to draw general conclusions concerning this topic, as the result depends largely on the specific case under examination. Still, in quantitatively distributed problems such as our case study, where no problem area is permanently prevailing, the social co-ordination approach based on structural co-operation of autonomous agents is advantageous.

Table 9.3. Comparison concerning architecture

	centralised (InTRYS)	decentralised (TRYSA$_2$)
a priori distribution	o	+
communication	o	o
robustness	–	+
scalability	o	o

From a knowledge-centred point of view, its scalability is a major benefit of the TRYSA$_2$ approach. When introducing a new agent into the system, agents still need to be informed about its capabilities and, if the newcomer may enact previously unknown signal plans, the interrelation of these plans with existing control actions is to be added to the agents' knowledge bases. Still, the introduction of the new agent produces a shift in the social equilibrium, leading to a new basic co-ordination without any further modifications to the agents' knowledge. In the centralised approach, however, this effect can only be achieved by completely reconsidering the priority relations that the corresponding KU of the co-ordinator hosts.

9.5.3 Architecture

The last evaluation criterion refers to the system architectures. Table 9.3 provides an overview of the different items of the comparative analysis and compiles our findings.

The first topic concerns the potential of exploiting *a priori distribution*. In principle, the agent-based characteristic of both systems makes it possible to locate traffic agents physically in the areas that they control, thus reducing the amount of sensor data to be transferred to the TCC[5]. However, the decentralised TRYSA$_2$ approach provides the potential to adapt to additional requirements that an a priori distribution may imply. Consider, for instance, a traffic management organisation that comprises different control centres (e.g. belonging to different public organisms, such as municipal and provincial authorities). Although both system architectures allow for locating agents physically at the different centres, only the TRYSA$_2$ approach is feasible. The centralised co-ordination paradigm of InTRYS will hardly be accepted, as neither organism will give up its autonomy and be co-ordinated by the other.

The above point gives rise to an analysis in terms of *communication* requirements. In the InTRYS approach, the *amount* of messages exchanged is rather limited: the co-ordinator instructs all traffic agents to perform local problem solving, and receives the set of all alternative complete local signal plans from

---

[5] The current implementation of InTRYS, which comprises all traffic agents as well as the co-ordinator in the same computational process, would obviously need to be redesigned.

every agent. Obviously, during the social interaction process of TRYSA$_2$ much more messages are exchanged. Still, these messages usually refer to one single portion of a global signal plan, so that the information *volume* of the messages is generally less in TRYSA$_2$ compared to InTRYS. However, co-ordination in both systems is performed in terms of signal plan interrelations, i.e. at the same high level of abstraction. So, the amount of inter-agent communication for co-ordination turns out to be minimal compared to the data volume sent from sensors to agents. So, a potential communication overhead of one approach does not provide any decisive argument in favour of the other.

The next criterion of comparison is *robustness*. As we have already mentioned, this is a major weakness of the centralised approach. Even though the InTRYS traffic agents and the co-ordinator were not part of the same computational process but independently running entities on different machines, the co-ordinator agent would remain the *conceptual* bottleneck. Its breakdown always renders the whole centralised system useless. The TRYSA$_2$ approach, by contrast, allows the system to recover from the failure of an agent. This argument does not only rely on computational aspects of the TRYSA$_2$ implementation. Most important, it arises *conceptually* from the autonomy of the traffic agents with respect to traffic management in their local problem areas. The autonomous TRYSA$_2$ agents may even "welcome" the failure of an acquaintance as this neutralises a possible source of negative interference. Still, the "cost" of robustness is an increased degree of redundancy.

Scalability from an architectural point of view is also an interesting topic to examine. The introduction of a new agent into the InTRYS system requires modifications only in the co-ordinator and is thus restricted to one component of the system. While it is true that all TRYSA$_2$ agents need to be adapted when the system is scaled up, research in open systems has demonstrated that this can be done adequately by introductory protocols, i.e. without the need of "manual" modifications.

Still, neither the architectural nor the computational (i.e. the "method complexity") point of view is decisive in order to scale-up systems comprising a limited amount of complex cognitive agents. Within this context, the essential problem of scalability refers to the requirements of co-ordination knowledge, which has been identified as an important strength of the TRYSA$_2$ approach in the previous section. It has to be acknowledged, however, that both systems will run into difficulties when being scaled-up to "hundreds" of traffic agents.

10 Conclusions

This book is concluded by reconsidering the scientific aims stated in the introduction. First, the contributions of this work are summarised. Subsequently, limitations of our approach are discussed. Finally, we point to the new lines of work that we suggest to follow in the future.

10.1 Contributions

One of the major challenges of this book has been to outline how a nexus between theory and practice in multi-agent system research can be achieved. We have complied with this objective throughout the preceding chapters: the whole process from the development of a multi-agent theory to the design of multi-agent application has been covered.

This book has reported how notions rooted in sociology can be adapted and transferred to societies of *artificial* agents, how they can be used to build and formalise a co-ordination mechanism within these societies, and how this mechanism is integrated in an experimental multi-agent system for urban road traffic management. In consequence, the book has approached the field of artificial agent societies from a variety of different perspectives. In the sequel, we will analyse the contributions of this work from these different viewpoints.

The major *conceptual* contribution of the present work lies in the study of the functionality of social structure in societies of autonomous problem-solving agents. This is reflected in two major points:

- a model of social co-ordination
  Computational co-ordination models usually rely either on a central co-ordinator that orchestrates the actions taken within the agent society, or on the replication of such a centralised mechanism in many agents' "heads". In this book, a model of social co-ordination has been developed: agents neither follow the instructions of a central co-ordinator, nor are they directly concerned with the welfare (i.e. the "global goals") of society. For this purpose, the notion of the functionality of social structure has been transferred from the sociological school of structural functionalism to Distributed Artificial Intelligence. The original descriptive aim of the structural functionalist approach has been turned upside down, giving rise to the prescriptive mechanism of structural co-operation. This mechanism has been developed by referring to structural no-

tions among artificial agents: the concepts of dependence structure, normative structure and social structure have been defined and a model of their interrelation presented.

- a model of autonomous agenthood in problem-solving contexts
  Problem-solving agents are traditionally modelled as benevolent or totally determined by prescriptions. In the field of multi-agent systems, work on autonomous agent interaction is usually not concerned with the emergent attainment of complex tasks, and is frequently not appropriate for problem solving. In this book, behaviour rules for problem-solving agents have been developed whose autonomy is bounded by social structure. A model of autonomous agent behaviour in a social context has been developed and the biasing effect of normative prescriptions on norm-abiding agents has been modelled. This notion of bounded autonomy has been related to structural co-operation.

Both conceptual contributions together provide a socially grounded metaphor for studying co-ordination in multi-agent problem-solving systems.

From a *formal* perspective, the contribution of this work consists in a mathematical framework for describing and analysing structural co-operation as well as in an operational model of the mechanism. These aspects are summarised as follows:

- a formal model of autonomous agent interaction based on bargaining theory
  Game theory, and bargaining theory in particular, usually model interactions within heterogeneous groups of self-interested agents. In this book, bargaining theory has been applied to autonomous problem-solving agents. We have presented a mapping from a *qualitative* model, intended to capture structural properties of artificial agent societies in reactive domains, to a *quantitative* model of social co-ordination. By associating bargaining scenarios with reactive co-ordination problems, we have managed to present an appropriate model of the outcome of social interaction in such scenarios. It has been demonstrated that, due to its formal properties, the Nash bargaining solution constitutes a convenient model of the result of autonomous agent interaction processes in our problem-solving context. The role of the disagreement point within bargaining models has been related to the biasing function of normative structure in social co-ordination models.

- the design and analysis of a social interaction strategy
  Models of social interaction strategies for autonomous agents usually set out from individual agent behaviour and rarely present results about the properties of the resulting global processes. The interaction protocols used in the field of distributed problem solving assume benevolence, hence ignore local autonomy. In this book, we have presented a social interaction strategy and have shown that the strategy encounters the outcome of autonomous agent interaction within the framework of structural co-operation. An asynchronous multi-stage algorithm based on distributed constraint optimisation has been devised. If fol-

lowed by all problem-solving agents, the corresponding local interaction strategies converge on the desired bargaining solution. Results about soundness and completeness as well as complexity considerations have been presented.

The above formal models go in line with the conceptual contributions mentioned above: social co-ordination by structural co-operation is expressed within bargaining theory, while the social interaction strategy provides a formal and operational model of the outcome of autonomous agent behaviour in a multi-agent problem-solving context.

The third part of this book comprises its *practical* contributions. They are essentially twofold:

- the ProsA$_2$ architecture
  Many agent architectures, in particular those aiming at autonomous agents, rely on layered architectures. Layering principles are usually functional or conceptual. In this book, the ProsA$_2$ layered agent architecture has been developed that is based on a *contextual* layering principle. The architecture comprises three layers that analyse a world model from three perspectives. These perspectives correspond to the different contexts within which structural co-operation unfolds. Contextual layering provides guidelines for the design of societies of autonomous problem-solving agents.

- the TRYSA$_2$ traffic management system
  Intelligent traffic management systems rarely support decisions at the strategic level. The InTRYS traffic management system, and the TRYS family of control systems in general, provide this support, but rely on a centralised control and co-ordination regime. In this book, InTRYS has been extended by our decentralised and social co-ordination mechanism, giving rise to the experimental TRYSA$_2$ traffic control system. TRYSA$_2$ applies the ProsA$_2$ agent architecture to the task of urban road traffic management in a real-world motorway network. It has been shown that structural co-operation is appropriate for this problem. A comparative analysis of both traffic management systems and their co-ordination architectures has been presented.

The ProsA$_2$ architecture and the instrumentation of structural co-operation within the TRYSA$_2$ traffic management system has shown that it is not just possible, but also advantageous to integrate aspects of autonomous agents, multi-agent systems and distributed problem solving, so as to build an operational framework of societies of autonomous problem-solving agents.

10.2 Limitations

There are assumptions intrinsic to the approach taken in this book that put limits to its applicability. Two topics deserve special consideration.

Structural co-operation, its formal model within bargaining theory as well as the social interaction strategy have been developed with respect to reactive co-ordination settings. Consequently, they have inherited the *reactivity assumption* of the domain, which gives rise to two major limitations.

Firstly, our model of structural co-operation relies on knowledge that defines a quantitative notion of "distance" to ideal states. On this basis, it has been possible to define a "utility" function. In some domains, however, it is hard to establish such quantitative measures with enough precision: the understanding of the domain might not be deep enough so as to map differences between world states accurately to numbers.

Secondly, the reactivity paradigm does not account for reconsidering plan choice during execution. This is not crucial in domains where complex plans can be generated incrementally, i.e. in a reactive fashion. Still, some domains intrinsically contain constraints that require non-reactive, strategic planning approaches. However, once plans are generated for larger time periods, their reassessment and re-coordination will be necessary. The extension of structural co-operation to such scenarios seems possible but is not straightforward.

Another important assumption underlying the present work is the hypothesis of *correlation between social and functional equilibrium*. Structural co-operation aims at providing a basic level of co-ordination, which corresponds to the social equilibrium among agents. This social equilibrium is determined by the agents' interests and their degree of autonomy, i.e. by the social structure and the corresponding bargaining scenario. The underlying idea is that agents are mutually dependent and that their social strength is similar in consequence. Still, the resulting "fair" solution needs to be close to the agreement that ensures effective co-ordination. If the best global co-ordination is usually achieved when one agent imposes its interest in a dictatorial fashion, the compromise that a social co-ordination model converges upon does not provide any benefit. The utility of structural co-operation is tied to domains where the social equilibrium correlates with the functional equilibrium that the co-ordination objective implies.

10.3 Future Work

Besides the results presented in the previous sections, this work has given rise to a variety of questions to be investigated. So, it does not surprise that there are prospective lines of research, that refer to almost every perspective taken in this book. Some of them will be described in the sequel.

In order to provide a formal and operational model of structural co-operation, in the book we have joined qualitative and quantitative approaches to social co-ordination. The former has been used to capture structural properties of agent societies, while the latter has been applied to determine the outcome of the dynamics of social co-ordination. Still, the last section has outlined that it is sometimes hard to come up with accurate quantitative measures in a variety of domains. So, a major research topic is to specify structural co-operation within a framework that relies completely on qualitative relationships in society, and that in addition provides an adequate model of the process and/or the outcome of social interaction. It has to be investigated as to how far the domain description for reactive co-ordination problems needs to be augmented with qualitative notions of the agents' preferences in order to refrain from the quantitative measure of distance between states.

With respect to the current instrumentation of structural co-operation, two topics are worth mentioning. The first refers to the social interaction strategy. The complexity of modelling the social interaction process as a distributed constraint optimisation is acceptable for agent systems comprising a limited number of complex, cognitive agents. Still, it is computationally prohibitive for large-scale agent societies. Therefore, it needs to be investigated as to how far decentralised social interaction processes and strategies can be developed that determine the solution to the bargaining scenario associated with the outcome of structural co-operation, but at the same time follow an *incremental* search regime.

A second line of work respecting the instrumentation of structural co-operation concerns the *integration of conflict detection and conflict resolution*. In relation to the complexity issues discussed above, the question arises as to whether the clear distinction between the detection of interrelations between individual plans and the decision about their management should be overcome. Especially in cases where there are many alternative individual plans it seems beneficial to use knowledge concerning the decision strategy already in the plan generation phase, so as to guide plan construction and filter out plans that will most probably be rejected during the co-ordination process.

Besides traffic management, it is interesting to study the *application* of structural co-operation to other types of problem domains, especially to *qualitatively distributed problems*. The traffic management scenario that has been described in this work is based on quantitative problem decomposition and does not provide positive interrelations between the agents' plans. Still, structural co-operation is also applicable to qualitatively distributed tasks, where agents play different functional roles within a common process, and helping behaviour becomes an important aspect of co-ordination. The domain of intelligent workflow management provides these characteristics. Some preliminary steps for the application of structural co-operation to intelligent workflow management have been made (Ossowski and García-Serrano 1996).

Finally, some thought should be given to a general and quite ambitious topic: what design methodologies and tools are necessary, in order that societies of autonomous problem-solving agents become a widely accepted paradigm for multi-agent application design? This book has focused on the operational aspect of social co-ordination. An operational model of co-ordination among autonomous problem-solving agents has been presented. For a particular case study in the domain of road traffic management, we have studied which type of co-ordination knowledge is necessary and how this knowledge can be used to achieve co-ordination among autonomous traffic control agents. In addition, a model of local problem solving for the case study has been presented. In general, however, we have abstracted from local problem solving and have assumed individual plans, preferences etc. to be given a priori. Most important, we have not tackled the many questions that arise in relation to knowledge acquisition and modelling already in the initial stages of (multi-agent) application design.

Therefore, maybe one of the most intricating lines of future work consists in the development of methodologies and tools that render support to all stages of multi-agent system design. In this book, we just have scratched the surface of the question by sketching some simple design guidelines. However, it is essential to make progress in this direction: only if the design of artificial agent societies stops giving the impression of a "black art", and moves towards a principled engineering process, the current success of agent technology can be consolidated.

Appendix

A. Proofs

This appendix comprises the proofs of theorems presented in the main text, maintaining their original numbering.

Theorem 6.1. Let $(S, \vec{d}\,)$ describe the *bargaining scenario* associated with a reactive co-ordination setting R. The only vector $\vec{\varphi}$ that complies with the Nash axioms N_1 to N_5 maximises the function

$$N(\vec{x}) = \prod_{i=1}^{n}(x_i - d_i) .$$

Proof. The theorem has been proven by Nash for bargaining problems in general. A simple, intuitive proof of his theorem for the two-agent case (i.e. $S \subseteq \Re^2$) is given by Thomson (1994). A detailed proof for the general case can be found in (Jones 1980). ❑

Theorem 7.1. Suppose a reactive co-ordination setting, where all agents apply the social interaction strategy. The following holds: after finite time Stage 1 terminates and the leader is endowed with a superset of all undominated, legally enactable multi-plans.

Proof. In order to prove Theorem 7.1 we will rely on three lemmas.

Lemma 1. Suppose a reactive co-ordination setting, where all agents apply the social interaction strategy. The following holds: if all agent processes are quiescent, then the agents' local values comprise a legally enactable multi-plan.

Proof. We first show that when an agent process is quiescent, its current value is locally consistent. This follows almost directly from the construction of agent programs. The options of an agent are given by those plans that comply with all constraints with higher priority agents, and the agent always chooses the option with highest local utility as its current individual plan.

Therefore, the assumption of the lemma implies that all agents are locally consistent. Now, we show by contradiction that under this assumption no constraint is violated. Suppose the opposite case. Hence, there is always one agent with lowest authority in the constraint and this agent is not locally consistent, which contradicts the assumption. So, the agents' values are globally consistent, which is a synonym for a legally enactable multi-plan. ❑

Corollary. Given that the agents set out from an undominated multi-plan, in a detached reactive co-ordination setting, the above multi-plan is also undominated.

Proof. It needs to be shown that in the multi-plan of Lemma 1 no agent can be better off without some other being worse. The highest priority agent always sets its most preferred plan, so cannot be better off. Suppose that any other agent α switches to a locally more preferred local plan. This implies that some constraint with a higher priority agent α' is violated. So, when α switches to a more preferred plan, α' cannot maintain its current value. Still, as in a detached reactive co-ordination setting there are no weak constraints, all values of α' that are consistent with the new value of α are necessarily worse for it. $\square$

Lemma 2. Suppose a reactive co-ordination setting, where all agents apply the social interaction strategy. The following holds: if all agent processes are quiescent, then this is detected by the leader agent.

Proof. The solution detection mechanism defines a degenerated tree among agents, where the leader agent is the root and all other agents are leaves. The Dijkstra-Scholten termination detection algorithm assures that a stable state is detected by the root node of such a tree. The lemma follows, in consequence, by the correctness of Dijkstra-Scholten termination detection. Proofs can be found in Ben-Ari (1990) and Dijkstra et al. (1980). $\square$

Lemma 3. Suppose a reactive co-ordination setting, where all agents apply the social interaction strategy. The following holds: either all agents become quiescent after finite time, or Stage 1 terminates.

Proof. First, we notice that every time that an agent changes its authority level, it generates a new nogood. Nogoods are only generated once. As the number of possible nogoods is limited by the finite number of multi-plans, the authority level remains constant after a finite number of changes.

It remains to be shown that from any situation characterised by some fixed total ordering of agents all agents eventually become quiescent, or termination of Stage 1 is detected. We provide a proof based on the ideas presented for asynchronous backtracking by Yokoo et al. (1992). It is based on induction over natural numbers k. Let us map the highest authority level to 1 and increment k for each agent while descending the total order that authority levels imply.

"$k=1$": As authority levels are assumed to be stable, the only situation for the highest authority agent to change values is given when it receives *nogood* messages from agents with less priority. If it has no possible value left, termination of Stage 1 is detected, otherwise it changes its current value. Still, this can only happen a finite number of times, as the number of potential nogoods is bounded. So, after some time, no more *nogood* messages arrive and the agent is continuously quiescent.

"$k-1{\rightarrow}k$": We assume that from time t on all agents with tag less than k are quiescent. Suppose that the agent tagged k is quiescent. As agents with lower tag do not change values by assumption, the argumentation of the base case applies: the only situation in which the agent becomes engaged is when *nogood* messages of agents with tag bigger than k arrive. This can only happen a limited number of times. So, from time $t'>t$ on, the agent is quiescent and neither receives *value* messages from higher priority agents by assumption, nor *nogood* messages from lower priority agents. ❑

We now proceed with the proof of Theorem 7.1. Lemma 3 ensures that either all agents eventually become quiescent or Stage 1 terminates after finite time. Lemma 2 tells us that this is detected by the leader agent. By Lemma 1, we can conclude that when this happens a legally enactable multi-plan has been found. So, if there exists a legally enactable multi-plan, it is found by the leader agent. Otherwise, Stage 1 is terminated. It remains to be shown that all undominated, legally enactable multi-plans are found in finite time.

When the leader agent detects a solution in a scenario S, it converts the current multi-plan into a solution constraint and "restarts" the algorithm. The new scenario S' is the same as S, except that the solution multi-plan, and in a detached setting also some of the multi-plans dominated by it, are excluded. This means in particular that either the detected solution constitutes an undominated, legally enactable multi-plan, or the set of undominated, legally enactable multi-plans in S and S' are the same. The above argument assures that also a solution to the reduced problem S' is detected. This gives rise to a sequence of problem scenarios of decreasing size, in the course of which all undominated, legally enactable multi-plans are eventually found by the leader. This sequence is bounded, as the number of legally enactable multi-plans is bounded. So, in finite time, a problem without solution is found. Consequently, Stage 1 terminates and the leader is endowed with a superset of all undominated, legally enactable multi-plans. ❑

Corollary. Given that the agents set out from an undominated multi-plan, in a *detached* reactive co-ordination setting, the leader hosts precisely the set of undominated, legally enactable multi-plans.

Proof. This follows directly from the corollary to Lemma 1, i.e. from the fact that when all agents are quiescent, in a detached reactive co-ordination setting an undominated, legally enactable multi-plan has been found.

Theorem 7.2. Suppose a reactive co-ordination setting, where all agents apply the social interaction strategy. The following holds: if Stage 2 is sound and complete, then the social interaction process is sound and complete with respect to the Nash solution.

Proof. It has to be shown that the social interaction process converges on the Nash solution. After finite time, Stage 1 returns a variable *UndominatedMPs*, which according to Theorem 7.1 contains all undominated, legally enactable multi-plans. The convex and comprehensive hull $cch\{UndominatedMPs\}$ of this set is a superset of the Pareto-surface. As Axiom N_2 (Pareto optimality) assures that the solution is located within the Pareto-surface, it is also located in $cch\{UndominatedMPs\}$. By Axiom N_5 (contraction independence) we get that a product-maximising vector of $(cch\{UndominatedMPs\}, \bar{d})$ coincides with the bargaining solution of the overall problem $(S, \bar{d})$. ❑

B. Examples of Knowledge Bases

B.1. A Specific Frame within the Problem Scenario KB

```
#---------------------------------------------------------------
# MARCO retenciones en A19 Mataro en salidas a Ronda Litoral
#---------------------------------------------------------------

DESCRIPCION

(A19 Mataro en Rambla Prim)
  velocidad= [media, baja]   [a],
  ocupacion= media           [b],
(A19 Mataro PK_3000)
  velocidad= [baja, media]   [c],
  ocupacion= [media, alta]   [d],
(A19 Mataro PK_3400)
  velocidad= [media, baja]   [e],
  ocupacion= [media, alta]   [f],
(A19 Mataro salida a Ronda Litoral direccion Llobregat)
  saturacion= [media, alta]  [g],
(A19 Mataro PK_3700)
  velocidad= baja            [h],
  ocupacion= [media, alta]   [i],
(A19 Mataro salida a Ronda Litoral direccion Trinidad)
  saturacion= [media, alta] [j],
(A19 Mataro PK_4000)
  velocidad= [media, baja]   [k],
  ocupacion= media           [l],

(seccion critica)
  localizacion= A19 Mataro PK_3700,
  estado= desbordamiento,
  categoria= problema,
  exceso= expresion(
              capacidad(A19 Mataro PK_3700) -
              capacidad(A19 Mataro salida a Ronda Litoral
                    direccion Trinidad) -
                  intensidad(A19 Mataro PK_4000)),
  itinerarios= {
    de Glories a Badalona por la A19            [15, 30],
    de Glories a Mataro por la A19              [35, 70],
    de Glories a  Ronda Litoral sentido Llobregat [15, 35] },


RELEVANCIA DE CARACTERISTICAS
a,c,e,g,h,j,k -> 90%.
b,d,f,g,i,j,l -> 90%.
(a;b),(c;d),(e;f),g,(h;i),j,(k;l) -> 100%.
```

B.2. A Generic Frame within the Problem Scenario KB

```
#-----------------------------------------------------------------
#
#  --\----\-  salida                      --/----/- entrada
#    \ o  \   sat = alta                  / oo / vel = baja,
#     \ o  \                              / oo /  ocu = alta,
#      \ o  \----\                        /----/ oo /
#       \ o o o \                         / ooooooo /
#---|---------- oo \--------------/oo ----------------|-----
#o  |o o o o o  o o ooooooooooooooo oooooooooooooooooo|ooooo
#---|------------------------------------------------|-----
# o |o o o o  o o o ooooooooooooooooooooooooooooooooo|ooooo
#---|------------------------------------------------|-----
# posterior                                 anterior
# vel = alta              <---              vel = baja
# ocu = baja                                ocu = alta
#
#-----------------------------------------------------------------
```

MARCO retencion por falta de capacidad en rampa de salida en
       zona de trenzado

DEFINICION
(<trenzado>)
   tipo = trenzado,
   seccion posterior = <posterior>,
   seccion anterior = <anterior>,
   seccion en rampa de entrada = <entrada>,
   seccion en rampa de salida = <salida>,

DESCRIPCION
(<anterior>)
   velocidad = baja [a],
   ocupacion = alta [b],
(<entrada>)
   velocidad = baja [c],
   ocupacion = alta [d],
(<salida>)
   saturacion = alta [e],
(<posterior>)
   velocidad= alta [f],
   ocupacion= baja [g],
(seccion critica)
   localizacion = <salida>,
   exceso = expresion(demanda(<salida>) - capacidad(<salida>)),
   estado = desbordamiento,
   categoria = problema,

RELEVANCIA DE CARACTERISTICAS
(a;b),(c;d),e,(f;g) -> 100%.
(a;b),e,(f;g) -> 90%.

B.3. A Frame within the Traffic Distribution Scenario KB

```
#-----------------------------------------------------------------
# MARCO DE USO DE ITINERARIOS aviso amplio de retencion en
#                                 avenida Meridiana
# TIPO uso de A17 entrada
#-----------------------------------------------------------------
```

SECCION DE ESTADO DE DISPOSITIVOS DE CONTROL

```
('A17/5-PIV-1')
   estado = retenciones en Meridiana
('A18/1-PIV-2')
   estado = retenciones en Meridiana
('A18/3-PIV-1')
   estado = retenciones en Meridiana
```

SECCION DE USO DE ITINERARIOS

```
(Girona -> Meridiana)
   [15,30] de Girona al area de Meridiana por las rondas,
   [70,85] de Girona al area de Meridiana por el desvio
(A18 -> Meridiana)
   [20,35] de A18 al area de Meridiana por las rondas,
   [65,80] de A18 al area de Meridiana por el desvio
```

SECCION DE ESTADO DE CIRCULACION

```
(A17 Barcelona del peaje al PK_8700)
   estado = libre
(A17 Barcelona de Asland al PK_7000)
   estado = libre
(A17 Barcelona de confluencia con A18 a Meridiana)
   causa = desbordado
(A17 Barcelona incorporacion desde A18)
   estado = libre
```

B.4. A Pattern within the Historic Demand KB

```
#================================================================
# ESTRUCTURA DE DEMANDA DE LA A2 DESDE MARTORELL A LITORAL
#================================================================


#----------------------------------------------------------------
# CLASIFICACION DE TIPOS DE DIA
#----------------------------------------------------------------

situacion en la semana {festivo, laboral, sabado}:
  DIA domingo -> festivo
 (FECHA 1/enero,      FECHA 6/enero,      FECHA 5/abril,
  FECHA 1/mayo,       FECHA 15/agosto,    FECHA 12/octubre,
  FECHA 1/noviembre, FECHA 6/diciembre, FECHA 8/diciembre,
  FECHA 25/diciembre) -> festivo
 (FECHA 8/abril,      FECHA 24/junio,
  FECHA 8/septiembre,FECHA 26/diciembre) -> festivo
 (FECHA 27/mayo,      FECHA 24/septiembre) -> festivo
 (DIA lunes, DIA martes, DIA miercoles, DIA jueves,
    DIA viernes) -> laboral
  DIA sabado -> sabado,

temporada {navidad, semana santa, verano, normal}:
  DESDE FECHA 22/diciembre HASTA FECHA 6/enero -> navidad
  DESDE FECHA 4/abril/1996 HASTA FECHA 7/abril/1996
      -> semana santa
  DESDE FECHA 1/julio HASTA FECHA 31/agosto -> verano
  resto -> normal.


#----------------------------------------------------------------
# PATRONES DE DEMANDA
#----------------------------------------------------------------

PATRON jornada laboral TIPO general:
  situacion en la semana: laboral,
  Martorell -> B30:          500 veh/h,
  Martorell -> Molins:       500 veh/h,
  Martorell -> Barcelona:   1500 veh/h,
  B30 -> Molins:             500 veh/h,
  B30 -> Barcelona:         1000 veh/h,
  Molins -> Barcelona:       500 veh/h.

PATRON sabado TIPO general:
  situacion en la semana: sabado,
  Martorell -> B30:          500 veh/h,
  Martorell -> Molins:       500 veh/h,
  Martorell -> Barcelona:   1500 veh/h,
  B30 -> Molins:             500 veh/h,
  B30 -> Barcelona:         1000 veh/h,
  Molins -> Barcelona:       500 veh/h.
```

A Pattern within the Historic Demand KB (continued)

```
PATRON festivo TIPO general:
  situacion en la semana: festivo,
  Martorell -> B30:                0 veh/h,
  Martorell -> Molins:             0 veh/h,
  Martorell -> Barcelona:       1000 veh/h,
  B30 -> Molins:                   0 veh/h,
  B30 -> Barcelona:             1000 veh/h,
  Molins -> Barcelona:             0 veh/h.

PATRON noche de jornada laboral TIPO jornada laboral:
  tramo horario: 21:30 - 6:30,
  Martorell -> B30:                0 veh/h,
  Martorell -> Molins:             0 veh/h,
  Martorell -> Barcelona:          0 veh/h,
  B30 -> Molins:                   0 veh/h,
  B30 -> Barcelona:                0 veh/h,
  Molins -> Barcelona:             0 veh/h.

PATRON entrada trabajo TIPO jornada laboral:
  tramo horario: 6:30 - 9:30,
  Martorell -> B30:             1000 veh/h,
  Martorell -> Molins:          1000 veh/h,
  Martorell -> Barcelona:       4000 veh/h,
  B30 -> Molins:                 500 veh/h,
  B30 -> Barcelona:             3000 veh/h,
  Molins -> Barcelona:          1000 veh/h.

PATRON entrada trabajo en sabado TIPO sabado:
  tramo horario: 6:30 - 9:30,
  Martorell -> B30:              500 veh/h,
  Martorell -> Molins:           500 veh/h,
  Martorell -> Barcelona:       3500 veh/h,
  B30 -> Molins:                 500 veh/h,
  B30 -> Barcelona:             2500 veh/h,
  Molins -> Barcelona:           500 veh/h.

PATRON vuelta de fin de semana TIPO domingo:
  tramo horario: 18:30 - 21:30,
  Martorell -> B30:                0 veh/h,
  Martorell -> Molins:             0 veh/h,
  Martorell -> Barcelona:       3500 veh/h,
  B30 -> Molins:                   0 veh/h,
  B30 -> Barcelona:             2500 veh/h,
  Molins -> Barcelona:             0 veh/h.

PATRON noche de festivo TIPO festivo:
  tramo horario: 21:30 - 21:30,
  Martorell -> B30:                0 veh/h,
  Martorell -> Molins:             0 veh/h,
  Martorell -> Barcelona:          0 veh/h,
  B30 -> Molins:                   0 veh/h,
  B30 -> Barcelona:                0 veh/h,
  Molins -> Barcelona:             0 veh/h.
```

B.5.   A Pattern within the Norm KB

```
#================================================================
# NORMAS DE LA A17
#================================================================


#----------------------------------------------------------------
# CLASIFICACION DE TIPOS DE DIA
#----------------------------------------------------------------

situacion en la semana {festivo, laboral, sabado, domingo}:
  DIA domingo -> festivo
 (FECHA 1/enero,     FECHA 6/enero,     FECHA 5/abril,
  FECHA 1/mayo,      FECHA 15/agosto,   FECHA 12/octubre,
  FECHA 1/noviembre, FECHA 6/diciembre, FECHA 8/diciembre,
  FECHA 25/diciembre) -> festivo
 (FECHA 8/abril,     FECHA 24/junio,
  FECHA 8/septiembre,FECHA 26/diciembre) -> festivo
 (FECHA 27/mayo,     FECHA 24/septiembre) -> festivo
 (DIA lunes, DIA martes, DIA miercoles, DIA jueves, DIA viernes)
            -> laboral
  DIA sabado -> sabado
  DIA domingo -> domingo,

temporada {navidad, semana santa, verano, normal}:
  DESDE FECHA 22/diciembre HASTA FECHA 6/enero -> navidad
  DESDE FECHA 4/abril/1996 HASTA FECHA 7/abril/1996 -> semana
santa
  DESDE FECHA 1/julio HASTA FECHA 31/agosto -> verano
  resto -> normal.


#----------------------------------------------------------------
# PATRONES DE IMPERATIVOS
#----------------------------------------------------------------

PATRON jornada laboral TIPO general:
  situacion en la semana: laboral,
  PERMISOS:      {}
  PROHIBICIONES: {}

PATRON sabado TIPO general:
  situacion en la semana: sabado,
  PERMISOS:      {B20/3-PIV-1, B20/6-PIV-1}
  PROHIBICIONES: {A18/3-PIV-1, A17/1-PIV-1}

PATRON festivo TIPO general:
  situacion en la semana: festivo,
  PERMISOS:      {B10/58-PIV-1, B10/53-PIV-1}
  PROHIBICIONES: {}
```

B.6. Rules within the Plan Relation KB

```
#===================================================================
# RELACION DE PLANES RESPECTO A A17
#===================================================================

[(Dispositivo, estado, Mensaje1), (Dispositivo,estado,Mensaje2),
 prueba(no(Mensaje1 = apagado)), prueba(no(Mensaje2 = apagado)),
 prueba(no(Mensaje1 = Mensaje2))]
=> [nogood].

[(Dispositivo, estado, apagado), (Dispositivo, estado, Mensaje),
 prueba(no(Mensaje = apagado)) ]
=> [(Dispositivo, estado, Mensaje)].

[(Dispositivo, estado, 'incidente proximo'),
 (Dispositivo, estado, 'incidente a un km') ]
=> [(Dispositivo, estado, 'incidente proximo')].

[(Dispositivo, estado, 'incidente proximo'),
 (Dispositivo, estado, 'incidente a dos km') ]
=> [(Dispositivo, estado, 'incidente proximo')].

[(Dispositivo, estado, 'incidente proximo'),
 (Dispositivo, estado, 'incidente a tres km') ]
=> [(Dispositivo, estado, 'incidente proximo')].

[(Dispositivo, estado, 'precaucion retenciones'),
 (Dispositivo, estado, 'retenciones hasta Meridana') ]
=> [(Dispositivo, estado, 'precaucion retenciones')].

[(Dispositivo, estado, 'precaucion retenciones'),
 (Dispositivo, estado, 'retenciones en A17 entrada') ]
=> [(Dispositivo, estado, 'precaucion retenciones')].

[(Dispositivo, estado, 'precaucion retenciones'),
 (Dispositivo, estado, 'retenciones en A17 salida') ]
=> [(Dispositivo, estado, 'precaucion retenciones')].
```

B.7. Rules within the Agent Dependence KB

```
#===================================================================
# DEPENDENCIA DE AGENTES DE A17
#===================================================================
[('A17/1-PIV-1',estado,_)] => [a18].
[('A17/5-PIV-1',estado,_)] => [dalta].
[('A18/3-PIV-1',estado,_)] => [a18,dalta].
[('B10/58-PIV-1',estado,_)] => [a18,dalta,litorala].
[('B10/53-PIV-1',estado,_)] => [a19,litorala].
[('B10/58-PIV-4',estado,_)] => [litorala].
[('B20/3-PIV-1',estado,_)] => [a18,litorala].
[('B20/6-PIV-1',estado,_)] => [dalta].
```

References

Agre, P.; Chapman, D. (1987): Pengi — An Implementation of a Theory of Activity. Proc. Int. Joint Conf. on Artificial Intelligence (IJCAI-87), Morgan Kaufmann, pp. 268–272

Aitken, J.; Schmalhofer, F.; Shadbolt, N. (1995): A Knowledge Level Characterisation of Multi-Agent Systems. In: Wooldridge and Jennings 1995, pp. 179–190

Auman, R.; Hart, S. (1992): Handbook of Game Theory (Vol. 1). Elsevier

Auman, R.; Hart, S. (1994): Handbook of Game Theory (Vol. 2). Elsevier

Avouris, N. (1995): Co-operating Knowledge-Based Systems for Environmental Decision Support. Knowledge-Based Systems 8 (1), pp. 39–54

Axelrod, R. (1984): The Evolution of Co-operation. Basic Books

Barbuceanu, M.; Fox, S. (1996): The Design of a Co-ordination Language for Multi-Agent Systems. Pre-Proc. ECAI Workshop on Agent Theories, Architectures and Languages (ATAL-96), pp. 263–278

Barceló, J.; Ferrer, J.; Grau, R. (1994): AIMSUN2 and the GETRAM Simulation Environment. Proc. 13th EURO Conf.

Barr, Cohen, Feigenbaum (1989). Blackboard Model of Problem Solving. In: Barr et al. 1989, pp. 4–82

Barr, Cohen, Feigenbaum (eds.) (1989). Handbook of AI. Addison Wesley

Befu, H. (1980): Structural and Motivational Approaches to Social Exchange. In: Gergen et al. 1980, pp. 197–214

Bel, G.; Thierry, C. (1993): A Constraint-Based System for Multi-Site Co-ordination and Scheduling. Proc. IJCAI Workshop on Knowledge-Based Production Planning, Scheduling and Control, pp. 1–10

Ben-Ari, M. (1990): Principles of Concurrent and Distributed Programming. Prentice Hall

Bendor, J.; Mookherjee, D. (1990): Norms, Third-Party Sanctions and Co-operation. Journal of Law, Economics and Organisation 6 (1), pp. 33–63

Benjamins, R. (1993): Problem-Solving Methods for Diagnosis. PhD Thesis, Univ. of Amsterdam

Bernold (ed.) (1986): Expert Systems and Knowledge Engineering. Elsevier

Bicchieri, C. (1990): Norms of Co-operation. Ethics 100, pp. 838–861

Bielli, M.; Ambrosino, G.; Boero, M. (eds.) (1994). Artificial Intelligence Applications to Traffic Engineering. VSP

Binmore, K.; Osborne, M.; Rubinstein, A. (1992): Non-Cooperative Models of Bargaining. In: Auman and Hart 1992, pp. 179–225

Bond, A. (1989): The Co-operation of Experts in Engineering Design. In: Gasser and Huhns 1989, pp. 463–484

Bond, A.; Gasser, L. (1992): A Subject-Indexed Bibliography of Distributed Artificial Intelligence. IEEE Transactions on Systems, Man and Cybernetics 22 (6), pp. 1260–1281

Bond, A.; Gasser, L. (eds.) (1988): Readings in Distributed Artificial Intelligence. Morgan Kaufmann

Bowers J.; Benford (eds.) (1991): Studies in Computer Supported Co-operative Work. North Holland

Bowers, J.; Button, G.; Sharrok, W. (1995): Workflow from Within and Without. Proc. Europ. Conf. on Computer Supported Co-operative Work (ECSCW-95)

Boyd, R.; Richardson, P. (1992): Punishment Allows the Evolution of Co-operation (or Anything Else) in Sizeable Groups. Ethology and Sociobiology 13, pp. 171–192

Brainov, S. (1996): Altruistic Co-operation between Self-Interested Agents. Proc. Europ. Conf. on Artificial Intelligence (ECAI-96), Wiley & Sons, pp. 519–523

Bratman, M. (1987): Intentions, Plans, and Practical Reasoning. Harvard Univ. Press

Bretherton, R.; Bowen, G. (1990): Recent Enhancements to SCOOT — SCOOT Version 2.4. Proc. Int. Conf. on Road Traffic Control

Bretherton, R.; Hunt, P.; Robertson, D.; Winton, R. (1981): SCOOT — A Traffic Responsive Method of Co-ordinating Signals. TRRL Rep. LR1014

Breuker, J.; van de Velde, W. (1994): CommonKADS Library for Expertise Modelling. IOS Press

Briggs, W.; Cook, D. (1995): Flexible Social Laws. Proc. Int. Joint Conf. on Artificial Intelligence (IJCAI-95), Morgan Kaufmann, pp. 688—693

Brodie, M.; Mylopoulos, J.; Schmidt, J. (eds.) (1984): On Conceptual Modelling — Perspectives from Artificial Intelligence, Databases, and Programming. Springer

Brooks, R. (1986): Achieving Artificial Intelligence through Building Robots. MIT Tech. Rep. AI Memo 899

Brooks, R. (1995): Intelligence without Reason. In: Steels and Brooks 1995

Burkhard, H.-D. (1994): On Fair Controls in Multi-Agent Systems. Proc. Europ. Conf. on Artificial Intelligence (ECAI-94), Wiley & Sons, pp. 254–258

Campbell, J.; Cuena, J. (eds.) (1989): Perspectives in Artificial Intelligence (Vol. 1). Ellis Horwood

Camphuis, E.; Kraemer, H.; Puente, A.; Sánchez, V. (1988): Elementos de Ingeniería de Tráfico. Tech. Univ. of Madrid, ITSICCP

Carley, K.; Gasser, L. (1998): Computational Organisation Theory. In: Weiß and Sen 1998, pp. 299–330

Carreiro, N.; Gelernter, D. (1989): Linda in Context. Communications of the ACM 32 (4)

Castelfranchi, C. (1994): Guarantees for Autonomy in Cognitive Agent Architectures. In: Wooldridge and Jennings 1994, pp. 56–70

Castelfranchi, C. (1995): Commitments — From Individual Intentions to Groups and Organisations. Proc. Int. Conf. on Multi-Agent Systems (ICMAS-95), AAAI/MIT Press, pp. 41–48

Castelfranchi, C.; Conte, R. (1996): Distributed Artificial Intelligence and Social Science — Critical Issues. In: O'Hare and Jennings 1996, pp. 527–542

Casti, J. (1994): Co-operation — The Ghost in the Machinery of Evolution. In: Casti and Karlqvist 1994, pp. 63–88

Casti, J.; Karlqvist, A. (1994): Co-operation & Conflict in General Evolutionary Processes. Wiley & Sons

Castillo-Hern, L. (1988): On Distributed Artificial Intelligence. Knowledge Engineering Review 3, pp. 21–57

Chaib-Draa, B. (1995): Industrial Applications of Distributed AI. Communications of the ACM 38 (11), pp. 49–53

Chaib-Draa, H.; Moulin, B. (1992): Trends in Distributed Artificial Intelligence. Artificial Intelligence Review 6, pp. 35–66

Chandy, K.; Lamport, L. (1985): Distributed Snapshots — Determining Global States of Distributed Systems. ACM Transactions on Computer Systems 3 (1), pp. 63–75

Clancey, W. (1991): The Frame of Reference Problem in the Design of Intelligent Machines. In: VanLehn 1991, pp. 357–423

Clarke, A.; Smyth, M. (1993): A Co-operative Computer Based on the Principle of Human Co-operation. Int. Journal of Man-Machine Studies 38 (1), pp. 3–22

Clearwater, S. (ed.) (1995): Market-Based Control — A Paradigm for Distributed Resource Allocation. World Scientific

Cockburn, D.; Jennings, N. (1996): ARCHON — A Distributed Artificial Intelligence System for Industrial Applications. In: O'Hare and Jennings 1996, pp. 319–344

Cohen, P.; Levesque, H. (1990): Intention is Choice with Commitment. Artificial Intelligence 41, pp. 213–261

Cohen, P.; Morgan, J.; Pollack, M. (eds.) (1990): Intentions in Communication. MIT Press

Collin, Z.; Dechter, R.; Katz, S. (1991): On the Feasibility of Distributed Constraint Satisfaction. Proc. Int. Joint Conf. on Artificial Intelligence (IJCAI-91), Morgan Kaufmann, pp. 318–324

Connolly; Edmonds (eds.) (1994): CSCW and Artificial Intelligence. Springer

Conry, S.; Kuwabara, K.; Lesser, V.; Meyer, R. (1991): Multistage Negotiation for Distributed Constraint Satisfaction. IEEE Transactions on Systems, Man and Cybernetics 21 (6), pp. 1262–1476

Conte, R.; Castelfranchi, C. (1995): Cognitive and Social Action. UCL Press

Conte, R.; Gilbert, N. (1995): Computer Simulation for Social Theory. In: Gilbert et al. 1995, pp. 1–18

Corkhill, D. (1979): Hierarchical Planning in a Distributed Environment. Proc. Int. Joint Conf. on Artificial Intelligence (IJCAI-79), Morgan Kaufmann, pp. 168–175

Crowston, K. (1994): A Taxonomy of Organisational Processes and Co-ordination Mechanisms. Tech. Rep. 174, Centre of Co-ordination Science, MIT

Cuena, J. (ed.) (1993): Knowledge Oriented Software Design. North-Holland

Cuena, J.; García-Serrano, A. (1993): Intelligent Computer Support. In: Power 1993, pp. 72–102

Cuena, J.; Garrote, L.; Molina, M. (1992): Combining Simulation Models and Knowledge Bases for Real Time Flood Management. Proc. Conf. on Hydraulic Engineering Software (HydroSoft-92). Computational Mechanics Publications, Wessex Inst. of Tech.

Cuena, J.; Hernández, J.; Molina, M. (1995): Knowledge-Based Models for Adaptive Traffic Management Systems. Transportation Research 3 (5), pp. 311–337

Cuena, J.; Hernández, J.; Molina, M. (1996): An Intelligent Model for Road Traffic Management in the Motorway Network around Barcelona. Proc. IFIP World Congress, Chapman & Hall, pp. 173–180

Cuena, J.; Hernández, J.; Molina, M. (1996): Knowledge-Oriented Design of an Application for Real Time Traffic Management — The TRYS System. Proc. Europ. Conf. on Artificial Intelligence (ECAI-96), Wiley & Sons, pp. 217–245

Cuena, J.; Molina, M. (1997): KSM — An Environment for the Design of Structured Knowledge Models. In: Tzafestas 1997, pp. 308–312

Cuena, J.; Ossowski, S. (1998): Distributed Models for Decision Support. In: Weiß and Sen 1998, pp. 459–504

David, J.; Krivine, J.; Simmons, R. (eds.) (1993): Second Generation Expert Systems. Springer

Davidson, P. (1996): Autonomous Agents & the Concept of Concepts. Ph.D. Thesis, Lund Univ., Dpt. of Computer Science

Davis, R.; Smith, R. (1983): Negotiation as a Metaphor for Distributed Problem Solving. Artificial Intelligence 20, pp. 63–109

Decker, K. (1995): Environment Centred Analysis and Design of Co-ordination Mechanisms. Ph.D. Thesis, Univ. of Massachusetts, Computer Science Dpt.

Decker, K.; Lesser, V. (1992): Generalising Partial Global Planning. Int. Journal of Intelligent Co-operative Information Systems, pp. 319–346

Decker, K.; Lesser, V. (1995): Co-ordination Assistance for Mixed Human and Computer Agent Systems. Univ. of Massachusetts, Computer Science Tech. Rep. 95-31

Decker, K; Li, J. (1998): Co-ordinated Hospital Scheduling. Proc. Int. Conf. on Multi-Agent Systems (ICMAS-98), IEEE, pp. 104–111

Demazeau, Y. (1995): From Interactions to Collective Behaviour in Agent-Based Systems. Proc. Europ. Conf. on Cognitive Science

Demazeau, Y. (ed.) (1991): Decentralised A.I. 2. North Holland

Dennet, C. (1987): The Intentional Stance. Bradford Books/MIT Press

Dijkstra, E.; Scholten, C. (1980): Termination Detection for Diffusing Computations. Information Processing Letters 11 (1), pp. 1–4

Dolado, F. (ed.) (1997): Análisis de Sistemas Complejos. Ed. Univ. Deusto

Durfee, E. (1988): Co-ordination of Distributed Problem Solvers. Kluwer

Durfee, E. (1996): Planning in Distributed Artificial Intelligence. In: O'Hare and Jennings 1996, pp. 231–245

Durfee, E. (1998): Distributed Problem Solving and Planning. In: Weiß and Sen 1998, pp. 121–164

Durfee, E.; Gmytrasiewicz, P.; Rosenschein, J. (1994): The Utility of Embedded Communications — Toward the Emergence of Protocols. Proc. Int. Distributed Artificial Intelligence Workshop, pp. 94–104

Durfee, E.; Lesser, V. (1987): Using Partial Global Plans to Co-ordinate Distributed Problem Solvers. Proc. Int. Joint Conf. on Artificial Intelligence (IJCAI-87), Morgan Kaufmann, pp. 875–883

Durfee, E.; Lesser, V.; Corkill, D. (1991): Trends in Co-operative Distributed Problem Solving. Kluwer

Durfee, E.; Montgomery, T. (1993): Co-ordination as Distributed Search in a Hierarchical Behaviour Space. IEEE Trans. on Systems, Man and Cybernetics 21, pp. 1363–1378

Durfee, E.; Rosenschein, J. (1994): Distributed Problem Solving and Multi-Agent Systems — Comparisons and Examples. Proc. Int. Distributed Artificial Intelligence Workshop, pp. 94–104

Easterbrook, S. (ed.) (1993): CSCW — Co-operation or Conflict? . Springer

Easterbrook, S.; Beck, E.; Goodlet, J.; Plowman, L.; Sharples, M.; Wood, C. (1993): A Survey of Empirical Studies of Conflict. In: Easterbrook 1993, pp. 1–68

Edmonds, E.; Vandy, L.; Jones, R.; Soufi, B. (1994): Support for Collaborative Design — Agents and Emergence. Communications of the ACM 37 (7), pp. 41–46

Ephrati, E.; Pollack, M.; Ur, S. (1995): Deriving Multi-Agent Co-ordination through Filtering Strategies. Proc. Int. Joint Conf. on Artificial Intelligence (IJCAI-95), Morgan Kaufmann, pp. 679–685

Ephrati, E.; Rosenschein, J. (1993): Multi-Agent Planning as a Dynamic Search for Social Consensus. Proc. Int. Joint Conf. on Artificial Intelligence (IJCAI-93), Morgan Kaufmann, pp. 423–429

Erman, L.; Hayes-Roth, F.; Lesser, V.; Reddy, D. (1980): The Hearsay-II Speech-Understanding System — Integrating Knowledge to Resolve Uncertainty. Computing Surveys 12 (2), pp. 213–253

Etzioni, O. (1993): Intelligence without Robots — A Reply to Brooks. AI Magazine

Fenster, M.; Kraus, S.; Rosenschein, J. (1995): Co-ordination without Communication — Experimental Validation of Focal Point Techniques. Proc. Int. Conf. on Multi-Agent Systems (ICMAS-95), AAAI/MIT Press, pp. 102–108

Ferber, J. (1996): Reactive Distributed Artificial Intelligence — Principles and Applications. In: O'Hare and Jennings 1996, pp. 287–314

Ferguson, I. (1995): Integrated Control and Co-ordinated Behaviour — A Case for Agent Models. In: Wooldridge and Jennings 1995, pp. 203–218

Filippi, G.; Theureau, J. (1993): Analysing Co-operative Work in an Urban Traffic Control Room for the Design of a Co-ordination Support System. Proc. Europ. Conf. on Computer Supported Co-operative Work (ECSCW-93), pp. 171–186

Finin, T.; Fritzson, R. (1994): KQML — A Language and Protocol for Knowledge and Information Exchange. Proc. Int. Distributed Artificial Intelligence Workshop, pp. 126–136

Fischer, K.; Müller, J.; Pischel, M. (1996): AGenDA — A General Testbed for DAI Applications. In: O'Hare and Jennings 1996, pp. 401–427

Fischer, K.; Müller, J.; Pischel, M.; Schier, D. (1995): A Model for Co-operative Transportation Scheduling. Proc. Int. Conf. on Multi-Agent Systems (ICMAS-95), AAAI/MIT Press, pp. 109–116

Franklin, S.; Graesser, A. (1996): Is it an Agent, or just a Program? — A Taxonomy for Autonomous Agents. Pre-Proc. ECAI Workshop on Agent Theories, Architectures and Languages (ATAL-96), pp. 193–206

García-Serrano, A.; Ossowski, S. (1997): Coordinación y Cooperación en Sistemas Distribuidos. In: Dolado 1997

García-Serrano, A.; Ossowski, S. (1998): Inteligencia Artificial Distribuida y Sistemas Multiagentes. Inteligencia Artificial — Revista Iberoamericana de Inteligencia Artificial No. 6, pp. 4–11

Gartner, N. (1983): OPAC — A Demand Responsive Strategy for Traffic Signal Control. Transportation Research Record 906

Gaspari, M.; Motta, E. (1994): Symbol-Level Requirements for Agent-Level Programming. Proc. Europ. Conf. on Artificial Intelligence (ECAI-94), Wiley & Sons, pp. 264–268

Gasser, L. (1991): Social Conceptions of Knowledge and Action: DAI Foundations and Open Systems Semantics. Artificial Intelligence 47, pp. 107–138

Gasser, L. (1993): Architectures and Environments for AI. Proc. Advanced Course on Artificial Intelligence (ACAI-93), ECCAI, pp. 1–42

Gasser, L.; Braganza, C.; Herman, N. (1989): MACE — A Flexible Testbed for Distributed AI Research. In: Gasser and Huhns 1989, pp. 119–152

Gasser, L.; Huhns, M. (eds.) (1989): Distributed Artificial Intelligence (Vol. 2). Morgan Kaufmann

Gasser, L.; Rouquette, N.; Hill, R.; Lieb, J. (1989): Representing Organisational Knowledge in Distributed AI Systems. In: Gasser and Huhns 1989, pp. 55–77

Gelernter, D.; Carriero, N. (1992): Co-ordination Languages and their Significance. Communications of the ACM 35 (2), pp. 97–107

Genesereth, M.; Ketchpel, S. (1994): Software Agents. Communications of the ACM 37 (7), pp. 48–53

Georgeff, M. (1983): Communication and Interaction in Multi-Agent Planning. Proc. Nat. Conf. on Artificial Intelligence (AAAI-83), pp. 125–129

Gergen, K.; Greenberg, M.; Willis, R. (eds.) (1980): Social Exchange — Advances in Theory and Research. Plenum Press

Gibbs, J. (1981): Norms, Deviance and Social Control. Elsevier

Gilbert, N.; Conte, R. (eds.) (1995): Artificial Societies — The Computer Simulation of Social Life. UCL Press

Glance, N.; Hogg, T. (1995): Dilemmas in Computational Societies. Proc. Int. Conf. on Multi-Agent Systems (ICMAS-95), AAAI/MIT Press, pp. 117–123

Glaser, N. (1996): Contribution to Knowledge Acquisition and Modelling in a Multi-Agent Framework — The CoMaMAS Approach. PhD Thesis, Univ. of Nancy I

Gmytrasiewicz, P.; Durfee, E. (1993): Reasoning about other Agents — Philosophy, Theory and Implementation. Proc. Int. Distributed Artificial Intelligence Workshop

Gmytrasiewicz, P.; Durfee, E.; Wehe, D. (1991): The Utility of Communication in Co-ordinating Intelligent Agents. Proc. Nat. Conf. on Artificial Intelligence (AAAI-91), pp. 166–172

Goldman, C.; Rosenschein, J. (1994): Emergent Co-ordination through the Use of Co-operative State-Changing Rules. Proc. Nat. Conf. on Artificial Intelligence (AAAI-94), pp. 408–413

Greenberg, M. (1980): A Theory of Indebtedness. In: Gergen et al. 1980, pp. 4–26

Greenberg, S. (ed.) (1991): CSCW and Groupware. Academic Press

Greif, I. (ed.) (1988): Computer-Supported Co-operative Work — A Book of Readings. Morgan Kaufmann

Gruber, T. (1993): A Translation Approach to Portable Ontology Specification. Knowledge Systems Laboratory Tech. Rep. KSL 92-71 (revised version), 1993

Haddadi, A.; Sundermeyer, K. (1996): Belief–Desire–Intention Agent Architectures. In: O'Hare and Jennings 1996, pp. 169–186

Haynes, T.; Lau, K.; Sen, S. (1996): Learning Cases to Compliment Rules for Conflict Resolution in Multi-Agent Systems. AAAI Spring Symposium on Adaptation, Co-evolution and Learning in MAS

Hendrikson, C.; Ritchie, S. (eds.) (1998): Applications of Advanced Technologies in Transportation. American Society of Civil Engineers (ASCE)

Hewitt, C. (1977): Viewing Control Structures as Patterns of Message Passing. Artificial Intelligence 8, pp. 323–364

Hewitt, C.; de Jong, P. (1984): Open Systems. In: Brodie et al. 1984, pp. 147–164

Holand, U.; Danielson, T. (1991): Describing Co-operation — The Creation of Different Psychological Phenomena. In: Bowers and Benford 1991, pp. 17–21

Holt, A. (1988): Diplans — A New Language for the Study and Implementation of Co-ordination. ACM Trans. on Office Information Systems, pp. 109–125

Huber, M.; Durfee, E. (1995): On Acting Together — Without Communication. Proc. AAAI Spring Symposium on Representing Mental States, pp. 60–71

Huberman, B. (ed.) (1988): The Ecology of Computation. Elsevier

Huhns, M. (ed.) (1988): Distributed Artificial Intelligence (Vol. 1). Morgan Kaufmann

Huhns, M.; Stephens, L. (1998): Multi-Agent Systems and Societies of Agents. In: Weiß and Sen 1998, pp. 79–120

Iglesias C.; Garijo, M.; González, J.(1998): An Overview of Agent-Oriented Methodologies. Pre-Proc. ICMAS Workshop on Agent Theories, Architectures and Languages (ATAL-98), pp. 185–194

Iglesias C.; Garijo, M.; González, J.; Velasco, J. (1996): A Methodological Proposal for Multi-Agent Systems Development extending CommonKADS. Proc. Banff Knowledge Acquisition Workshop (KAW-96)

Jennings, N. (1992): A Knowledge Level Approach to Collaborative Problem Solving. Proc. AAAI Workshop on Co-operation Among Heterogeneous Intelligent Agents, pp. 52–62

Jennings, N. (1992): Towards a Co-operation Knowledge Level for Collaborative Problem Solving. Proc. Europ. Conf. on Artificial Intelligence (ECAI-92), Wiley & Sons, pp. 225–228

Jennings, N. (1993): Commitments and Conventions: the Foundation of Co-ordination in Multi-Agent Systems. Knowledge Engineering Review 8 (3), pp. 223–250.

Jennings, N. (1996): Co-ordination Techniques for Distributed Artificial Intelligence. In: O'Hare and Jennings 1996, pp. 187–210

Jennings, N.; Campos, J. (1997): Towards a Social Level Characterisation of Socially Responsible Agents. IEE Proc. on Software Engineering, 144 (1), pp. 11–25

Jennings, N.; Faratin, P.; Johnson, M.; O'Brian, P.; Wiegand, M. (1996): Using Intelligent Agents to Manage Business Processes. Proc. Int. Conf. on Practical Applications of Intelligent Agents and Multi-Agents (PAAM-96), pp. 345–360

Jennings, N.; Mamdani, E. (1992): Using Joint Responsibility to Co-ordinate Problem Solving in Dynamic Environments. Proc Nat. Conf. on Artificial Intelligence (AAAI-92), pp. 269–275

Jennings, N.; Wooldridge, M. (eds.) (1998): Agent Technology — Foundations, Applications, and Markets. Springer

Jones, A. (1980): Game Theory — Mathematical Models of Conflict. Ellis Horwood

Kautz, H.; Selman, B.; Coen, M. (1994): Bottom-Up Design of Software Agents. Communications of the ACM 37 (7), pp. 143–146

Kephart, J.; Hogg, T.; Huberman, B. (1989): Dynamics of Computational Ecosystems — Implications for DAI. In: Gasser and Huhns 1989, pp. 79–95

Kinney, D.; Georgeff, M.; Rao, A. (1996): A Methodology and Modelling Technique for Systems of BDI Agents. In: van de Velde and Perram 1996, pp. 56–71

Klein, M.; Methlie, L. (1995): Knowledge-Based Decision Support Systems (2nd edn.). Wiley & Sons

Krogh, C. (1996): Normative Structures in Natural and Artificial Systems. Ph.D. Thesis, Univ. of Oslo, Dpt. of Philosophy

Kuper, A. (1973): Anthropologists and Anthropology — The British School 1922–72. Penguin Books

Kurz, M. (1994): Game Theory and Public Economics. In: Auman and Hart 1994, pp. 1153–1192

Kusiak, A. (ed.) (1988): AI Implications for CIM. Springer

Lander, S. (1994): Distributed Search and Conflict Management Among Reusable Heterogeneous Agents. PhD Thesis, Univ. of Massachusetts, Computer Science Dpt.

Lander, S.; Lesser, V. (1992): Customising Distributed Search Among Agents with Hetero-geneous Knowledge. Proc. Conf. on Information and Knowledge Management, pp. 335–344

Lemaître, C.; Sanchez, V.; Loyo, C. (1993): Co-operative Open Systems Architecture. In: Verdejo and Cerri 1993, pp. 126–141

Lesser, V. (1991): A Retrospective View of FA/C Distributed Problem Solving. IEEE Trans. on Systems, Man and Cybernetics 21 (6), pp. 1347–1361

Lesser, V.; Corkhill, D. (1981): Functionally Accurate, Co-operative Distributed Systems. IEEE Trans. on Systems, Man and Cybernetics 11 (1), pp. 81–96

Lesser, V.; Corkhill, D. (1983): The Distributed Vehicle Monitoring Testbed — A Tool for Investigating Distributed Problem-Solving Networks. AI Magazine 4 (3), pp. 81–93

Levesque, H.; Cohen, P.; Nunes, J. (1990): On Acting Together. Proc Nat. Conf. on Artificial Intelligence (AAAI-90), pp. 94–99

Logi, F.; Ritchie, S. (1998): A Distributed Approach to Network-Wide Traffic Control Management. In Hendrikson and Ritchie 1998, pp. 83–90

Lowrie, P. (1982): The Sydney Co-ordinated Adaptive Traffic System — Principles, Methodology, Algorithms. Proc. IEE Int. Conf. on Road Signalling

Lux, A.; Steiner, D. (1995): Understanding Co-operation — An Agent's Perspective. Proc. Int. Conf. on Multi-Agent Systems (ICMAS-95), AAAI/MIT Press, pp. 261–268

Malone, T. (1987): Modelling Co-ordination in Organisations and Markets. Management Sciences 33 (10), pp. 1317–1332

Malone, T. (1988): What is Co-ordination Theory. MIT Sloan School of Management, Working Paper no. 2051/88

Malone, T.; Crowston, K. (1990): What is Co-ordination Theory and How Can It Help Design Co-operative Work Systems. Proc. Int. Conf. on Computer Supported Co-opera-tive Work (CSCW-90), pp. 357–370

Malone, T.; Crowston, K. (1994): The Interdisciplinary Study of Co-ordination. Computing Surveys 26 (1), pp. 87–119

Marshak, J.; Radner, R. (1972): Economic Theory of Teams. Yale Univ. Press

Mauro, V; di Taranto (1989): UTOPIA. Proc. IFAC/IFORS Conf. on Control, Computers and Communications in Transport

McCarthy, J. (1979): Ascribing Mental Qualities to Machines. Tech. Rep. Memo 326, Stanford Univ., AI Lab

Minsky, M.; Papert, S. (1969): Perceptrons — An Introduction to Computational Geome-try. MIT Press

Mintzberg, H. (1988): La Estructuración de las Organizaciones. Ariel

Molina, M.; Cuena, J. (1995): Knowledge-Oriented and Object-Oriented Design — The Experience of KSM. Proc. Banff Knowledge Acquisition Workshop (KAW-95)

Montanari, U.; Rossi, F. (1996): Graph Rewriting and Constraint Solving for Modelling Distributed Systems with Synchronisation. Proc. Int. Conf on Co-ordination Languages and Models (Coordination-96), Springer, pp. 12–27

Montgomery, T.; Durfee, E. (1990): Using MICE to Study Intelligent Dynamic Co-ordin-ation. Proc. IEEE Conf. on Tools for AI, pp. 438–444

Mor, Y.; Rosenschein, J. (1995): Time and the Prisoner's Dilemma. Proc. Int. Conf. on Multi-Agent Systems (ICMAS-95), AAAI/MIT Press, pp. 276–282

Moulin, B.; Chaib-Draa, B. (1996); An Overview of Distributed Artificial Intelligence. In: O'Hare and Jennings 1996, pp. 3–56

Mullen, T.; Wellman, M. (1995): A Simple Computational Market for Network Information Services. Proc. Int. Conf. on Multi-Agent Systems (ICMAS-95), AAAI/MIT Press, pp. 283–289

Müller, H.-J. (1996): Negotiation Principles. In: O'Hare and Jennings 1996, pp. 211–225

Müller, J. (1996): A Co-operation Model for Autonomous Agents. Pre-Proc. ECAI Workshop on Agent Theories, Architectures and Languages (ATAL-96), pp. 135–147

Müller, J. (1996): An Architecture for Dynamically Interacting Agents. Ph.D. Thesis, DFKI, Univ. of Saarbrücken

Müller, J. (1998): The Right Agent (Architecture) to Do the Right Thing. Pre-Proc. ICMAS Workshop on Agent Theories, Architectures and Languages (ATAL-98), pp. 1–16

Müller, J.; Pischel, M.; Thiel, M. (1995): Modelling Reactive Behaviour in Vertically Layered Agent Architectures. In: Wooldridge and Jennings 1995, pp. 261–276

Nash, J. (1950): The Bargaining Problem. Econometrica 28, pp. 155–162

Neches, R.; Fikes, R.; Finin, T.; Gruber, T.; Patil, R.; Senator, T.; Swartout, W. (1991): Enabling Technology for Knowledge Sharing. AI Magazine 12 (3), pp. 36–56

Newell, A. (1982): The Knowledge Level. Artificial Intelligence 18 (1), pp. 82–127

Newell, A. (1993): Reflections on the Knowledge Level. Artificial Intelligence 59, pp. 31–38

Norman, T.; Jennings, N.; Faratin, P.; Mamdani, H. (1996): Designing and Implementing a Multi-Agent Architecture for Business Process Management. Pre-Proc. ECAI Workshop on Agent Theories, Architectures and Languages (ATAL-96), pp. 149–162

Nwana, H. (1996): Software Agents — An Overview. Knowledge Engineering Review 11 (3), pp.1–40

O'Hare, G.; Jennings, N. (1996): Foundations of Distributed Artificial Intelligence. Wiley & Sons

Ossowski, S. (1997): Contribución al Estudio Funcional de las Sociedades Artificiales de Agentes. Ph.D. Thesis, Tech. Univ. of Madrid, Artificial Intelligence Dpt.

Ossowski, S. (1998): A Structural Functionalist Conception of Artificial Agent Societies. Proc. KI Workshop on Socionics, pp. 48–59

Ossowski, S.; Cuena, J.; García-Serrano, A. (1998): A Case of Multi-Agent Decision Support — Using Autonomous Agents for Urban Traffic Control. Proc. Ibero-American Conf. on Artificial Intelligence (Iberamia-98), Springer

Ossowski, S.; García-Serrano, A. (1995): A Knowledge-Level Model of Co-ordination. In: Zhang and Lukose 1995, pp. 46–57

Ossowski, S.; García-Serrano, A. (1996): A Model of Co-ordination Support for Unanticipated Situations. Proc. IFIP World Computer Congress, pp. 516–524

Ossowski, S.; García-Serrano, A. (1997): Social Co-ordination Among Autonomous Problem-Solving Agents. In: Wobcke et al. 1997, pp. 134–148

Ossowski, S.; García-Serrano, A. (1998): La Coordinación en Sociedades de Agentes. Inteligencia Artificial — Revista Iberoamericana de Inteligencia Artificial No. 6, pp. 46–56

Ossowski, S.; García-Serrano, A. (1998): Social Structure in Artificial Agent Societies — Implications for Autonomous Problem-Solving Agents. In: Pre-Proc. ICMAS Workshop on Agent Theories, Architectures and Languages (ATAL-98), pp. 353–368

Ossowski, S.; García-Serrano, A.; Cuena, J. (1996): Emergent Co-ordination of Flow Control Actions through Functional Co-operation of Social Agents. Proc. Europ. Conf. on Artificial Intelligence (ECAI-96), Wiley & Sons, pp. 539–543

Ossowski, S.; García-Serrano, A.; Cuena, J. (1997): Coordinación Descentralizada en Siste-mas de Agentes Autónomos para Resolución de Problemas — Aplicación a la Gestión de Tráfico. Proc. Spanish Conf. on Artificial Intelligence (CAEPIA-97), pp. 551–560

Ossowski, S.; García-Serrano, A.; Cuena, J. (1998): "From Theory to Practice in Multi-Agent System Design — The Case of Structural Co-operation". Proc. German Annual Conf. on Artificial Intelligence (KI-98), Springer, pp. 105–116

Owen, G. (1995): Game Theory (3rd edn.). Academic Press

Parunak, H. (1988): Distributed Artificial Intelligence Systems. In: Kusiak 1988, pp. 225–251

Parunak, H. (1988): Manufacturing Experience with the Contract Net. In: Huhns 1988

Pattison, H.; Corkill, D.; Lesser, V. (1988): Instantiating Descriptions of Organisational Structures. In: Huhns 1988, pp. 59–96

Pollack, M. (1992): The Uses of Plans. Artificial Intelligence 57, pp. 43–68

Pollack, M; Ringuette, M. (1990): Introducing Tileworld — Experimentally Evaluating Agent Architectures. Proc. Nat. Conf. on Artificial Intelligence (AAAI-90), pp. 183–189

Power, R. (ed.) (1993): Co-operation Among Organisations — The Potential of Computer Support Co-operative Work. Springer

Pruitt, D. (1981). Negotiation Behaviour. Academic Press

Puppe, F. (1993): Systematic Introduction to Expert Systems. Springer

Radcliffe-Brown, A. (1952): Structure and Function in Primitive Society. Cohen & West

Rao, A.; Georgeff, M. (1995): BDI Agents — From Theory to Practice. Proc. Int. Conf. on Multi-Agent Systems (ICMAS-95), AAAI/MIT Press, pp. 312–319

Rizzo, P.; Cesta, A.; Miceli, M. (1995): On Helping Behaviour in Co-operative Environ-ments. Proc. Int. Workshop on the Design of Co-operative Systems, pp. 96–108

Robinson, M. (1993): Design for Unanticipated Use. Proc. Europ. Conf. on Computer Supported Co-operative Work (ECSCW-93), pp. 187–202

Rosenschein, J.; Zlotkin, G. (1994): Designing Conventions for Automated Negotiation. AI Magazine 15 (3), pp. 29–46

Rosenschein, J.; Zlotkin, G. (1994): Rules of Encounter — Designing Conventions for Automated Negotiation among Computers. MIT Press

Rumbaugh, J.; Blaha, M.; Premerlani, W.; Eddy, F.; Lorensen, V. (1991): Object-Oriented Modelling and Design. Prentice-Hall

Russell, S.; Norvig, P. (1995): Artificial Intelligence — A Modern Approach. Prentice-Hall

Sandholm, T. (1996): Negotiation among Self-interested Computationally Limited Agents. PhD Thesis. Univ. of Massachusetts, Computer Science Dpt.

Sandholm, T. (1998): Distributed Rational Decision Making. In: Weiß and Sen 1998, pp. 201–258

Sandholm, T.; Lesser, V. (1995): Equilibrium Analysis of the Possibilities of Unenforced Exchange in Multi-Agent Systems. Proc. Int. Joint Conf. on Artificial Intelligence (IJCAI-95), Morgan Kaufmann, pp. 694–701

Schaerf, A.; Shoham, Y.; Tennenholz, M. (1995): Adaptive Load Balancing — A Study in Multi-Agent Learning. Journal of Artificial Intelligence Research 2, pp. 475–500

Schreiber, G.; Akkermans, H.; Wielinga, B. (1990): On Problems with the Knowledge Level Perspective. Proc. Banff Knowledge Acquisition Workshop (KAW-90)

Searle, J. (1969): Speech Acts. Cambridge University Press

Searle, J. (1990): Collective Intentions and Actions. In: Cohen et al., 1990, pp. 401–416

Sekaran, M.; Sen, S. (1995): To Help or not to Help. Proc. 17th Annual Conf. of the Cogni-tive Science Society, pp. 736–741

Shehory, O.; Kraus, S. (1995): A Kernel-Oriented Model for Autonomous Agent Coalition Formation in General Environments. In: Zhang and Lukose 1995, pp. 31–45

Shehory, O.; Kraus, S. (1996): Co-operative Goal Satisfaction without Communication in Large-Scale Agent Systems. Proc. Europ. Conf. on Artificial Intelligence (ECAI-96), Wiley & Sons, pp. 544–548

Shehory, O.; Sycara, K.; Chalasani, P.; Somesh, J. (1998): Increasing Resource Utilisation and Task Performance by Agent Cloning. Pre-Proc. ICMAS Workshop on Agent Theories, Architectures and Languages (ATAL-98), pp. 305–318

Shoham, Y. (1993): Agent-Oriented Programming. Artificial Intelligence 60 (7), pp. 51–92

Shoham, Y.; Tennenholz, M. (1992): On the Synthesis of Social Laws for Artificial Agent Societies. Proc. Nat. Conf. on Artificial Intelligence (AAAI-92), pp. 276–281

Shoham, Y.; Tennenholz, M. (1994): Co-Learning and the Evolution of Social Activity. Stanford Univ., Tech. Rep. CS-TR-94-1551

Shoham, Y.; Tennenholz, M. (1995): On Social Laws for Artificial Agent Societies — Off-Line Design. Artificial Intelligence 73, pp. 231–252

Sichman, J. (1995): Du Raisonnement Social Chez des Agents. Ph.D. Thesis, Institut National Polytechnique de Grenoble

Sichman, J.; Demazeau, Y. (1995): Exploiting Social Reasoning to Deal with Agency Level Inconsistencies. Proc. Int. Conf. on Multi-Agent Systems (ICMAS-95), AAAI/MIT Press, pp. 352–359

Sichman, J.; Demazeau, Y.; Conte, R.; Castelfranchi, C. (1994): A Social Reasoning Mechanism Based on Dependence Networks. Proc. Europ. Conf. on Artificial Intelligence (ECAI-94), Wiley & Sons, pp. 188–192

Simmons, R. (ed.): Second Generation Expert Systems. Springer

Singh, B. (1992): Interconnected Roles — A Co-ordinated Model. MCC Tech. Rep. CT-84-92

Singh, M.; Huhns, M.; Stephens, L. (1993): Declarative Representation of Multi-Agent Systems. IEEE Trans. on Knowledge and Data Engineering 5 (5), pp. 721–739

Smith, R. (1980): The Contract Net Protocol — High-Level Communication and Control in a Distributed Problem Solver. IEEE Trans. on Computers 29 (12), pp.1104–1113

Staniford, G. (1994): Multi-Agent System Design — Using Human Societal Metaphors and Normative Logic. Proc. Europ. Conf. on Artificial Intelligence (ECAI-94), Wiley & Sons, pp. 289–293

Steeb, R.; Cammarata, S.; Hayes-Roth, F.; Thorndyke, P.; Wesson, R. (1981): Architectures for Distributed Air Traffic Control. In: Bond and Gasser 1988

Steels, L. (1990): Components of Expertise. AI Magazine, pp. 28–49

Steels, L. (1994): Emergent Functionality in Robotic Agents through On-Line Evolution. Proc. Alife IV

Steels, L. (ed.) (1995): The Biology and Technology of Intelligent Autonomous Agents. Springer

Steels, L.; Brooks, R. (eds.) (1995): The Artificial Life Route to Artificial Intelligence. Lawrence Erlbaum

Stefik, M. (1986): The Next Knowledge Medium. AI Magazine 7 (1), pp. 34–46

Steiner, D. (1996): IMAGINE — An Integrated Environment for Constructing Distributed Artificial Intelligence Systems. In: O'Hare and Jennings 1996, pp. 345–364

Sycara, K. (1989): Argumentation — Planning Other Agents' Plans. Proc. Int. Joint Conf. on Artificial Intelligence (IJCAI-89), Morgan Kaufmann, pp. 517–523

Sycara, K. (1989): Multi-Agent Compromise via Negotiation. In: Bond and Gasser 1989, pp. 119–137

Sycara, K. (1998): Multi-Agent Systems. AI Magazine 19 (2), pp. 79–92

Sycara, K.; Roth, S.; Sadeh, N.; Fox, M. (1991): Distributed Constrained Heuristic Search. IEEE Trans. on Systems, Man and Cybernetics 21 (6), pp. 1446–1460

Tel, G. (1994): Introduction to Distributed Algorithms. Cambridge Univ. Press

Thomas, R. (1995): The PLACA Agent Programming Language. In: Wooldridge and Jennings 1995, pp. 355–370

Thompson, G. (1967): Organisations in Action. Mac Graw Hill

Thomson, W. (1987): Monotonicity of Bargaining Solutions with Respect to the Disagreement Point. Journal of Economic Theory 42, pp. 50–58

Thomson, W. (1994): Co-operative Models of Bargaining. In: Auman and Hart 1994, pp. 1238–1284

Tuomola, R. (1996): Philosophy and Distributed Artificial Intelligence — The Case of Joint Intentions. In: O'Hare and Jennings 1996, pp. 487–504

Tzafestas, S. (ed.) (1997): Knowledge-Based Systems — Advanced Concepts, Techniques and Applications. World Scientific

Ullmann-Margalit, E. (1977): The Emergence of Norms. Clarendon Press

Van de Velde, W. (1993): Issues in Knowledge Level Modelling. In: Simmons 1993, pp. 211–231

Van de Velde, W.; Perram, J. (eds.) (1996): Agents Breaking Way. Springer

VanLehn, K. (ed.) (1991): Architectures for Intelligence — 22nd CMU Symposium on Cognition. Lawrence Erlbaum

Verdejo, F.; Cerri, S. (eds.) (1994): Collaborative Dialogue Technologies in Distance Learning. Springer

Vernadat, F. (1996): Enterprise Modelling and Integration — Principles and Applications. Chapman & Hall

Vidal, J.; Durfee, E. (1995): Recursive Agent Modelling Using Limited Rationality. Proc. Int. Conf. on Multi-Agent Systems (ICMAS-95), AAAI/MIT Press, pp. 377–382

Vlahavas, I; Bassileiades, N.; Sakellariou, I.; Molina, M.; Ossowski, S.; Futo, I; Pasztor, Z.; Szeredi, J.; Velbitskiyi, I.; Yershov, S.; Golub, S.; Netesin, I. (1998): System Architecture of a Distributed Expert System for the Management of a National Data Network. Proc. Int. Conf. on Artificial Intelligence — Methodology, Systems, Applications (AIMSA-98), Springer

Von Martial, F. (1992): Co-ordinating Plans of Autonomous Agents. LNAI 610, Springer

Von Martial, F. (1992): Einführung in die Verteilte Künstliche Intelligenz. Künstliche Intelligenz 1, pp. 6–11

Von Wright, H. (1970): Norma y Acción — Una Investigación Lógica. Technos

Walker, A.; Wooldridge, M. (1995): Understanding the Emergence of Conventions in Multi-Agent Systems. Proc. Int. Conf. on Multi-Agent Systems (ICMAS-95), AAAI/MIT Press, pp. 384–389

Weiß, G.; Sen, S. (eds.) (1998): Multi-Agent Systems — A Modern Approach to Distributed Artificial Intelligence. AAAI/MIT Press

Wellman, M. (1995): Market-Oriented Programming — Some Early Lessons. In: Clearwater 1995

Wielinga, B.; Schreiber, A.; Breuker, J. (1992): KADS — A Modelling Approach to Knowledge Engineering. Knowledge Acquisition 4, pp. 5–53

Winograd, T. (1988): A Language/Action Perspective on the Design of Co-operative Work. In: Greif 1988, pp. 623–653

Wobcke, W.; Pagnucco, M.; Zhang, C. (eds.) (1997): Agents and Multi-Agent Systems — Formalisms, Methodologies and Applications. LNAI 1441, Springer

Wöhe, G. (1986): Einführung in die Betriebswirtschaftslehre (16th edn.). Vahlen

Wooldridge, M.; Jennings, N. (1994): Towards a Theory of Co-operative Problem Solving. Pre-Proc. Europ. Workshop on Modelling Autonomous Agents in a Multi-Agent World (MAAMAW-94), pp. 15–26

Wooldridge, M.; Jennings, N. (1995): Intelligent Agents — Theory and Practice. Knowledge Engineering Review 10 (2), pp. 115–152

Wooldridge, M.; Jennings, N. (1998): Pitfalls of Agent-Oriented Development. Proc. Int. Conf. on Autonomous Agents (Agents-98), pp. 385–391

Wooldridge, M.; Jennings, N. (ed.) (1995): Intelligent Agents. LNAI 890, Springer

Yang, H.; Zhang, C. (1995): Definition and Application of a Comprehensive Framework for Distributed Problem Solving. In: Zhang and Lukose 1995, pp. 1–15

Yokoo, M. (1994): Weak Commitment Search for Solving Constraint Satisfaction Problems. Proc. Nat. Conf. on Artificial Intelligence (AAAI-94), pp. 313–318

Yokoo, M. (1995): Asynchronous Weak Commitment Search for Solving Distributed Constraint Satisfaction Problems. Proc. Int. Conf. on Principles and Practice of Constraint Programming (CLP-95). LNAI 976, Springer, pp. 88–102

Yokoo, M.; Durfee, E. (1991): Distributed Constraint Optimisation as a Formal Model of Partially Adversarial Co-operation. Univ. of Michigan, Tech. Rep. CSE-TR-101-91

Yokoo, M.; Ishida, T. (1998): Search Algorithms for Agents. In: Weiß and Sen 1998, pp. 165–200

Yokoo, M.; Ishida, T.; Durfee, E.; Kuwabara, K. (1992): Distributed Constraint Satisfaction for Formalising Distributed Problem Solving. Proc. Int. Conf. on Distributed Computing Systems, pp. 614–621

Zhang, C.; Lukose, D. (1995): Distributed Artificial Intelligence — Architecture and Modelling. LNAI 1087, Springer

Zlotkin, G.; Rosenschein, J. (1991): Incomplete Information and Deception in Multi-Agent Negotiation. Proc. Int. Joint Conf. on Artificial Intelligence (IJCAI-91), Morgan Kaufmann, pp. 225–231

Lecture Notes in Artificial Intelligence (LNAI)

Lecture Notes in Computer Science